PRAISE FOR | **"The Utes Must Go!"**
American Expansion and the Removal of a People

"The story develops with the fatal inevitability of a train wreck which we watch and are powerless to prevent. And still, after all these years, the real question is whether we are capable of truly understanding the terrible American truths that lie embedded in the events Peter Decker narrates so skillfully."

—Frederick Turner, author of *Beyond Geography:*
The Western Spirit Against the Wilderness

"This is a powerful story, told with craft and gripping narrative. ... The book is splendid at giving [the reader] a brilliant critical understanding of all the characters involved and the unmitigated politics, as well as crucial miscalculations, that extracted penalties from Utes at almost every turn of events."

—Syd Nathans, associate professor
of history, Duke University

"A well-researched history of a critical time in the life of the Ute Nation. Decker brings their tragic story to life, correcting errors and folklore that have clustered about the final conflict that drove them to Utah—an important contribution to western history."

—Vine Deloria Jr., Native American
scholar and author of *God Is Red*

"THE UTES MUST GO!"

American Expansion and the Removal of a People

Peter R. Decker

FULCRUM PUBLISHING

For Brian Cockburn and his family

Library of Congress Cataloging-in-Publication Data

Decker, Peter R., 1934-

  "The Utes must go!" : American expansion and the removal of a people /

Peter R. Decker.

    p. cm.

Includes bibliographical references and index.

  ISBN 1-55591-465-9

  1. White River Massacre, Colo., 1879. 2. United States. Office of
Indian Affairs. White River Agency (Colo.)--History. 3. Ute
Indians--Wars, 1879. 4. Ute Indians--Relocation--Colorado--Ute Indian
Reservation. 5. Ute Indian Reservation (Colo.)--History. I. Title.

  E83.879.D43 2004

  973.8'5--dc22

                              2003023775

ISBN 1-55591-465-9

Printed in the United States of America

0 9 8 7 6 5 4 3 2 1

Editorial: Faith Marcovecchio, Katie Raymond

Design: Ann Douden, Jack Lenzo

Cover image: Henry Farney painting, "The Old Buffalo Trail."

Painting copyright © American Heritage Center, University of Wyoming.

Back cover photo: "The Utes Must Go!"
   Courtesy of the Colorado Historical Society, #F-44177

Fulcrum Publishing

16100 Table Mountain Parkway, Suite 300

Golden, Colorado 80403-1672

(800) 992-2908 • (303) 277-1623

www.fulcrum-books.com

Contents

Foreword

The experience of the Ute Indians in the face of the westward push of the burgeoning American republic, like that of the Indians generally, is a sad and often bloody chapter frequently marked by the racism of a predominantly white European culture over a marginalized native population.

Westward expansion brought frequent clashes between Indians and whites and, as Robert Utley aptly put it, is really the history of two peoples in physical union due to the frontier but culturally, socially, and intellectually apart—in a state of "mutual unintelligibility."

Despite the passage of time, in many respects Indian-white relations remain unintelligible.

Nonetheless, the Ute Indians are not only still with us but also are thriving, albeit not in their original locations. The fact is that though the Utes' land and traditional way of life were taken, their steel spirit is intact.

In *"The Utes Must Go!"*, Peter Decker follows Utley's tradition in painting a picture of the Ute Indians that in large part is typical of the Indian experience in America.

Hundreds of books have been written about the sad and often bloody history of Indian people during the westward expansion of North America. Few have been able to tell the story of how that history affected the lives and destinies of one people—in this case the Utes—as Peter Decker does in this book.

In this meticulously researched narrative spanning the period from the mid-1800s to 1881 when the Utes were forced into Utah, Decker focuses on the cause and effects, both small and large, that the expansion of the new nation had on the Ute Indians.

In hindsight, the eras of American history we have come to know so well appear to fit neatly into discrete time frames and transition, one to the other, almost seamlessly.

When Columbus arrived, the land the natives had known for millennia was "discovered" by the Europeans. Thus began a three-hundred-year effort, under a variety of rationales, to push the Indian from his land and to occupy it in the name of God, progress, and nation.

From the earliest colonial period of Jamestown and Plymouth to the post-Revolutionary years and the beginning of westward expansion, America saw the country's natives largely in terms of an "Indian problem" and went about separating the Indian from the land so coveted—and necessary—for the growing young nation.

With thoughts of a permanent Indian settlement in present-day Oklahoma, the removal of the Indians east of the Mississippi became the official policy of the United States in the 1830s until it became obvious that more land was needed.

In quick succession Texas was annexed (1845), Utah, Arizona, Nevada, western Colorado, New Mexico, and California were added with the Treaty of Guadalupe Hidalgo (1848), and Ute life changed forever.

Skirmishes and massacres between settlers, pioneers, miners, and the Indians were unfortunately not rare. In 1864 Chivington and his Colorado Militia slaughtered innocent Cheyenne men, women, and children at Sand Creek, despite the fact that the Cheyenne were not engaged in hostilities and were flying the American flag as a sign of their friendliness.

The Civil War period brought temporary relief to wholesale westward migration as Federal and Confederate forces fought each other for five long years.

The post–Civil War era brought long and bloody Indian wars in the southern plains and with the Sioux. Having secured the bulk of the Indian land base, in 1870 the United States ended the practice of treaty-making and chose instead to deal with the Indians through executive order or federal legislation, markedly different in terms of Indian involvement and ability to affect outcomes.

In the summer of 1876, Americans read with horror the fate of General Custer and the Seventh Cavalry at Little Bighorn and witnessed with wonder the travails of the Nez Perce and Chief Joseph a year later.

In 1887, in a well-intentioned yet disastrous policy stroke, Congress passed the General Allotment Act intending to Christianize and civilize the Indian, break up the Indian landmass, encourage individual Indian ownership of land and agriculture, and, in the process, bring an end to Indian culture. Perhaps more than any other of the many ill-conceived Indian policies, the General Allotment Act has caused great harm to Indian people and culture.

Many scholars perceive the 1890 battle at Wounded Knee as the crescendo to this tableau of events, policy twists, cultural resistance, and military episodes.

As Decker points out, all of these events are echoed in American dealings with the Utes. How did it happen?

The American legal system evolved from a point of recognizing Indian tribes as sovereign nations with which it was necessary to enter legally enforceable contracts in order to secure title to their lands to an interim phase where tribes were held to be domestic, dependent nations—in essence wards of the federal government.

From the guardian-ward era it was not a big policy stretch to push for the assimilation of the Indian and make him "more like us"—white Christian farmers.

On the other hand, American settlers—the very people the Indians were meant to simulate—felt their only obstacle to a country of infinite resources was the presence of the Indians.

In accounts that mirror countless other tribes' experiences, when the pressure mounted on the Utes, they appealed to Washington—usually without success—to honor the agreements it had struck.

Witness the corrupt and ineffective Indian Bureau focused more on benefiting special interests and profits than on benefiting the Indians.

For those wanting to peel back the pages of history and see what Manifest Destiny meant to the small bands of Ute Indians, Decker has created the kind of readable and hard-hitting narrative that belongs in the ranks of great western scholars.

The bottom line is that the peopling of America by white pioneers necessitated some answer to the "Indian problem," and the U.S. response varied in tactics but never lost its focus on the ultimate goal: elimination of the Indian from the western landscape either by assimilation or warfare.

Peter Decker correctly shows that the guiding principle toward the Indian people was that they should stand aside, be overwhelmed or, as he puts it, simply "must go."

For their part the Indians, fairly consistently, wanted to be left alone or, having struck what they thought were solemn agreements with the Great White Father, wanted the benefit of the what they thought they had bargained for.

Unfortunately, for the Utes and the Indians generally, neither proved to be the case as continued white encroachment onto Indian lands necessitated the involvement of U.S. agents and troops that ultimately were not there to protect the Indians or their rights, but to ensure that what evolved on the ground in terms of land losses to the Indians would not be undone.

Through it all, the Utes—like the Cherokee, Chippewa, Cheyenne, Sioux, Navajo, Mission Indians, and hundreds of other Indian tribes—showed the kind of tenacity and will to survive rarely seen in human history. The Indian spirit, like the Utes', survives still.

Ben Nighthorse Campbell
United States Senator

Preface

Indian Country once included my ranch. It does no longer. I was reminded of this a few years ago when I discovered that a fence behind my office needed repair. A fierce spring wind had uprooted a massive tree and downed about twenty feet of an old fence that had stood, out of habit, longer than the quarter of a century I had occupied the ranch. Building or fixing a barbed-wire fence is not, for me, an enjoyable activity. So with some wire, two replacement posts, a shovel, fencing pliers, staples, and a wire stretcher, I trudged up the hill to attend to the unpleasant chore. After digging two new postholes, I sat to rest on the hilltop in the cooling breeze and drank tepid water from a canvas water bag. There on the ground was an arrowhead, broken at the tip and unfinished at its shank. Beside it lay small chips of chert stone and another imperfectly completed head. I scratched around in the dirt and discovered more chips and broken heads. An Indian, I thought to myself, had sat here beneath the piñon tree, fashioning his weapons, while he spotted game up and down the valley from this perfect lookout.

I wanted to know more about this Indian who, along with his Ute band, had lived and hunted on my ranch little more than a century ago. How long had he and his ancestors, who called themselves the Nuche ("the People"), occupied this land? Clearly longer than the Anglos who arrived here in the 1880s. Where had he gone and why had he left? Surely he had not departed voluntarily this land—rich in game, grass, timber, and water. I, like my neighbors, knew the Utes had lived here before us: their arrowheads and teepee rings lay scattered on our hay and cattle pastures; their paths had become our roads and highways; and their sacred hot springs we visited to soak our recreational aches and pains.

After their departure and in their memory, we made little effort to honor them except for a small, underfunded museum, a monument or two, and a few historical road markers. Yes, we named a town and later a county after their chief, Ouray, but less to celebrate him than to protect ourselves from attack by playing to his vanity. In our nod toward a sense of history, we even kept some Ute place names, such as the Uncompahgre River, all the while finding it, as President William Taft had said in 1909 during a visit to the area, impossible to pronounce and even more difficult to spell. And finally, to advance our commercial endeavors, we used Ute identities for our cafes, motels, campgrounds, realty companies, sports teams, and innumerable "Indian" gift shoppes.

The old-timers, mostly deceased now, still remember the presence of those Utes who did not stay put in the outdoor pens we designed for them, called reservations. They played with them as children, learned of their trails through the forest, and trapped and shot game with them at their favorite hunting sites. The first- and second-generation white settlers hired Utes to work on hay crews or help in their town shops. A local family in my home-town of Ridgway, Colorado, can remember how, in the 1930s, a few Utes who continued to survive in the area would gather in their kitchen every morning, sit silently on the floor around the stove, await their daily cup of coffee, and then leave without a word. They'd walk by their sacred hot springs nearby and then disappear into the timber. Today the Utes are no more a part of our human landscape here in western Colorado, their tradi-tional homeland, than are the Pequots in Massachusetts or the Potawatomi in Kansas. Fewer and fewer Utes appear at the annual local powwow in nearby Delta, Colorado. Occasionally some Utes can be seen in their pickups as they pass through this area on their way to or from their reservations in Utah and southern Colorado. Their hunting grounds are now ski resorts and cattle ranches, where some people own trophy homes larger than the president's ("Great White Father's") home in Washington, D.C., and decorate them with expensive Indian artifacts. Or, more likely, their land has been transformed into gated ranchettes with names such as Whispering Pines or Ute Acres, suggesting a rural Arcadia connected, if only tangentially, to what is perceived as a simple and romantic Indian past.

When I embarked on this book, like most whites, I had only a vague sense of Indian history, and even less of the particular history of the Utes. The smattering of things I learned was either vaguely gathered through tedious "social science" classes or absorbed through Hollywood and its trivialization of American history. In the American West, where Indians are most in evidence, even our best efforts to record their history have resulted in narratives that usually serve as a brief background for someone else's story. Until relatively recently, our white narratives of western settlement have usually followed a familiar and heroic theme: that of God-fearing pioneers facing bravely the hardships of an inhospitable frontier, including those brutal and incessant attacks by Indians. When seen through a screen of gauzy nostalgia, the hearty pioneers inevitably endure victorious over the environment and "the savages," the former defeated by true grit and technology, the latter conquered by the army and superior Christian values. In these epic success stories, the Indian is almost always portrayed as the inevitable victim and, if not for the enlightened vision of a Christian nation, fortunate to have survived a fate worse than a reservation. Thankfully, recent scholarship has corrected these simplistic myths.

I set out, therefore, to learn about Utes, or at least to know more about their experience with the U.S. government in the years leading up to their forced departure from their homeland, an area in the early nineteenth century of more than one hundred thousand square miles—larger than New England and New York combined. The land they ceded—virtually all of western Colorado with its wealth of timber and minerals and five fertile river valleys—for a reservation in Utah, was not an equal exchange, nor was it a voluntary one.

Friends ask: "Why investigate the Utes? We know the outcome." "Of course we took their land," they say, "so what else is new?" We wanted their land, we thought we had an inalienable right to it, and we seized it. The outcome was predictable from the day the first colonists stepped off their boats in the Massachusetts Bay Colony. So why bother with the details? Such facile disregard of the Indian experience suggests that it is remembered, if at all, as little more than a footnote in our national history. By such treatment, individual tribal experiences differ only in unimportant details. The massive removal of Indians from their land, along with the frequent attempts to eradicate "the savages" from the American landscape, is hidden beneath the more glorious story of the American Experience.

When, in our historical treatment of the Indian experience, the story carries the interpretive burden of an inevitable outcome, the Indian becomes little more than a passive subject unable, if not unwilling, to struggle against the historical forces aligned against him. He is seen as a helpless victim—weak in spirit and unimagined in action. And when a preordained outcome is combined with a passive subject, there are no reasons to look for, or even consider, alternative policies that might have changed the predicted outcome. Nor is there any sense of culpability. If, as many nineteenth-century leaders believed, the ultimate fate of the Indian was ordained by God, then there was nothing that whites could have done, or should have done, to stop the train. There were no options, only the intractable cycle of history, which predetermined the ultimate victory of white Americans and the tragic fate of those we had to destroy to preserve and advance our own welfare. Gen. William T. Sherman, who signed the final order to expel the Utes from their home, put it bluntly in a letter to his friend, President Ulysses S. Grant: "Both races cannot use this country in common, and one or the other must withdraw. We cannot withdraw without checking the natural progress of Civilization."[1]

Even today there are historians who continue to argue that the "irreconcilable differences" between Native Americans and white settlers preordained that one group would "have to give way to the other." "It is easy today to sit back and criticize ... the settlers and frontiersman for what they did to the Native Americans," Stephen Ambrose writes, "but for them the choices were to go back to where they came from or to go forward and seize what they wanted or needed."[2] That they could not, or rather would not, go back meant that whites would take by military force what they could not acquire by peaceful negotiation.

If, as the political philosopher Isaiah Berlin suggested, one sees the world so intractable and human options so narrow, the perpetuators of war are no longer responsible for their own actions. For those who believe in a preordained outcome, it is not only easy for them to wreck considerable havoc on whomever they wish, but also to dissociate themselves from any personal responsibility for the destructive outcome.[3] By virtue of the universal law that civilization must win over savagery, a force so strong that humans have no choice but to follow and assist it, the perpetrators lose all freedom of choice.

Therefore, they cannot be blamed for the natural consequences of the law. "Agonizing doubts about the conduct of individuals caught in historical crisis, and the feeling of hope and despair, guilt, pride and remorse which accompanies such reflections, are taken from us, like soldiers in an army driven by forces too great to resist." "Where there is no choice," Berlin writes, "there is no anxiety ... [only] a happy release from responsibility."[4] When it came to Anglo actions against the Indians, we absolved ourselves of all responsibility. In short, this universal law came to be "the great alibi."

In our enthusiasm to both defend and boost our national self-righteousness, we have infrequently looked into the darker, less virtuous layers of our national history. On those occasions when we have peered into our past and discovered that our history has not conformed to the myths we have created for our personal comfort and self-esteem, historical amnesia has, too often, resulted. In such investigations, sometimes, there are no heroes, only men less evil than others.

This is not an uplifting story. The deceitful and violent manner in which the U.S. government treated the Utes may seem a small part of our national history, but it does, I believe, further illuminate this nation's racial attitudes in the nineteenth century. This is not to suggest the Utes did not also have blood on their hands. There is enough evidence of unprovoked and murderous attacks on innocent whites for us to know that Utes, like some other tribes, were both capable of and willing to commit violent crimes. Too often these attacks are dismissed by their white defenders as retaliatory raids against Anglo provocations. But the Utes did steal livestock, burn off-reservation homesteads, and on occasion, take white captives for ransom. To deny these crimes is to oversimplify their world, while romanticizing their life. They did not always live peacefully in a benign state of nature while, as Hollywood would have it, participating in "Dances with Wolves." And while this book does not absolve the Utes of initiating occasional preemptive bloodshed, nonetheless it is the white response to the very existence of the Utes, on land coveted by whites, that drives this story.

This narrative covers the events affecting the Utes primarily between the mid-nineteenth century and 1881, when a majority of the tribal survivors were forced into Utah. Various books have appeared over the past thirty years describing the Ute experience during this time period, but none, I believe, see the actions against the Utes as interrelated. Nor are the racial attitudes of the whites closely examined. In the end, this story is as sad for its deadly and racist outcome as it is for the options barely considered and not taken. There are few heroes. Only some Ute chiefs and a German émigré fought against the forces allied against the Utes. Mostly this is the story of countless hateful, dishonest, and corrupt men and their insensitive and often brutal actions against an Indian tribe that wanted only to be left alone. But they were not to be left alone. Americans wanted their land and took it. In losing their ancestral home, the Utes left behind their sacred burial grounds, and, in Southern Colorado, one Ute left some arrowheads on a hilltop.

Acknowledgments

For a researcher, there is no finer place to work than the Denver Public Library, a cultural jewel. Its Western History/Genealogy Department, with its superb collections and professional staff, provided me with constant assistance in locating critical primary and secondary sources for this book. I owe a special thanks to Barbara Walton, Phil Panum, Bruce Hanson, Jim Kroll, James Jeffrey, John Irwin, and Joan Harms.

Other libraries and their staffs rendered additional assistance. I wish to thank the archives staff at the Colorado Historical Society, Bruce Kirby at the Library of Congress, Murney Gerlack and Nan Card at the Rutherford B. Hayes Presidential Center, Mary Frances Morrow and Michael Musik at the National Archives, Lynn Brittner at the Southern Ute Cultural Center, and Frances O'Donnell, who led me into and through the American Unitarian Association Collection at the Andover-Harvard Theological Library (Harvard Divinity School).

Individual scholars also provided me with helpful critiques of individual chapters and suggestions for further research. Anne Scott, Syd Nathans, and Peter Wood, three former colleagues at Duke University, all read portions of the manuscript and provided important additions and corrections. William deBuys, Claudio Saunt, Duane Smith, Sam Maynes, James Gross, Robert Utley, Mark Miller, and John Kessell offered many helpful leads to materials I would have otherwise missed. Andrew Gulliford and his staff at the Center for Southwest Studies at Fort Lewis College lent assistance at critical stages of the book. I wish also to acknowledge the valuable interviews given to me by Ute tribal members Roland McCook; Lance Nightwalker; Jim Jefferson; Becky Hammond; Lynn Brittner at the Southern Ute Museum; and Leonard Burch, the recently deceased tribal chairman of the Southern Utes. Roger Echo-Hawk, formerly at the Denver Art Museum, provided me an important perspective on Indian history as I worked through the nineteenth century history of the Utes.

In the selection of photographs, I was assisted by Vyrtis Thomas and Paula Richardson Fleming at the archives of the National Anthropological Archives at the Smithsonian Institution, Joanna Stull in the archives of the City of Greeley Museums, Jennifer Brathovde at the Library of Congress, Judy Prosser-Armstrong at the Museum of Western Colorado, Todd Ellison at Fort Lewis College, Coi Drummond-Gehrig at the Denver Public Library, Eric Paddock at the Colorado Historical Society, Cindy Brown at the Wyoming State Archives, Robert Lewis of Denver, and Leonel and Ilean Silva of Centennial, Colorado.

Many friends lent assistance and support in ways often invisible but always critical. I am particularly grateful to Maxine Grofsky, Win Knowlton, Richard and Julia Moe, Ted Moews, Tom Noel, Kathleen Kelley, Joe Sullivan, Ethel Starbuck, Fred Turner, Steve Cox, Sally Pearce, George Carey, Gene Rooke, Larry Kelly, Terry Minger, Doris Gregory, P. David Smith, and Steve Horn. My golfing buddies—Kent Parkison, Gary Christy, Ed Barlow, Jeff Markel, Daniel Wolf, "Chips" Barry, Glynn Williams, and Sam Wagonfeld—constantly reminded me that a "birdie" from time to time provided a pleasant relief from working with microfilm and "Endnotes" through Windows. And finally thanks to some medical folks who kept most of my critical body parts functioning throughout stages of this book: Richard Murdoch, Stuart Frankel, David Tanaka, Richard Hughes, and Paul Gross.

When I first thought about assembling the history of Ute-Anglo conflicts, I had a long meeting with Vine Deloria. His initial encouragement and support was critical from the very beginning, as was that of Bob Baron at Fulcrum Publishing. The manuscript was considerably improved at Fulcrum with the editorial assistance of Marlene Blessing, Katie Raymond, Faith Marcovecchio, and Sam Scinta. My secretary, Anne Price, with care and exquisite patience, was asked to correct some confusing syntax, all the while providing me cover from annoying interruptions. But most important of all, Bill Adler lent his considerable editorial skills to the manuscript by adding clarity and focus, too often missing in earlier drafts.

Finally my wife, Deedee, picked up all the ranch chores and many of the family responsibilities I left unattended throughout the research and writing of this book. To her and my immediate family—Karen, Chris, Hilary, Kristin, Pete, and the two Bens—I am forever grateful.

Introduction

An early spring in 1882 ended a long and monotonous winter schedule for the U.S. Army troops at Wyoming's Fort Washakie. Relieved of hauling feed to their mounts and chopping wood for themselves, the small cavalry contingent posted on the Wind River Indian Reservation began the work of preparing their horses for summer reconnaissance maneuvers among the Shoshone Indians. The troops of the Third Cavalry could focus once again on their main mission: to keep the Indians within the confines of their reservation, a mission similarly performed by scores of small army units throughout the West. The Indians, and particularly the Utes, a tribe to the south in Colorado, refused to be confined to the outdoor holding pens the U.S. government designed for them. The Utes had only recently been moved from Colorado into a reservation in Utah, but some refused to stay put, including their war chief, Nicaagat—Green Leaf, or "the one with the ring in his ear." Whites called him "Captain Jack."

The previous November, after Jack failed to present himself in Utah for his food rations and clothing annuity, the army had sent an undercover agent to find the "troublemaker." The rumor circulated among some Utes that he wanted to arrange an alliance with a few Cheyenne and Shoshone bands and reopen hostilities with the army. Two years earlier in northern Colorado, Jack had led his Ute band in one of the longest Indian battles in U.S. history. Out-numbered by a far superior army force, his braves killed or wounded more than fifty U.S. soldiers in the course of the seven-day battle. At an investigative hearing in Washington, he did not hesitate to call the Indian Bureau a pack of liars and then, for good measure, bragged about killing the senior officer of the combined army command. The agent had tracked Jack to Rawlins, Wyoming, where Jack worked briefly as a teamster, and then in the spring of 1882 to the Shoshone's reservation on the Wind River. The bureau wanted Jack returned to Utah where his movements could be monitored. For if Jack and his band were not made to stay in Utah and kept out of Colorado, war would again be a certainty.[1] The army hunted down Jack and, instead of returning him to Utah, murdered him. The army had its revenge. The armed resistance of the Utes had ended.

It had taken the U.S. government almost thirty years to subdue the Utes and far longer to clear the continent of Indian tribes that stood in the way of the nation's Manifest Destiny. The purchase of the Louisiana Territory in 1803 from France had almost doubled the nation's size and moved its western borders from the Mississippi River to the Rocky Mountains—a massive expansion of the continental empire envisioned by President Thomas Jefferson. Echoing the calls from the pulpit, President John Quincy Adams soon thereafter proclaimed the "proper dominion" of the United States to be the entire North American continent. The "laws of nature" as "commanded by God the Almighty" dictated the westward expansion of the United States. We must, proclaimed Adams, subdue the earth, make it "blossom as the rose" and, referring to the western territory's Indian tribes, take on the added responsibility of raising "inferior peoples" to a higher level of civilization. In the 1820s, Senator Thomas Hart Benton of Missouri, a strong proponent of the idea of Manifest Destiny, added to Adams's territorial obligation his own racial imperative that only the white race had "received the divine command to subdue ... the continent."[2] If Manifest Destiny suggested inevitable progress for whites, it came to be a story of cultural destruction for Indians.

As white settlement moved across the continent, new western voices added some unique background music to the national chorus singing the praises of Manifest Destiny and its attendant benefits. William Gilpin, Colorado's first territorial governor, observed that as the nation subdued the continent and freed American Indians and other unspecified continental residents from their cultural "darkness," the nation would, in its Christian spirit, "shed a new and resplendent glory upon mankind and shed blessing around the world."[3]

It was a tall order for a nation so young but not without hubris.

On the receiving end of these Christian goals, the West's Indians gradually came to understand in the nineteenth century what the eastern tribes had learned from the British and American colonists in the seventeenth and eighteenth centuries. The white man's sense of entitlement to the American continent guaranteed to the Indian physical displacement, deadly diseases, and attempted genocide.

Armed with moral justification to fulfill its destiny and committed to the myth of its own virtue and innocence, the United States amassed additional western lands with both the annexation of Texas in 1845 and, a year later, the acquisition of the Oregon Territory from Great Britain. The final and critical piece of the trans-Mississippi West region quickly fell into place with the military victory over Mexico. In 1848, the United States took title to present-day Utah, Arizona, Nevada, the western portions of Colorado and New Mexico, and California—including the latter's valuable fifteen-hundred-mile Pacific coastline.

With the American continent finally under one flag, the nation quickly set out to "make the wilderness blossom." Aided by government subsidies for new canals, turnpikes, and railroads, settlers moved west to plow additional farmland and discover new mineral deposits. Not only would the nation's wealth increase but, with the spread of agriculture, democracy would flourish. Even the Great American Desert, earlier thought to be a worthless expanse of mountains and "unfruitful plains ... an uninhabited and dreary waste," was soon found to include rich minerals and fertile valleys.[4] Thousands of white settlers also discovered the presence of more than thirty distinct Indian tribes that did not wish to move from, or be disturbed on, their traditional homelands. The nation quickly recognized that it was far easier to overcome the West's physical obstacles than to conquer the region's human barrier—the Indians.

By the nineteenth century, the issue of race, of course, had confronted the United States for more than two centuries. When Grant entered the White House in 1869, the United States had only recently won a war generated by the issue of one race making slaves of another. Having freed blacks from slavery, however, the nation felt no compunction about taking land from Indians. Presidents before Grant, and the colonists before nationhood, had systematically eradicated or removed Indians from their homelands, usually into the more remote and isolated regions of the West.

Even Thomas Jefferson, the spokesman for individual liberties and virtuous government, failed to include Indians within his vision for an egalitarian society. These "merciless savages," he observed, had yet to learn the precepts of white "civilization," Jefferson's code word for farming. When and if Indians stopped being hunters and gatherers and learned to be cultivators of the earth, they could "incorporate with us." Assimilation, however, did not mean for Jefferson equality or citizenship for the Indian. They needed to be moved out of the way so as not to block the westward movement of Jefferson's hero, the white yeoman farmer—the conveyor of agriculture and democracy. Clearly for Jefferson these "merciless savages" possessed more land than they needed. To one Indian delegation, Jefferson said in 1802 that he wanted them to "cultivate the earth, to raise herds of useful animals and to spin and weave."[5] For if the Indians abandoned the hunt, raised domestic animals, and took to farming, they would more easily give up their excess land and make room for the yeoman Anglo-Saxon farmer.

Regardless of government policy, most Americans thought the "Indian problem" would take care of itself. Unwilling to accept and appreciate modern civilization, Indians would, as a matter of course, disappear and become extinct. They would either be decimated by disease (as occurred among eastern tribes earlier), commit racial suicide through intertribal warfare, or be killed off by whites. For Jefferson, however, the latter was neither a pleasant alternative nor a necessity. The newly acquired Louisiana Purchase provided ample space in which to place eastern tribes, under the protection of the army. The problem remained: how to get the Indians to give up their lands and move, either voluntarily or by force if necessary, to the territorial holding pens (now called "reservations") devised for them by whites?[6]

Jefferson's Indian policy became, in many ways, a model for subsequent presidents, particularly Andrew Jackson, well into the nineteenth century. The first step involved establishing an unequal trade relationship with Indian tribes. As the Indians became increasingly dependent upon Anglo trade—especially food, clothing, and weapons—Washington frequently interrupted the flow of goods in order to leverage the Indians' removal from their land. The invitation to visit with the president in Washington to witness firsthand his overwhelming military power was another ploy, coupled with gifts and bribes as means to achieving "peace"—the equivalent of a real estate transaction. A not-so-subtle hint of war accompanied the unequal negotiations.

The war threat carried its own scenario. As whites encroached on and attacked Indian lands, unimpeded by—and, indeed, encouraged by—government authorities, Washington had only to await the inevitable Indian retaliation. Such response gave them the perfect excuse to invade—or threaten to do so—in order to punish the "savages" and protect innocent white settlers. In such scenarios, the U.S. Army would prevail against the Indians and their primitive weaponry.[7] No longer would it be necessary to adopt the strategy of Lord Jeffrey Amherst, the commander of British forces in North America during the French and Indian War, whose officers distributed among their Indian foes "gifts" of handkerchiefs and blankets—infected with the deadly smallpox virus.[8]

Following Jefferson's Indian policy and to advance his own political career, President Andrew Jackson, the Tennessee frontiersman, began in 1830 the removal of 45,000 Indians from the southern frontier east of the Mississippi River to the newly created Indian Territory (present-day Oklahoma). Jackson claimed to be protecting the security of white settlers, while simultaneously preventing his loyal constituents from conducting genocide. Lewis Cass, whose Department of War was responsible for managing "the Indian problem," said Indians had no right to their lands, because God "intended the earth should be reclaimed from a state of nature and cultivated" and "the uncivilized tribes" had no option but to yield to civilized society.[9] By the end of Jackson's administration and with the concurrence of Congress, the United States had acquired roughly 100 million acres of Indian land, two-thirds of it east of the Mississippi.[10] And to ensure the Indians remained in place, the army began an intensive effort to build forts on the boundaries of Indian lands, which they used as trading posts, meeting places for treaty negotiations, depots for rations, and sallying points for punitive expeditions.

Indians, Washington believed, lacked any physical or cultural connection to a permanent home and, like migratory livestock connected to no particular piece of ground, they could be moved about the continent. A line was drawn approximately along the eastern edge of the Great Plains, and every tribe east of it would be removed to an allotment of land west of it. Within a decade of the Removal Act of 1830, eighty thousand Indians had been pushed to the trans-Mississippi West. The program to create a clear separation of the Indians from Anglo-Europeans, said one historical geographer, "entirely reshaped the human geography of the nation."[11]

Some Americans viewed the Indian through a very different set of lenses. One view as expressed by some eastern clergy and notable writers, in particular James Fenimore Cooper, pictured the Indian as the "noble savage," an innocent child of nature uncorrupted by the vices of civilized society—God's uncorrupted human—permanently "bathed in righteousness and free of oppression." He lived the simple life in harmony with nature and took from the earth only what he needed to survive and no more.[12] True, said mid-nineteenth-century scientists, but the Indian along with the Negro had been created an inferior creature, unenlightened, lazy, undisciplined, and capable of outbursts of hideous savagery.[13] Most scientists and theologians did admit, however, that the Indian possessed the mental capacity to forego his "primitive" ways, and once he did and learned the skills of agriculture, the Indian might be transformed from a hunter-gatherer to the "half-civilized state" of the Chinese. With further training in the arts and sciences, he could eventually attain the "civilized" state. However, the final "enlightened" (white European) status, where humans attained the greatest perfection, was beyond the Indian's capacity.[14]

In the early nineteenth century, as the United States moved toward an industrial society, nature (the home of Indians) needed to be conquered, not admired or romanticized as an abstract idea. Indians would have to be sacrificed. And with the nation's increasing demand for land and the attendant ruthless conquering of nature, Indians came to be viewed as an enemy. What better way to create an enemy than to demonize the Indian by stripping "noble" from the "savage"? "Few will see their extinction without regret," Francis Parkman wrote in 1852.[15] Indian-haters had only to add Darwin's scientific theory of evolution to their arsenal to prove the Indians' genetic inferiority. Did not the inferior "blood-thirsty savages" continue to commit atrocities against whites? Nothing should stand in the way of a superior race as it fulfilled its divinely ordained destiny.

In the West, the prevailing nineteenth-century racial attitudes translated into a strong rationale for the Indian's "extinction," or what we today call "ethnic cleansing." One group of western boosters in Cheyenne, Wyoming Territory, the Big Horn Association, announced in 1870:

> The rich and beautiful valleys of Wyoming are destined for the occupancy and sustenance of the Anglo-Saxon race. The wealth that for untold ages has lain hidden beneath the snow-capped summits of our mountains has been placed there by Providence to reward the brave spirits whose lot it is to compose the advance

guard of civilization. The Indians must stand aside or be overwhelmed by the ever advancing and ever increasing tide of immigration. The destiny of the aborigines is written in characters not to be mistaken. The same inscrutable Arbiter that decreed the downfall of Rome has pronounced the extinction upon the red men of America.[16]

The "doom of extinction" so confidently prophesied by scores of Anglo-Saxons reflected a racism so pervasive, so harsh, and ultimately so violent that it was the rare individual who raised his or her voice in the West to defend the Indians. Having defined Indians as inferior, Anglo-Saxon Americans used their power to enforce and make permanent their degraded status. Lowlier even than the lowly black, whom the constitution recognized as three-fifths of an individual for purposes of allocating representatives to Congress, Indians counted for nothing. As individuals they existed only as members of a tribe, and as tribes they remained wards of the nation. And when, after the Civil War, blacks were granted limited constitutional protection, Indians possessed fewer rights than former slaves. Personal prejudice and group intolerance had enlisted the overwhelming power of the state to expropriate their land and threaten their existence in much the same way similar forces combined to enslave blacks. Racism had triumphed, all in the name of God, natural law, and modern science.[17]

The history of the Utes is not much known in the nation or the West—including Colorado, New Mexico, and Utah, their traditional home. Small by comparison with other tribes, particularly the Plains tribes, they lived relatively undisturbed until white settlers and miners expanded into the heart of the Rocky Mountains after the Civil War. The Utes lived and hunted as separate bands, each with its own hierarchy of chiefs and sub-chiefs, though all sharing the same language (Uto-Aztecan language group). The Utes also possessed a keen sense of their tribal genetic purity and knowledge of each band's geographical boundaries. The individual bands traded with each other and often intermarried, but they remained in separate, distinct regions and, when necessary, fought their own battles against intruders—the Spanish, other tribes, and later the Americans.

Individual bands arranged themselves geographically within various protected river valleys, the location of their permanent winter homes. The adjacent mountains or high plateaus served as seasonal hunting grounds, always carefully guarded by each band as part of its territorial homeland.

The six Utah bands who, it is believed, had migrated into the Great Basin area from southern California and Arizona, probably in the tenth century, occupied all the major river drainages from Utah's Wasatch Mountains east to the Uintah basin along the Colorado border. In Colorado, it is thought the Utes had expanded from their Utah base around A.D. 1300. Different bands settled throughout the major river valleys of the Colorado Rockies as far north as Wyoming adjacent to the Shoshone, and east to the edge of the plains up against the Arapaho and Cheyenne. Generally referred to as the northern Utes, these two Ute bands took their names from the river drainages along which they lived. The Uncompahgres (meaning "running red water"), the largest of the bands with as many as 1,100 members, controlled the San Juan Mountains south to the Dolores River and the major river valleys flowing west 150 miles into eastern Utah.[18] The White River band, a combination of the Grand River and Yampa (the "root eaters") bands, had by the mid-nineteenth century united into a loosely confederated unit and located themselves in Colorado's northern Rockies, between the Yampa (Bear) River and the White River. Their hunting grounds extended west through the river valleys leading into northeastern Utah, east into North Park and Middle Park in Colorado, and north into the high plateau country of southern Wyoming. Other bands moved into southern Colorado from Utah, and possibly Arizona, along the rivers flowing out of the southern Rockies, and into northern New Mexico, settling close to the Navajo, Apache, and Pueblo Indians. The three Colorado bands, originally named by the Spanish for their own convenience and later Anglicized, included the Muache (the "cedar bark" people) and the Capote (the "blanket" or "cloak" people), who had spread along the Front Range of the Rockies, throughout the San Luis Valley and down the Rio Grande Valley into northern New Mexico. Farther to the west, toward the Utah border, the third southern band, the Weeminuche ("long time ago" people), controlled the Animas, Mancos, and La Plata River drainages that flowed south out of the Rockies into the San Juan River basin of northern New Mexico and Arizona. By the 1850s, the estimated total population of the northern and southern Utes in Colorado was thought to be 4,500 to 5,000.

Well into the nineteenth century, the Utes prospered as a hunter–gatherer tribe. They lived in both wickiups and hide-covered teepees, fashioning the conical-shaped wickiups out of lodgepole pines or large willows that they covered with boughs, branches, and juniper bark and often weatherproofed with mud or hides. The larger teepees consisted of lodgepole pines covered by six to ten elk hides, lined inside with cedar bark, with buffalo or bear robes covering the earth floor. Less mobile than the traditional teepee, wickiups tended to be more permanent structures and were used, in addition to rock caves and alcoves, as seasonal shelters when the Utes hunted away from their winter headquarters. In addition they built lean-tos, sweat lodges, and menstrual huts.

The tribe survived and sometimes thrived on a diet of fresh and dried meat, fish, wild roots, fruits, and vegetables. They stored fresh game by wrapping it in thick coatings of green grass, soaked in water, and hung from a tree. As the water evaporated, it kept the meat cool. Other meats were cut in long, thin slices and air-dried atop a tall tree, then jerked down ("jerked meat") to be cleaned and scraped. They snared rabbits, grouse, quail, and sage hen in fences made from sage brush and soap weed or in nets fabricated from tree and plant fibers. Buffalo, venison, elk, antelope, bear, mountain sheep, and wild turkey were stalked and ambushed on horseback or foot, assisted by dogs and often utilizing camouflaged hunting pits and blinds made from rock or brush. They tracked the more elusive elk on snowshoes and brought them down in deep snowdrifts with arrows or ropes made from sinew, rawhide, and hair. To drive and encircle game into strategic hunting locations, and to enhance forage for livestock and wild game, they set fires on open plateaus and mountainsides.

If necessary, they ate rattlesnakes and lizards, but avoided dogs, coyotes, wildcats, lions, wolves, and their revered horses. In the rivers and lakes, they used arrows, spears, weirs, and willow nets to catch native trout, and duck decoys to attract waterfowl. They supplemented their diet with wild currants and berries (fresh and dried) and fresh roots, piñon nuts, the tuber of the yampa plant (a wild carrot), and the blossoms and fruit of the yucca. The Utes also harvested wild potatoes and onions and ground up the seeds from pigweed, rice grass, and sunflowers, and captured grasshoppers, which they dried and pulverized into a mixture with berries. They traded with the southern bands for maize, and once they learned how to grow it in their cooler climes, it became a dietary staple. In times of shortages, the Utes survived on the inner bark from ponderosa pine, which provided them with a critical source of minerals and vitamins. The bark, combined with roots, served as an effective purgative and remedy for wounds and fevers.[19]

By Anglo standards, Indian medicine appeared primitive, if not sometimes cruel. John Wesley Powell, the famous explorer–geographer who had spent the winter with the White River Utes before descending the Colorado River in the spring of 1868, reported on their "barbaric medical practices." Powell reported that to rid the body of evil spirits, which the Utes believed was the cause of all illness, the medicine man and his assistants placed live coals on the sick person's flesh, fanning the coals until they raised blisters. The medicine man then jumped up and down on the patient's body, beat the patient with clubs, and with a stone knife carved crude incisions to drive out the evil spirits. In one elaborate treatment Powell witnessed in the teepee of a local chief, the medicine man "howled, chanted, blew smoke, sucked at the patient's heels, and appeared to extract the guilty spirit through the navel, carrying it outside and burying it in the ground." When Powell later dug up the offending spirit, he found it to be "nothing more than a fossil shell."[20]

The Utes' unique attire, their lodge furnishings, and their primitive weapons all reflected the natural environment in which they survived. Women fashioned clothing from the skins of buffalo, deer, elk, rabbit, coyote, badger, and, where available, beaver, otter, and muskrat. The men wore their hair in two braids with otter or weasel skins woven into the ends for decoration. Shaved hair indicated mourning. Small tattoos, made with porcupine quills or cactus thorns dipped in cedar leaf ashes, often marked their cheeks and foreheads to indicate, with a common design (usually an animal), their family clan. Both men and women wore necklaces of animal claws, bone beads, stones, and juniper seeds. Women decorated hides with bright colors available from plant dyes, animal blood, and nearby minerals. Clay pottery served for cooking, storing, and hauling water; squaw brush, willows, or hides were fashioned into baskets and mats; cups and ladles came from the horns of mountain sheep or buffalo; and bowls and platters were made from turtle shells or carved from abundant cottonwood and spruce. For their weapons, they cut four-foot bows from the branches of chokecherry or mountain mahogany and arrows from the hard wood of oak; chert stone provided the material for arrowheads, and the feathers of owls, hawks, and eagles gave guidance to their deadly aim; stone war clubs wrapped in rawhide, wooden spears, buffalo hide shields, and flint knives completed their arsenal. Their horses carried wooden saddles covered with rawhide, horsehair bridles and saddle blankets, and twisted rawhide mouth bits. Most of their weapons would be replaced later with metal spear tips, steel knives, and guns acquired from the Spanish and white trappers who hunted, usually with permission, in Ute territory, and later from the white settlers.[21]

The Utes, similar to all Indians, held deep respect for the powerful and creative acts of nature. All natural events in the universe—a sunrise, lightning and thunder, a blossoming tree—possessed for them inherent and important explanations. Anglos failed to understand and certainly did not believe this "savage" frame of reference. Ceremonies, including hunting, played an important role in the life of the Utes. An Indian hunted as much for its ritual importance as for a source of food. Animals, considered the equal of man, had come to the land as envoys from another world, carrying with them their own powerful and truth-telling myths. They provided Indians with sustenance to their lives and hence they were accorded great respect, if not reverence. In nature's world, a buffalo gave his life so that Utes might live and survive. To indiscriminately slaughter a buffalo (or any other animal) only for the sake of killing or for its hide or tongue was both a crime against nature and an act of massive disrespect.[22]

In the spring, when the bear emerged from his den, the Indians danced to give thanks to the Creator for allowing them to survive the winter. The Sun Dance served as a curing ritual for the performer to acquire and maintain good health for himself and his community. On both occasions, Indians of all ages participated in games: archery, ring spearing, foot races, wrestling, and shinny (similar to field hockey), played with curved wooden sticks and a buckskin ball stuffed with deer hair.

The Utes made no economic distinctions among individuals within a band since they owned almost all property in common. John Wesley Powell observed that the Indian "has no word signifying rich or poor in the ordinary sense— that is, having much or little property; but when an Indian says, 'I am rich,' he means, 'I have many friends,' or 'I am poor: I have but few.'"[23] The primary basis of authority was age rather than gender. They organized subsistence tasks around the extended, multigenerational family, where the elders guided tribal activities. In the family, women's views were given equal weight to men's, and in battle women played a critical role in gathering loot and attending to the wounded. Because they were the givers of life, women were honored and celebrated, though they did not participate in the important council decisions made by the male elders. Their skills at tanning, making clothes, preparing food, and repairing leather goods were recognized as vitally important tasks.[24]

The Utes, similar to other tribes, selected their chiefs and sub-chiefs for their demonstrated courage in the hunt and in battle. Leaders had to be smart, good talkers, and wise and pragmatic decision-makers. They were expected to know and decide where and when to hunt, with what tribe to ally and trade, and when to do battle. In addition, and of equal importance, a band selected its chief for his knowledge of its distinct history. The chief knew from memory the important myths and tales of his band, all passed down to him by former chiefs and elders. A band's cultural memory resided with its chief, the one who constantly taught and reminded his band, through word and action, the lessons of the past. These tales of past heroes and stories connecting the band to the natural world gave definition and purpose to their collective lives. As the final arbiter of internal and external disputes, a chief's decisions and authority were rarely questioned. At death, chiefs were buried in caves along-side their favorite horses, which would provide them with transportation for their afterlife.[25]

While some of the cultural history of the Utes has been described and documented, what is forgotten is the Utes' history of accommodation with the eighteenth-century Spanish settlers, a history that would reverberate a century later in the tribe's negotiating tactics with their American aggressors. When whites did appear in growing numbers, the Utes sought not immediate war but, at critical junctures, peaceful coexistence with the invaders. It is the warring tribes, such as the Sioux and others, who have generally captured the most attention and notoriety from historians, not those tribes, such as the Utes, who sought to avoid military engagement. In the end, however, the Utes resorted to warfare, not out of choice but as a last resort. The few government accounts in the nineteenth and twentieth century either explain away or eradi-cate the record of the Utes' painful experience. More recent studies fail to admit or even recognize in the Ute ordeal the American experiment at ethnic cleansing, i.e., the involuntary removal of an ethnic minority from a piece of territory it considers its common and historical home. The Ute removal was neither the nation's first attempt at removal nor its last, but it may stand as our most ambitious effort. And if genocide is the intentional killing off of all or part of a minority, the Utes, a tribe that stood stubbornly in the way of the nation's Manifest Destiny, became a major target for eradication. That the Utes persevered through the white efforts to eradicate them is testimony less to the Christian principles of their enemy than to the superb survival strategies, astonishing staying power, and immense courage of the tribe.[26]

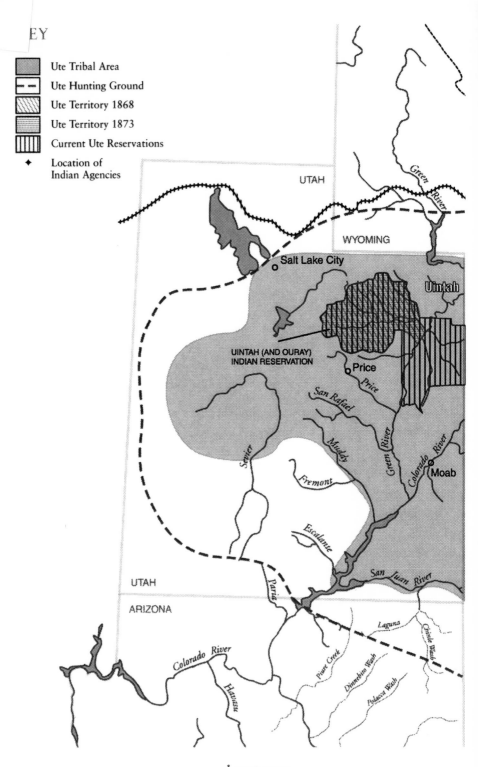

EY

Ute Tribal Area

Ute Hunting Ground

Ute Territory 1868

Ute Territory 1873

Current Ute Reservations

◆ Location of
Indian Agencies

UTAH

WYOMING

o Salt Lake City

Uintah

UINTAH (AND OURAY)
INDIAN RESERVATION

o Price

Price

San Rafael

Green River

Muddy

Colorado River

o Moab

Sevier

Fremont

Escalante

San Juan River

UTAH

ARIZONA

Paria

Laguna

Chinle Wash

Colorado River

Havasu

Piute Creek

Dinnebito Wash

Polacca Wash

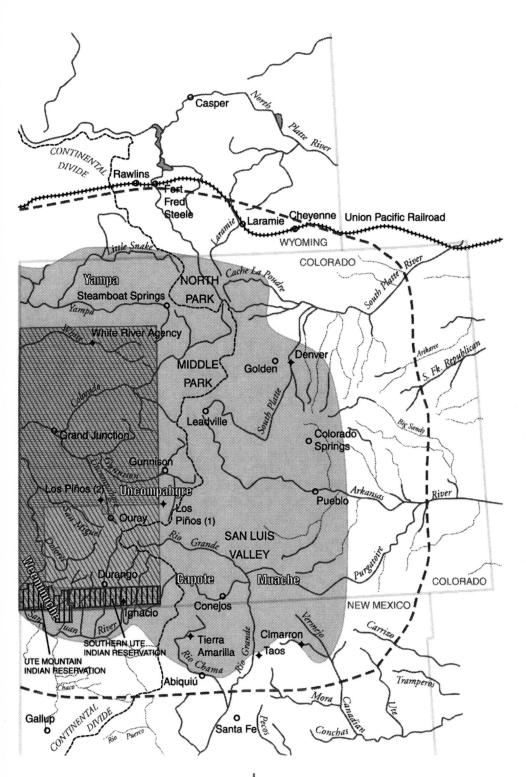

ONE | *From Spanish Neighbors to an American Reservation*

In the spring of 1874 near the present-day town of Chama, New Mexico, a northbound wagon train attracted the attention of Ignacio, the headman of the Utes' Weeminuche band. Encumbered by baggage and trailing livestock, the train appeared to Ignacio larger than normal, not the usual four or five New Mexican traders headed for the mines in southern Colorado, but rather an entourage of families moving north, looking to settle along New Mexico's San Juan River. Only the year before, the Utes had ceded the immediate area to the United States. But Ignacio's band continued to live in the area where, for a decade, it had collected annuity disbursements at the Tierra Amarilla Agency. They watched closely and with suspicion other Indians, Spaniards, or Anglos moving in on their traditional lands.

As Ignacio and his men rode up on the New Mexicans, their leader, Francisco Manzanares, moved forward on his horse to engage the Ute leader. They immediately greeted each other warmly, conversing at length in Ute. Manzanares had been born a Ute, captured by a New Mexican as a young boy, and then taken into the José Antonio Manzanares home as a servant. He had worked off his indenture, and now with his New Mexican wife, two sons, and two daughters accompanied by their New Mexican husbands, he and his family sought a new home for themselves. José Salome Jaquez rode forward to join the two men and also extended greetings in Ute. The Utes had raised him in captivity until his parents found the means to ransom him. Manzanares's

Spanish sons-in-law, who also spoke Ute, joined the discussion. Ignacio welcomed the party to his region in much the same manner other Utes had, on occasion, encouraged New Mexicans to settle Colorado's San Juan Valley over the past few decades. The men, women, and children gathered around Manzanares's wagons near the New Mexico–Colorado border represented a racial, ethnic, and linguistic mix that, if not the norm, was by no means an exception within the southwest border country of the mid-eighteenth century.[1]

The complex cultural fabric of Indians and Spaniards along the ragged edges of colonial New Mexico has always defied a simple description. The Spaniards had, in their two-century presence in the southwest borderland, murdered, captured, and enslaved thousands of Indians. Later they had also baptized, married into, and traded with these same tribes. The Utes, like other tribes, survived the Spaniards' sporadic efforts to subjugate them and by 1750, both groups had arranged, out of necessity, a peaceful coexistence, encouraged and sustained by a flourishing trade.

Spain's primary imperial interests lay elsewhere, not along the dry and barren borderland of northern New Mexico. Yes, Indians' souls needed to be saved, but not at the expense of more important missionary and commercial interests in fertile California. Not wanting to add to their military and administrative burdens by sending soldiers into the isolated interior of the Southwest, Spain never controlled the region they claimed for the crown. The successful revolt of the Pueblo Indians against the Spaniards in 1680 had taught Spain a bloody lesson about colonial control in the New World. Better a policy of "paternal pacification" than to continue their earlier efforts at military subjugation.[2] Maintaining trade with the Indians, if properly conducted and directed, would supply a profitable stream of Indian captives to the mines and rancheros of Mexico and valuable animal hides to the Spanish settlements at Santa Fe and Taos.

Spanish New Mexicans much admired the tanned hides of deer, elk, sheep, antelope, and buffalo the Utes offered for trade. In return for their hides and dried meat, the Utes received horses, weapons, grains, cloth, metal tools and knives, ammunition (ten charges for a sheepskin), tobacco, awls, and decorative beads from the Spanish. A good, stout, young pony traded for twenty *antas blancas*, the highly prized, soft, bleached-white elk hides brought to the trade fairs in northern New Mexico. Among the southern Utes, a captured Indian child from the Navajo or the Paiute tribe commanded from the Spaniards a premium—at least two ponies and maybe a spotting glass. From an occasional white trapper, they'd receive flour, cloth, tobacco, weapons, and ammunition in return for hides and safe guidance through their mountainous territory.

The most-prized trade items, however, continued to be slaves. Long before the arrival of the Spaniards, the Utes had captured and traded slaves with other neighboring tribes. The arrival of the Europeans only increased the demand, raised the stakes, and spread the practice widely among the Southwest's Indian tribes. The Utes immediately recognized the added trade value of young Indian boys and girls, whom they and the Spanish captured from the Pueblo and Apache. The Spaniards sent the young Indian boys to mines or to farms as field hands or herders. Young Indian maidens commanded the highest premium as domestic servants at the fledging trade fairs in Santa Fe, Taos, Abiquiú, and Picuris.

By the 1750s, a flourishing trade in slaves and other commodities had grown between the Spaniards and their Ute neighbors to the north. The Utes remained wary, however, about the territorial inroads of the Spanish. The Indians conducted minor forays into a few, small isolated outposts that had sprung up in the northern reaches of the territory, particularly north of the San Juan River. But the local Spanish authorities retaliated not with calls for war, but with overtures for peace. They wanted their trade, but more importantly, they needed Ute warriors as allies against more warlike tribes.

Surrounded as they were by a sea of hostile tribes, the Spanish never exercised strong economic or political control in New Mexico. Spain's continued demand for slaves and their encroachment on Indian lands only served to provoke Indian hostility. Even after the Spanish outlawed the slave trade, they could not enforce the prohibition in their American colonies. To maintain a semblance of peace with the tribes, therefore, the Spanish attempted, with some success, to play one tribe off against another by entering into trade agreements with individual tribes in order to prevent the threat of a multitribal alliance against the European interlopers. Unwilling to commit a large military force or an adequate administrative system, they allowed different economic and political arrangements in the New World than they allowed in other colonies. Left very much to their own devices in a different and distant environment, the Spanish colonists along the northern border of New Spain learned to live with the Indians.[3]

Indian servant girls adopted by Manuel and Ruperta Archuleta. Maria Dolores Archuleta and Juana Neporena Archuleta are pictured at their first communion at Our Lady of Guadalupe Church in Conejos, Colorado, circa 1874. (Courtesy of Ilene and Leonel Silva)

With a renewed Spanish alliance, the Utes received increasing gifts of food, horses, and weapons from the authorities in Santa Fe, and welcomed temporary visits of Spanish traders and occasional explorers into their communities. And to prevent troublesome traders from stirring up trouble with the Utes, the Spanish were careful to license only those merchants whom they thought "honest." They also banned (but could not enforce) Spanish settlers from moving north into Ute territory in search of good farm and pastureland and, if fortunate, a rich mine or two. The Utes, for their part, generally accepted the presence of these peaceful reconnoitering parties and horse traders, though on some occasions it remained unclear to the Utes if the visitors wished to trade or to plunder.

In some cases, the Spaniards only wanted to explore for the rumored gold and silver thought to be embedded in the mountains to the north. To this end, Tomas Vélez Cachupin, governor of New Mexico, sent Juan Maria de Rivera on an expedition into present-day Colorado. In 1765 Rivera traveled north into the heart of Colorado's Rocky Mountains, where he noticed the "outcropping of metallic ore," an enticement for future expeditions into Ute territory.[4] He exchanged gifts with the Utes, whom he reported to be peaceful and helpful, and encouraged their presence at the popular New Mexico trade fairs.

Nine years later, on the eve of the American Revolution, two Spanish missionaries, Fray Francisco Atanasio Domínguez and Fray Silvestre Vélez de Escalante, left Santa Fe in search of not gold, but a direct land route to another small Spanish settlement at Monterey in Alta California. With primitive maps, and encumbered by a pack train, the small expedition slowly made its way north up the headwaters of the Rio Grande before heading west into the center of Ute territory within the Colorado plateau country. Two Ute guides directed them to a safe crossing through the high and formidable Rockies, while the two Franciscans mapped and reported for a wider audience their territorial discoveries. In the midst of the mountains, the missionaries took the opportunity to preach to a group of curious Utes about how they should accept Christianity, thereby saving their souls. The friars promised the heathens they would arrange upon their return for the Utes "a mode of living" to prepare them for baptism. The friars also exhorted the Indians to take no more than one wife. It is doubtful the Utes totally comprehended the lectures about Christian salvation and polygamy, but they did not hesitate to accept some glass beads and lame horses in return for dried buffalo meat and healthy

From Spanish Neighbors to an American Reservation

ponies. The friars never reached their destination but, with Ute assistance, they returned safely to New Mexico.[5] The few Spanish expeditions through Ute territory later in the century were designed not to reconnoiter the region for conquest, but rather to encourage Colorado Ute bands to trade into New Mexico.

During the later years of Spanish presence in the Southwest, the growing trade with the Indians encouraged many Utes, Navajo, Apache, and Comanche to integrate peacefully within the outlying Hispanic towns north of Santa Fe. On one occasion, for example, a band of more than four hundred Utes from northern Colorado spent a peaceful winter near Abiquiú and took up temporary residence in the small town. Some Indians, brought into the New Mexico trade fairs as captives by other Indians or by the Spanish, either for ransom or sale, voluntarily gave up or were stripped of their tribal affiliation and lived in Spanish homes. Often Indian slaves managed to work off their indenture over ten to twenty years to gain their independence. And not infrequently, Spanish residents adopted or redeemed Indians, mostly children, from their captors, and brought them into their homes. Some were baptized and almost all took on the name of their new Spanish family. With their newly adopted surnames, their status as *genizaros* allowed the Indians to integrate slowly and successfully into the social fabric and political culture of northern New Mexico. By the mid-eighteenth century in Abiquiú, *genizaros* made up approximately 10 to 15 percent of the town's population, and in Taos they composed 35 percent of all families.[6] The Spanish allowed them to marry up and out of bondage, testify in court, and own property, though the *genizaros* were among the lowest on the social scale. Those who intermarried with the Spanish residents gained additional rights and status as a *vecino*, or neighbor and citizen. In Abiquiú, *genizaros* shared in community functions and mixed freely with the Spanish and those of mixed Spanish-Indian ancestry *(mestizos)*. The Spanish, and later the Mexican authorities, encouraged *genizaros* to settle new frontier communities north of Santa Fe and Taos, outposts that would serve as the first line of defense against hostile tribes or the perceived military threat from French or British territories to the north. The acquisition of property by *genizaros* and *mestizos* blurred the distinctions of class and caste in towns of the Chama Valley and farther north into Colorado's San Luis Valley, where individual southern Utes received from the Spanish and, later, the Mexicans small land grants.[7]

The Utes continued to trade with Mexico after it won its independence from Spain in 1821. In a major effort to generate critical income, the new nation promoted the growing commercial trade with the United States flowing from Saint Louis down the Santa Fe Trail while also encouraging Utes to increase their trade traffic to the northern New Mexico trade fairs. But the Mexicans, with fewer military resources and even weaker administrative control than Spain, could not prevent a new wave of Hispano settlers from moving north into Ute territory. Almost bankrupt, the new nation abruptly halted all gifts to the Utes and, as a consequence, the old Spanish–Ute alliance unraveled, and sporadic violence broke out in the northern province.

From their homeland in Colorado, the Utes, now well mounted and armed, attacked the growing trade traffic along the Santa Fe Trail and renewed their raids against the Navajo and the Pueblo. Recognizing their new military strength and with tactics learned from the Spanish, the well-mounted Utes in the 1820s and 1830s expanded their sphere of influence into central Utah and northern Arizona where, for the first time, they raided the Paiute, capturing slaves, and, on occasion, continued west into California to steal horses. Despite the feeble efforts of the Mexican and American authorities to halt the slave trade, the Utes continued the practice as much for profit as to replenish their own warrior ranks, depleted by increasing disease and intermittent warfare.[8]

What becomes clear throughout the eighteenth and well into the first half of the nineteenth century is that the Utes experienced recurring cycles of violent conflict that came with European colonialism. They armed themselves, as did other Southwest tribes that came in contact with the Spanish, and by so doing became a feared military force of their own. The powerful Utes, usually portrayed as passive and peaceful, survived and, most important of all, adapted to their Spanish and Mexican neighbors.

Neighboring tribes recognized the Utes as skilled warriors and superb horsemen. When they believed their home territory or property (particularly their highly regarded horses) to be threatened by the Spanish, the Mexicans, other Indian tribes, and later the Americans, the Utes did not hesitate to go on the warpath. Like most tribes, they avoided standing battles, preferring a more fluid and mobile engagement from horseback. Because their existing lands contained most, if not all, of their food requirements, the Utes had little reason to expand their homeland or hunting grounds against the Spanish or other tribes. Prior to the mid-nineteenth century, only a few foreigners had

From Spanish Neighbors to an American Reservation

made any serious attempt to settle permanently on Ute lands, and those who did settled at the invitation of the Utes.

The Utes inherited two important legacies from the Spanish and the Mexicans. One almost eliminated the tribe entirely; the other totally transformed the Utes' mobility and hence their geographical expansion over the western landscape.

In their initial contact with the Spanish, the Utes, like other tribes, were introduced to European diseases—smallpox, typhus, influenza, diphtheria, syphilis, mumps, and measles—against which Indians possessed no natural immunities. We have no clear estimate of the Ute population before Spanish contact, but some anthropologists suggest that North American Indian tribes in the first 130 years of contact with Europeans lost as much as 95 percent of their early-seventeenth-century population. Other scholars ("the low counters") estimate a smaller loss, generally around 50 percent. Using the more conservative estimate, four thousand Utes may very well have died from disease between 1600 and the mid-eighteenth century, a death rate far lower than experienced by the Plains Indians—the Sioux, Blackfoot, Assiniboine, Cheyenne, Arapaho, Mandan, Gros Ventres, Arikara, and Pawnee—most of whom had more contact with Europeans than did the Utes. It is likely that another five thousand to six thousand Utes lost their lives in the next hundred years, during which their contact with Europeans significantly increased.[9]

Living isolated in the inaccessible Rocky Mountains, the northern Ute bands had, until the mid-nineteenth century, insulated themselves from the ravaging diseases. But the southern Ute bands, with their increasing contact with Europeans, experienced the full brunt of the smallpox epidemics that devastated southern Colorado and the valleys and plains of northern New Mexico. The Americans, with their increased contacts with the Utes, only added to the germ pool—sometimes, the Utes charged, intentionally.

In 1854, Kit Carson reported that on the way to Ute hunting grounds to the north, smallpox broke out among a Ute band, taking the life of its leader. The Utes believed Colorado's superintendent of Indian affairs to be responsible for the disease when he collected infected blankets and had them distributed among the band. In retaliation, the Utes joined the Apache in a raid on a Hispano community in the San Luis Valley, where they "murdered citizens as they be found."[10]

The second Spanish legacy, the horse, allowed the Utes, and soon all western Indian tribes, to expand their hunting grounds beyond the boundaries previously limited by foot travel and what the Indians, aided by the dog travois, could carry with them. From the horse, and armed with new weapons, they would hunt buffalo in greater numbers, move more quickly into and out of new hunting grounds and, with the horse as barter, trade to an advantage with other tribes. Throughout the seventeenth and eighteenth centuries, the horse allowed the Utes to expand their food base and population. Utes also extended their geographical universe in the Southwest—from the Wasatch Mountains in central Utah all the way to the eastern plains in Colorado, and north from the Colorado Rockies into the southern portions of Wyoming.

If the horse aided the mobility of the Utes, so too did it allow other mounted tribes to move more easily into the rich hunting grounds of the Utes. The tribes of the Great Plains, under increasing competition from white hunters for the valuable buffalo, began to invade the rich hunting grounds of the Utes along the Front Range of the Rockies. The Arapaho, Cheyenne, Kiowa, and Comanche all coveted Ute ground, particularly the San Luis Valley, as much for its large buffalo herd as for the additional grassland required for their expanding horse population. The northern Ute bands, more often than not outnumbered by the larger Plains tribes, retreated to the isolated safety of the Rockies, while the southern bands sought help from Hispano settlers. Accordingly, the Utes invited a few select Hispano farmers to settle in their valley to assist with the protection of the rich valley and to help them supplement their food source.[11]

Traditional Ute culture, isolated as it was in its Utah/Colorado/New Mexico homeland, soon came under attack—first from the south, and later from all directions. When Mexico, after its independence from Spain in 1821 encouraged immigration to Ute hunting grounds in Colorado's San Luis Valley, the univited Hispano settlers met immediate resistance. By the 1840s, two southern Ute bands, the Capote and Muache, quickly recognized the difference between traders and settlers and promptly raided the latter. The Mexicans could do nothing to protect either their citizens or the Utes. And when, with the annexation of Texas in 1845 and the victory over Mexico, the Indian-white violence took on a new importance, the United States took possession of all of Mexico's land in North America (California, Arizona, Utah, Nevada, southwest Wyoming, and the western portions of Colorado and New Mexico) and jurisdiction over all the Indians living therein.

The United States's military defeat of Mexico in 1848, and particularly the Treaty of Guadalupe–Hidalgo that ended it, radically changed the world of the Utes. Before the war they experienced no formal relationship with the United States. For more than 200 years, the Utes had forged a generally peaceful relationship with the Spanish and Mexicans, not one of equality but at least one of mutual accommodation. But with the treaty, which placed the Utes under U.S. authority, suddenly and without warning, the climate of accommodation disappeared. The United States looked upon all Indians, including the *genizaros*, not as human beings with certain inalienable rights, but as "savages" to be controlled and, in some instances, eliminated.

The Utes realized almost immediately that they had lost the rights, and often the title, to lands allowed, granted, and "inviolably respected" by the Spanish and later by Mexicans. They would also soon discover that under U.S. jurisdiction their new landlord would demonstrate little eagerness for their assimilation but rather considerable enthusiasm for their eradication.

To protect themselves, many Utes gave themselves Spanish surnames in the hope that their Indian identity might be camouflaged from their new land-lord. They hoped and believed that their old relationship with the Hispanos might be carried forth and possibly even replicated throughout the new south-west territories now claimed by the United States. Soon after the United States took possession of New Mexico and Washington began to impose its dominance over both the Indians and the Hispanos, one experienced Hispano Indian agent reminded his superiors in Washington that "these Indians have been very good friends of the people of New Mexico for many years, and if any tribe deserves the favor of the Indian Department, it is the Utes ... "[12]

Before a peace treaty could be signed with Mexico, the United States actively encouraged white settlement onto traditional Ute land. With an increasing number of Hispanos and Anglos moving into the San Luis Valley, the Utes escalated their raids. The United States responded in 1849 by calling for a parley with the Utes at Abiquiú, New Mexico, to arrange a "friendship" treaty with the Ute southern bands that occupied lands in the Chama and Rio Grande Valleys in northern New Mexico.

Mistakenly, as it turned out, Washington believed the Treaty of 1849 set a precedent with all the Utes (though the treaty was only agreed to by the Muache band), where the band agreed to: (1) recognize U.S. sovereignty and jurisdiction (and its laws) over their area; (2) allow U.S. military posts and agencies on Ute land (unspecified); (3) live within boundaries (yet to be determined and agreed upon) and "not to depart from their accustomed homes or localities unless specifically permitted by an agent;" (4) "cultivate the soil, and pursue such other industrial pursuits"; (5) "abstain ... from all depredations; to cease [their] roving and rambling habits ... [and] confine themselves strictly to the limits which may be assigned them"; and finally (6) "to support themselves by their own industry, aided and directed ... by the wisdom, justice and humanity of the American people." With its attempts to alter Ute behavior, the United States tried to accomplish by the law what it hoped to avoid by force.[13]

To both "protect" and placate the Utes, the federal government established in 1852 a new Indian agency at Taos, where they appointed Kit Carson, a friend of the Utes, as agent. Other agencies were opened at Abiquiú, Tierra Amarilla, and Cimarron. Responding to calls from Anglo and Hispano settlers and unable to confine southern Utes to a reservation, the United States built its first military outpost in Colorado—Fort Massachusetts (later relocated and named Fort Garland in 1858)—in the center of the southern Ute territory. The post signaled to the Indians that they now lived under a new landlord that would monitor the Utes' "rambling habits," while providing protection to its new American citizens—a legal category that excluded Indians.[14] The U.S. military presence, however, only increased the Utes' anger. They retaliated with raids on the new settlements, killing some settlers at Fort Pueblo, Colorado, on Christmas Day 1854, and capturing livestock in what became known as the Ute War of 1854–55. When the U.S. Army sent six companies of troops against the Indians, killing forty warriors at present-day Salida, the Utes sued for peace and the short war ended in a standoff. In response, the handful of American citizens in the area increased their calls for the federal government to remove the Utes or, at a minimum, to somehow keep them confined on a reservation and at peace. But before action could be taken, the Civil War intervened; at the same time, the Indian Bureau in Washington had to focus on the Mormons in Utah and their continuing conflict with the Ute bands in that territory.

The arrival of the Mormons into Utah in the 1840s put the "Saints" in direct conflict with the Utes, who historically had occupied most of the central and eastern portions of the new territory (23.5 million acres or 45 percent of Utah). By 1850, more than ten thousand of Brigham Young's followers had migrated across the country from Illinois and Missouri into Utah's Great Basin. They immediately occupied and usurped much of the Utes' traditional grazing and hunting grounds. In 1851, the Indian superintendent in Utah reported, "The Indians have been driven from their lands and their hunting grounds destroyed without compensation, wherefore they are in many instances reduced to a state of suffering, bordering on starvation. In this situation some of the most daring and desperate [Utes] approach the settlements and demand compensation for their lands, where upon the slightest pretexts, they are shot down or driven to the mountains."[15]

As the Ute attacks increased in frequency and bloodshed, Young, the ex-officio superintendent of Indian affairs in Utah by virtue of his appointment as territorial governor, directed the Indians to move out of the way and, with all due speed, sell their land to the United States. Young, an imperious man not given to ethnic or religious tolerance in his semi-autonomous kingdom, informed the Indians, "If you do not sell your land to the Government [,] they will take it, whether you are willing to sell it or not. ... and it won't make a particle of difference whether you say they may have the land or not, because we [Mormons] will increase, and we shall occupy this valley and the next and the next, and so on until we occupy" the entire region.[16] Move the Utes to eastern Utah, Young demanded of Washington. President James Buchanan, however, was in no mood to placate unreformed polygamists who, in some cases, owned Indian slaves. Instead, he ordered a detachment of three thousand federal troops to Utah to establish federal authority in the semi-independent Mormon State of Deseret. Young and his followers persisted in their demands for the removal of the Utes to an area of 2 million acres in eastern Utah, which he had surveyed specifically for the Utes. It was, Young reported, "one vast 'contiguity of waste,' and measurably valueless, except for nomadic purposes, hunting grounds for Indians, and to hold the world together."[17] Lincoln acceded to Young's request and signed an executive order in 1861 authorizing the establishment of the Uintah Reservation. By 1867, virtually all the Ute bands in Utah had moved, under threat of Mormon violence, to their new reservation home. But as one legal scholar noted, "it was a homeland of force and deceit as well as soil."[18]

The displacement of the western Ute bands, a repetition of the Americans' two-hundred-year-old habit of removing Indians from their homelands, reflected the stereotypical values shared by the vast majority of Americans.

All Indians were alike and, as tribes, they possessed no real distinctive history. And because they were primitive, nomadic hunters and gatherers, they held no attachment to the soil. Because Anglo-Americans believed Indians "so loosely bound were they to any locality," one historical geographer asserted, "they could be shifted about without serious disruption; pleas about the pain of leaving their homelands and the bones of their forefathers could be dismissed as a ploy to impede negotiations." After all, had not European Americans, for generations, moved to lands an ocean away?[19] Further, American law had redefined the Indians' status. Rather than being recognized as sovereign and independent nations, their status had changed, by virtue of a U.S. Supreme Court decision during the administration of President Andrew Jackson, to that of "domestic dependent nations." The federal government, the Indians' guardian, would henceforth treat Indian tribes as wards.

The same "savage" stereotypes and legal precedents came into play beginning in 1858 with the arrival of gold seekers and the settlers who followed them into the front range of the Rockies in and around Denver. A year later, fifty thousand people responded to the call of "Pike Peak or Bust." By 1861, the newly created Territory of Colorado counted more than thirty-five thousand residents, excluding Indians. The miners quickly spread south into Colorado's Arkansas valley and west into the heart of Ute country. At first the Utes were more stunned than aggressive, but as the intruders spread over more and more territory, the Utes responded with swift raiding parties against the small, unprotected mining camps. In response, the *Rocky Mountain News* editorialized that the Indians "are a dissolute vagabondish, brutal and ungrateful race and ought to be wiped from the face of the earth."[20]

With calls for protective action, Washington attempted once again to consolidate the Utes into one definable area. The Indian Bureau believed the Utes had agreed to such an arrangement in 1849, but President Lincoln, with the army engaged in the Civil War, was unwilling to enforce the provision. At the urging of Colorado's territorial politicians, Lincoln called for another meeting with the Utes in 1863 to see if they could be enticed to sell all the land east of the Continental Divide and confine themselves to a reservation. But the chief of the Capote band whose lands, in particular the San Luis Valley, would be most affected by the proposed sale, refused to accompany Colorado's territorial governor, Governor John Evans. Ouray, chief of the Uncompahgre band, did attend to give some credence to the proceedings, but he carried no authority from the other bands to represent their interests. To ease the negotiations and to empower Ouray, Lincoln appointed Ouray chief of all Utes, with the grand title of head chief of the Confederated Ute Nation of Colorado. The Utes were neither confederated, a political term they failed to understand, nor a unified nation. Nor did the autonomous Ute bands, particularly the southern Utes, recognize Ouray as their chief. To the consternation of two southern bands in attendance, Ouray consented to a defined reservation for the Utes, an agreement that particularly angered the Capotes and Muaches. Ouray's concession to Washington would forever poison his relationship with the southern Utes.

The U.S. Senate ratified the treaty in 1864, but Congress failed to appropriate funds for the promised annuities. Lincoln, not wishing to antagonize the Utes by forcing the issue of a reservation and possibly pushing them into a military alliance with Colorado secessionists, did not press the issue. After the Civil War, the U.S. government continued to face the problem of how to confine the six geographically dispersed bands of Colorado Utes without resorting to force, a measure thought to be an unattractive alternative for the smaller post-war army.

The problem was compounded by a bloody massacre suffered by two other Indian tribes on Colorado's eastern plains. In 1864 the Colorado militia conducted a vicious and unprovoked attack on five hundred Southern Cheyenne and about fifty Arapaho at Sand Creek, about seventy miles east of Denver. Colorado's second governor, John Evans, had set the stage for the massacre, announcing in 1863 that citizens needed "to kill and destroy" all Indians "wherever they may be found." No peace offers were to be accepted and no distinctions were made between "hostiles" and "friendlies." All Indians, Evans insisted, must return to their reservation on the Arkansas River or face the consequences. On a cold November morning, Col. John M. Chivington, who in his civilian life served as a Methodist minister in Denver, launched a surprise attack with more than seven hundred cavalry troops (a mixture of territorial militia and federalized volunteers)—"The Bloody Third"—against the Cheyenne and Arapaho encampment at Sand Creek, where the Indians believed civilian authorities had promised them a safe winter refuge from the military.

From atop his teepee, Cheyenne Chief Black Kettle flew the American flag to signify his friendship with the United States but the flag failed to prevent one of the most bloody and brutal Indian battles of the nineteenth century. Chivington's army, under orders to take no prisoners, slaughtered more than

ATTENTION!
INDIAN
FIGHTERS

Having been authorized by the Governor to raise a Company of 100 day

U. S. VOL CAVALRY!

For immediate service against hostile Indians. I call upon all who wish to engage in such service to call at my office and enroll their names immediately.

Pay and Rations the same as other U. S. Volunteer Cavalry.

Parties furnishing their own horses will receive 40c per day, and rations for the same, while in the service.

The Company will also be entitled to all horses and other plunder taken from the Indians.

Office first door East of Recorder's Office.

HAL SAYR.

Central City, Aug. 13, '64.

Colonel John Chivington's broadside for recruits to the Third Colorado Volunteer Cavalry Regiment, the unit responsible for the 1864 Sand Creek Massacre. (Courtesy of the Colorado Historical Society, #F-42630)

one hundred men, women, and children. When a cavalry officer reminded Chivington that the Cheyenne had been given assurances of safety by Colorado and federal authorities, Chivington responded, "I have come to kill Indians, and believe it is right and honorable to use any means under God's heaven to kill Indians!"[21]

In the process of the short battle, the Colorado troops "desecrated the bodies of the Indian wounded and dead, bashing in the skulls of babies, mutilating and cutting up corpses, and taking scalps, skin, and genital organs as souvenirs."[22] One militia major, a lawyer in civilian life admitted at the congressional investigation following the massacre, "I think and earnestly believe the Indians to be an obstacle to civilization, and should be exterminated."[23]

Chivington returned to a hero's welcome in Denver. For the white population of miners and merchants, regardless of their faith or the lack thereof, Chivington had performed a necessary and heroic service. Citizens flocked to a local theater and city saloons to witness the proud display of Indian scalps hoisted atop bloody sabers by Chivington's troops and the assortment of rings and earrings still attached to fingers and ears. To the horror of the local residents, the troops also exhibited the scalps of white settlers found in the teepees at Sand Creek. Indians in Denver and throughout the Territory of Colorado could not fail to acknowledge the threat to their lives and their traditional homeland. The massacre and its aftermath served as a graphic lesson to Indians throughout the West, and particularly in Colorado, that the promises and "peaceful" intentions of the territory's white authorities could not be trusted.

The young "Queen City of the Plains" had always demonstrated little tolerance for Indians despite the fact that it had only recently lobbied Washington successfully for the establishment of an Indian agency.[24] The agency for the "Denver Utes," as they were called, served as something of a pork-barrel project, a source of federal dollars for a town desperately short of capital. It also served to help feed and clothe the town's two hundred or so Indians (mostly Utes), a measure, the town fathers believed, that would help prevent the Indians from begging on city streets or raiding neighboring farms. Also, some even believed that "Indian parents might become wise unto salvation, and gradually be brought under the refining influences of civilization."[25]

That Denver thought of itself as something of a center of "civilization" said as much about the town's pretentiousness as it did about its hatred and fear of its Indian residents. Most citizens agreed with the city's leading newspaper editor, William Vickers, that the Indians were "disagreeable neighbors" and should be removed as soon as possible. Even a few of the city's Indian missionaries, who might have been expected to possess some sympathy for the objects of their Christian teaching, had difficulty defending the presence of "savages" in Denver. One Congregational missionary wrote toward the end of the Civil War, "We who have seen and live [with] Indians know that, as a whole, they are a filthy, lazy, treacherous, revengeful race of vagabonds. ... The grace of God may indeed be sufficient for them; and yet, humanely speaking, there seems to be no better destiny in store for them, than to fade away before the white man."[26]

Denver, along with the rest of the nation after the Civil War, insisted to Washington that all western tribes, wherever they existed, needed to be pacified, controlled and, if necessary, eradicated if white civilization, with its commercial development, was to expand into and across the western territories. Railroads required safe passage, farmers and miners demanded protection, and all wanted land—land promised by the Homestead Act of 1862 and advertised widely by numerous land companies. Territorial, state, and national politicians could no longer dismiss the calls to end, once and for all, the "Indian problem."

To this end, Washington began serious peace initiatives in 1868 with a number of Indian nations. The Indian Bureau arranged a treaty with the Sioux on the northern plains guaranteeing to them a reservation in the western half of the Dakota Territory. The government had only recently removed the Arapaho and Southern Cheyenne to the Indian Territory by the Treaty of Medicine Lodge. For the Utes, the only remaining tribe in Colorado, the Indian Bureau ordered its agents in Colorado to bring Ute tribal leaders to Washington yet again in order to negotiate, if possible, a treaty that would permanently confine all the Utes within a defined reservation.

Again the problem arose: how to entice Ute chiefs to Washington when they did not wish to negotiate with the "Great White Father." The southern Utes said, as they had in 1864, that they wanted no part of any U.S. effort to sell, trade, or be removed from their lands. The northern Utes, especially the Uncompahgres under Chief Ouray's leadership, were more amenable to Washington's overtures, in part because of Ouray's recognition of the overwhelming military power of his American adversary.

Ouray had both knowledge of and connection with the southern Utes. He was born in 1833 near Taos, the son of a Jicarilla Apache father who had been captured by the Utes and later raised by a Hispano family (Guero) and also an Uncompahgre (Tabeguache) mother, a *genizaro*. It is believed he was educated by Catholic friars in Taos; possibly baptized in the Catholic church; and, after his mother died and his father left to join his deceased wife's family in the Uncompahgre Valley, raised by a Spanish family within the Hispano/*genizaro* culture of Abiquiú. Ouray spoke Spanish fluently, some English, witnessed firsthand the conflict between the Utes, the Mexicans, and the Spanish, but also no doubt recognized the possibilities of Indian coexistence with Hispanos. Would it not be possible, Ouray may have wondered, for such a relationship to be extended and expanded for Utes to live peacefully among Americans? Ouray, on the other hand, also witnessed the impressive firepower of the U.S. Army under Gen. Stephen W. Kearny's command as it passed through Taos and Santa Fe in 1846 on its way to do battle in the Mexican War. Ouray also knew of the Americans' deadly retaliatory raid against the Taos Pueblo Indians for the death of New Mexican Territorial Governor Charles Bent and was keenly aware of the Sand Creek Massacre four years before his trip to Washington.

The short, barrel-chested, muscular young chief had gained his position among the Uncompahgres after moving to the valley to join his father in the 1840s. Following his father's lead, Ouray gained membership in the band and within a short time earned a reputation on hunting trips to the eastern plains as a superb horseman, brave fighter, and effective leader against the Cheyenne and the Arapaho. It was on one of these trips that the Arapaho captured his young son and only child, Paron, by his first wife, Black Mare. In 1859, Ouray remarried a daughter of a Kiowa Apache, Chipeta. The Utes had raised her too after an Indian raiding party had killed her parents. By 1864, Ouray had emerged as the leader of the Utes' largest band. He traveled and hunted throughout the Rockies, into the valleys of the Rio Grande, San Juan, Dolores, Uncompahgre, Gunnison, White, Yampa, Arkansas, and Cache la Poudre Rivers—an area only somewhat smaller than New England. He came to know many of the chiefs and sub-chiefs from other bands, particularly the White River band from which his sister had married a medicine man. The Indian agents in Colorado knew Ouray personally and recognized the respect accorded him by the northern bands and even a few of the southern leaders. And so, with his elevated status and considerable language skills (Ute, Spanish, English, and Apache), Ouray went to Washington at the president's invitation as the chief spokesman and negotiator for all seven of the Ute bands.

Presidents had long believed that by bringing Indian leaders to Washington the chiefs would be so impressed by Washington's buildings, monuments, the "Great White Father's" house, and his attending army that they would be discouraged from entering into any warlike scheme. "In this respect inviting Indian delegations to Washington has been found to be one of the most effective peace measures which the Government has ever adopted," one observer noted. In addition, the government would be saved thousands of dollars and hundreds of lives if it averted war.[27]

The tactic of inviting chiefs to Washington, however, was only part of a larger reservation policy put in place prior to the Civil War. For as more and more whites moved in on lands traditionally occupied by Indians, the incidence of Indian–white conflict increased. To avoid these conflicts, which often escalated into small but expensive wars and loss of life, the federal government, from the time of Jefferson, believed it necessary to remove and relocate Indians to protected enclaves safe from trespass by whites. The Indians' removal would also have the added benefit (for many it was the primary purpose) of freeing up lands desired by white settlers—farmers, miners, and land speculators. Allowing the Indians to continue to occupy their lands while awaiting their demise from starvation, disease, or both was not a considered option, if for no other reason than the Indian penchant for survival would only further delay their inevitable fate.

Of course, they could be eradicated, as some suggested, but as the nation began to decommission its army after the Civil War, Washington had little appetite for continued bloodshed. The Utes could be removed to the Indian Territory to join with the Cherokee and other tribes, an attractive cost-saving alternative for the government. In such a scenario, the United States would be spared the cost of additional agents. It would also allow for more effective military control. But, as the Ute Indian agents reported to Washington, the Indians would resist and fight. And to remove them to another political jurisdiction would only raise the ire of other state and territorial governors who did not wish their lands to be the dumping ground for unwanted "savages."

Best then, according to the politicians, to let them remain in Colorado on lands not presently wanted by whites, distant from white settlements, and separated from and uncontaminated by the corrupting influence of white contact. On their own reservation, the theory went, the Utes would be protected and,

Chief Ouray of the Uncompahgre Utes,
appointed chief of the Ute tribe by the
U.S. government in 1868.
(Courtesy of the Denver Public Library,
Western History Collection, #WHJ-10328)

if at all possible, partially supported and trained in agricultural techniques by Indian agents until they might become self-sufficient and assimilated into American society. Efforts toward assimilation would, as we shall see, create a whole new set of debates within both the ranks of government and the American public and eventually lead to a major military conflict.

The liberal editor of the *Springfield Republican* (Massachusetts), Samuel Bowles, summed up what most Anglo-Americans thought of Indians and why they felt their present lands needed to be appropriated and the Indians moved and confined to reservations. White Americans possessed a superior claim to the continent's land because God gifted the earth to whites "for its improvement and development." They must say to the Indian, Bowles wrote, "you are our ward, our child, the victim of our destiny, ours to displace, ours to protect. We want your hunting grounds to dig gold from, to raise grain on, and you must MOVE on." On the designated reservations, you must stay put. When, in the future, "the march of our empire demands this reservation of yours, we will assign you another; but so long as we choose, this is your home, your prison, your playground." If the Indians failed to agree to this arrangement peacefully, the United States had every right to use all necessary force to enforce their removal. Indians needed to be treated, the editor advised his readers, "just as a father would treat an ignorant, undeveloped child." Whatever training was given the Indian would be wasted, for in the end, he would die off regardless of what efforts were made on his behalf. The world for the Indian was now changed, Bowles declared, and "it is his destiny to die; we cannot continue [to protect his] ... barbaric life, [and] he cannot mount to that of civilization; the mongrel marriage of the two that he embraces and must submit to is killing him—and all we can do is to smooth and make decent the pathway to his grave."[28] The respected editor had defined for his readers a popular nineteenth-century form of euthanasia.

In such a racial climate, the United States brought to Washington in the winter of 1868 Colorado Territorial Governor Alexander Hunt; Kit Carson, who had advised the Utes in the Treaty of 1863–64; ten Ute chiefs and sub-chiefs representing five Colorado Ute bands (the Uncompahgre, Muache, Capote, Weeminuche, and Yampa [or White River]); and the Uintah from Utah. As for how to overcome the underrepresentation of the southern bands, President Andrew Johnson followed Lincoln's lead and once again appointed Ouray chief of all the Utes. The southern Utes complained, but Ouray represented the largest band and held the respect of the other northern bands, which together controlled the largest area of Ute territory. Washington officials believed Ouray could, through the force of his reputation, bring the smaller and relatively weak southern bands into a negotiated settlement.

By the Treaty of 1868, the Utes agreed to confine themselves within the western portion of Colorado. They surrendered in eastern Colorado, southern Wyoming, and northern New Mexico well over half of their traditional hunting grounds. In return, the U.S. government guaranteed to the Utes approximately one-third of the landmass of present-day Colorado (16,500,000 acres) or about 4,500 acres for each man, woman, and child. The reservation included all lands in Colorado west of longitude 107 degrees, a line extending from a point eighty miles south of the Wyoming border down through the Rocky Mountains, passing just west of present-day Steamboat Springs, Aspen, Gunnison, and on down through Pagosa Springs to the New Mexico border. The treaty guaranteed the Utes "absolute and undisturbed use" of the reservation lands (except for government officials and their agents), a prohibition against whites (e.g., miners) "to pass over, settle upon, or reside in" the reservation. Two new agencies were to be created, one on the White River to serve the northern bands, and another near Gunnison at Los Piños (on the "River of the Pines") for Ouray's Uncompahgre band and the three southern bands. Any white accused of crimes against the Utes would be tried, after investigation, in the U.S. court system; Utes charged with violations of U.S. laws were to be tried before the Indian Bureau. To encourage Utes to give up their hunting culture and help move them toward assimilation, heads of families would receive title to 160 acres, as well as farm implements, seeds, and instruction if they declared willingness to farm. To assist in this endeavor, the new agencies were to receive teachers, millers, farmers, and blacksmiths, and each lodge was to receive "a gentle American cow" (as opposed to the wild Texas or Mexican variety) and five head of sheep. The United States agreed to build a school-house for every thirty children who might be "induced" to attend instruction. In addition, the Utes were to receive $30,000 per year in clothing, blankets, and "other articles of utility (annuities)," and another $30,000 a year in food (rations specified as beef, mutton, wheat, flour, beans, and potatoes) until such time as they "shall be found to be capable of sustaining themselves." All appropriations for annuities and rations would be divided proportionately among the seven Ute bands. If a chief or any band made war, that chief forfeited

Brunot Treaty (1873) delegation to Washington.
Chipeta and Chief Ouray are in the front row,
flanked by two Uncompahgre sub-chiefs. Second row
(left to right), agents Uriah Curtis, J. B. Thompson,
General Charles Adams, and interpreter Otto Mears.
Back row, Sub-chief Washington, Susan (Ouray's sister),
Sub-chief Johnson, and two unidentified sub-chiefs.
(Courtesy of the Denver Public Library,
Western History Collection, #X-30679)

From Spanish Neighbors to
an American Reservation

his position and all rights to any benefits, but all "peaceful" Utes would maintain their benefits. In return, the Utes relinquished all land claims in the United States, including the northwest corner of Colorado, the entire San Luis Valley, and all lands in New Mexico. The relinquishment diminished the Utes' traditional homeland by about half, to a total of approximately 16.5 million acres.

The maps, claiming to be accurate, and the treaty's descriptive narrative with its latitudinal and longitudinal descriptions, were incomprehensible to the Utes and to most whites when translated to actual boundaries on the ground. The eastern boundary, for example, did not follow any distinctive geographical pattern such as a mountain range or river and led to considerable misunderstanding. The Utes had been led to believe that the new north–south boundary in Colorado followed along the axis of the Continental Divide and that everything west of that line fell within the confines of the reservation. In fact, the boundary line was well west of the divide and took from the Indians their critical hunting grounds in Middle and North Parks and the Yampa Valley, lands already settled by whites. Because of the inaccurate maps, one of the two new agencies, Los Piños in the central Rockies, was sited off the reservation and required the southern Utes to travel over a hundred fifty miles into unfamiliar and mountainous territory for their annuities and rations.

Through the summer and into the fall of 1868, government agents met with the various bands to secure additional signatures of chiefs and sub-chiefs required to agree to the treaty. However, the southern Utes remained distrustful of Ouray, a half-blood Ute. He had no authority, despite his designation by Washington as the head chief, to speak for all the Utes. They so distrusted him that they refused to accept Ouray as an interpreter and requested, and received, one of their own choosing.[29]

Ouray, however, more than any of the other Ute leaders, recognized that the tribe would be safer on a protected reservation, as promised in the treaty, than it would by having to fight a well-armed U.S. Army to protect its traditional lands. If Ouray and his band had no land to lose in the bargain (unlike all other bands), he had, at a minimum, prevented inevitable bloodshed in the short run. To gain the support of the other bands, Ouray and Kit Carson assured the other Ute leaders that the treaty guaranteed to the Utes "forever" a secure homeland, an area of rich valleys and ample game, protected from white incursion and settlement. To assist in the process of collecting signatures for the treaty's approval, a provision was inserted in the treaty at the last hour gifting to Ouray $1,000 a year for life as an inducement to him to use his influence with the other band leaders to gain their signatures. By late autumn of 1868, forty-seven chiefs and sub-chiefs, representing all bands, had signed. But among the southern Utes, they remained bitterly divided and resentful of Ouray's role in agreeing to abandon much of the southern Ute territory.[30]

By ultimately agreeing to the relinquishment, Ouray's standing with the southern bands would forever be compromised. When southern bands learned of the specific treaty provision handing over the San Luis Valley to the United States, the southern leaders verbally attacked the reputation and motives of the Uncompahgre leader. Ouray defended himself by suggesting that the Utes had no alternative. It was "such an agreement as the buffalo makes with the hunter when his hide is pierced by arrows," Ouray explained. "All he can do is lie down and cease every attempt at resistance."[31] But if Ouray's response suggested to white leaders and his fellow tribesmen a passive and powerless chief, he was, in fact, an astute and assertive leader who realistically recognized the benefits of a treaty over the inevitability of a war.

The majority of the Utes, particularly the northern bands who resided within the heart of the Rockies, probably thought themselves protected, if not by the treaty, then certainly by geography. The major overland trails skirted the northern and southern flanks of the new reservation so as to avoid the heart of the Rockies. The Union Pacific Railroad, under construction and wanting to avoid the mountains, had reached into southern Wyoming, but well north of the reservation. By 1868, the United States had secured a political union at great cost but had not yet fulfilled its Manifest Destiny as a continental nation. Within two years, Colorado's growing white population came to view the 16.5 million-acre Ute Reservation not as part of the "Great American Desert," but as land, rich in natural resources, "too valuable" for occupation by a small group of "roaming savages."

TWO | *"Conquer by Kindness"*

The provisions of the Treaty of 1868 with the Utes reflected both the older U.S. Indian policy of placing Indians within ethnic enclaves free from trespass by whites, and a new emphasis on training and educating the Indians for "civilization and ultimate citizenship." Reformers believed that once the Utes had learned the virtues of industry and hard work and the "arts of agriculture," they would then possess the mental tools to become self-sufficient farmers. Transformed from hunters and gatherers into agriculturalists, the Indians would no longer need to roam at will off the reservation, bothering and scaring whites in settlements. Everything the Utes needed for their short-term survival and their eventual secular salvation was present on the reservation: food, clothing, teachers, tools, seeds, and farming equipment—all supplied to them by a paternalistic government. Finally, once the Indians became self-sufficient farmers, the government, reeling from Civil War debt, would be relieved of this additional financial burden.

Those who believed in the possibility of the Indians' conversion—a powerful group of church leaders, newspaper editors, writers, and philanthropists—came out of the abolitionist wing of the Republican Party. Some, such as William Lloyd Garrison, Rev. Henry Ward Beecher, Wendell Phillips, and the authors John Greenleaf Whittier and Harriet Beecher Stowe, considered themselves social radicals. Their ranks also included church and lay groups such as the Society of Friends, The Universal Peace Society, Union League Club of

New York, the Women's National Indian Association, and the New England Indian Rights Society.

The reformers recognized that the Indians must accept white civilization, flee before it, or perish. A new way of life must be devised for the Indian, based, one historian noted, "on the values of an idealized middle-class, nineteenth-century Easterners—law abiding, morally Christian, and politically democratic."[1] They maintained the government must halt its destructive policy against the Indians who, as innocent victims, suffered from the dishonesty of the government and its cronies—private land speculators, government contractors, and agents. Because the reformers believed God had "made man of one blood," Indians, similar to blacks, were brothers and sisters to whites, endowed with the virtues of loyalty, integrity, and bravery, and therefore capable of cultural and material advancement.

For the reformers, reservations would serve as the appropriate educational training ground for the Indians' advancement. In these holding pens, the "savages," in a controlled environment, "may be taught a better way of life ... and be made to understand and appreciate the comforts and benefits of a Christian civilization, and thus be prepared ... to assume the duties and privileges of civilization."[2] To this end, the Indians had to be schooled in the virtues of individual ownership and initiative, a strong work ethic, and guidance in American law and conversion to Christianity. Most importantly, the Indian had to be educated in the manual arts, particularly those related to agriculture. And to speed the process of transforming the Indians from hunters and gatherers to self-sufficient farmers, the reformers pressed for the destruction of the Indians' basic food source, the buffalo. Once dependent upon the government for food, the Indians would have no choice but to give up their hunter-gatherer existence and gradually learn agricultural skills. "The Indian will never be reclaimed," one reformer preached, "till he ceases to be a communist."[3]

In the eyes of the reformers, Indians lacked the values embedded in the Protestant Ethic: they had to be taught to think and act like whites. One Indian reformer, Merrill E. Gates, the president of Amherst College, believed that if an Indian owned a parcel of land, for example, he would become more ambitious and hence self-sufficient. "To bring [the Indian] out of savagery into citizenship we must make the Indian more intelligently selfish before we can make him unselfishly intelligent. We need to *awaken in him wants*. In his dull savagery he must be touched by the wings of the divine angel of discontent. ...

Discontent with the teepee and starving rations ... is needed to get the Indian out of the blanket and into trousers—and trousers with a pocket ... that aches to be filled with dollars. ...!"[4] To fill these pockets, reformers planned to provide Indians with proper instruction in a healthy, progressive, and Christian environment. By transforming Indians into Jeffersonian, self-sufficient yeoman farmers, the reformers also hoped their efforts would alter white attitudes. Once reformed, whites would accept Indians, not necessarily as equal citizens with voting rights, but as adolescents on a path toward assimilation.

But beneath all their proclamations about the need for the "savages" to become farmers, the reformers' actions belied their Christian rhetoric. By attempting to destroy tribal culture with their paternalistic policies, the reformers forced upon their wards a life they did not want with methods they did not understand. That the Indians reacted sometimes with violence, the reformers would not admit; and if violence was recognized, they tended to excuse it because Indians "were more sinned against than sinning."[5] Few reformers would ever admit, of course, that much of the violence could be explained by their beloved reservation system in which they wished to confine Indians.

In the West, however, few residents believed the Indian either capable or deserving of reform. For westerners, who referred to reformers as the "eastern sentimentalists," any effort to train and educate the "savages" was a waste of time and money. The continuing settlement of the West meant the slow elimination of Indians' hunting grounds and hence their food supply; besides, the Indians were thought mentally incapable of civilized behavior. If kept on their reservation by the army and allowed to live out their pastoral lives, the Indians would slowly, and inevitably, starve to death.

The more bellicose westerners, however, called for an immediate military solution to the Indian "problem." Forget the useless philanthropic efforts by easterners, who failed to understand the Indians' barbaric nature. As for relying on the Indian Bureau to protect whites against Indian attacks, it was as corrupt and incompetent a bureaucracy as it was useless and expensive. One newspaper in the heart of Colorado's mining district editorialized, "That war to the knife is the only way of avenging the many depredations that are daily being committed on the border ... we of the West, who live in Indian country, are the best judges of what is slaughter and useless bloodshed."[6] Further, went the refrain of the hard-line westerners, all Indians caught off the reservation should be escorted by military force back to their homeland. If they refused to return, then they should be exterminated. Colorado's territorial governor, Edward McCook, suggested that if the eastern philanthropists were so committed to raising the Indians to a "higher standard of civilization," maybe instead of isolating them on reservations, "these untutored tribes [should settle] in the vicinity of, say, Boston, where they would be thrown in contact with what is claimed to be the most 'civilized' community on the continent."[7]

The army found itself caught between those westerners who wanted the Indians eliminated and those Eastern reformers who wished to guide the Indian toward assimilation. Gen. of the Army William T. Sherman, who privately despised the "Indian Lovers," nevertheless understood, as did Grant, that these reform forces could not simply be dismissed out of hand. While he feared the army might be hindered in its operations by the reformers' allies in the Indian Bureau, Sherman's strategy remained one of caution and patience. He believed that because of their inferior nature and the hostility of whites, the Indians were doomed to die. But in the meantime, the army must monitor their movements from nearby military posts so as to keep the "savages" on their reservations, isolated from whites, and at a safe distance from the "roads of commerce." Also, Sherman noted, the army must remain on the alert for any excuse to "destroy the hostile Indians in detail as opportunity affords." Let the Indian Bureau do their day-to-day job on the reservations. In the meantime, the military had to be prepared to fight the Indian when and where necessary. The more immediate matter, for which Sherman asked Grant for clarification, was to "clearly define the duties of civil and military agents of government so that we won't be quarreling all the time as to whose business it is to look after them."[8]

But as his army found itself increasingly involved in Indian skirmishes and battles, and as its reputation suffered (particularly after Custer's defeat in 1876), Sherman lost all patience with the reformers and came to resent their meddling in military affairs. He believed that his army was up against a savage hunter-warrior culture, which could not be civilized or "rescued from destruction." Eventually all Indians, said the army's ranking general, would "have to be killed or be maintained as a species of paupers" because their "attempts at cultivation are simply ridiculous."[9] Sherman complained to Grant somewhat disingenuously, "There are two classes of people, one demanding the utter extinction of the Indians, and the other full of love for their conversion to civilization and Christianity. Unfortunately the army stands between and gets

"THE UTES MUST GO!"

the cuff from both sides."[10] Best for the army, said Sherman, to encourage and guard the new western railroads, and the "battle of civilization with barbarism" would be won.[11]

Sherman recognized the limits of his army to engage in major battles against strong well-armed tribes, either singularly or in alliance with each other. Immediately after the Civil War until 1871, Congress cut the army's size by about half when they slashed the military appropriations and mandated demobilization measures. Southern Democrats wished to shrink the size of the federal government's military occupation force in the South, while other military critics wished to halt the progression of army officers into politics.

Despite a smaller budget, Congress continued to expect the army to protect new rail lines, and the settlers who followed them, into the western territories. Frontier army units maintained approximately one hundred posts, forts, camps, or cantonments, all of which suffered supply problems and severe manpower shortages. Most cavalry units reported vacancies of anywhere from 30 to 80 percent. Reliable horses, sufficient ammunition, and new weapons were in short supply. Officers and noncommissioned officers aged without promotion, and throughout the ranks low pay accounted for poor morale. In addition, when soldiers did receive their pay, often delayed by up to six months due to congressional politics, they received paper currency, which they then had to convert into specie at a discount. To fill the depleted personnel ranks, frequently caused by a desertion rate of more than 25 percent, the army was forced to recruit more and more from the ranks of foreign-born Americans— predominately the Irish. The *New York Sun* characterized army recruits as "bummers, loafers, and foreign paupers."[12]

President Grant, always sympathetic to the difficult Indian mission faced by Sherman's army, also recognized that white settlers on the frontier caused as many, if not more, problems on the frontier than did Indians. "I do not believe," Grant wrote to a friend in the West, "our Creator ever placed the different races on this earth with a view to having the strong exert all his energies in exterminating the weaker."[13] The major impediment to peace with the Indians, thought Grant, rested with the quality of the Indian agents. He wished to rid the Indian Bureau of unqualified agents—including numerous congressional political appointees—who came under constant attack from the eastern press for their well-deserved reputation for harsh treatment toward the Indians. To pacify his political critics among the reform element of the Republican

Party, Grant initiated his Indian "Peace Policy." The army would be kept in readiness, but in the background, ready when called upon to keep whites off the reservations and Indians on them.

Grant, at the instigation of the Quakers, instituted a novel policy to break the political patronage system favored by congressmen. The president asked the Society of Friends to nominate Indian agents as a way to improve the quality of agents. The experiment with the Quakers proved such a success that the president invited other interested Christian sects to nominate additional Indian agents. The Unitarians arranged with the Indian Bureau, for example, to look after the northern Utes while the Evangelical Lutherans selected the southern Utes. Some close observers of Grant, however, questioned the sincerity of Grant's reform, contending that his "Peace Policy" was generated more by politics than any genuine concern for Indians. Grant, his critics pointed out, did not hesitate to appoint ex-military officers, some of whom he knew personally from the Civil War, to agencies where he expected trouble, particularly among the Indian tribes on the northern plains. Congress, fearful of losing its traditional patronage when it came to selecting Indian agents, tried time and again to undermine the president's reform appointments. Sherman, in his *Memoirs*, reported the rationale behind Grant's counter plan. The president, said Sherman, told a group of angry congressmen, "Gentlemen, you have defeated [for lack of appropriations] my plan of Indian management; but you shall not succeed in *your* purpose, for I will divide these appointments up among the religious churches, with which you dare not contend."[14]

In another concession to the "eastern sentimentalists," the president urged Congress to create a Board of Indian Commissioners, a watchdog group of twelve eminent philanthropists, to oversee the operation of the Interior Department's Indian Bureau and make recommendations regarding Indian policy. In its first report to the President, the commission suggested that the United States should inaugurate a "hitherto untried policy of endeavoring to conquer by kindness."[15]

"Kindness" only extended, however, to those "good" Indians, those such as the Cherokee, Choctaw, Chickasaw, and Creek, who engaged in agriculture and attended white-run schools to learn useful trades. The "bad" Indians— those "wild" ones who "lived by the chase" and who demonstrated little interest in "the pursuits of civilized life" or the education of their children— had to be watched constantly until they were civilized. To those "good" Indians would be sent ministers who, by definition, qualified as agents. For the "wild" Plains Indians—Cheyenne, Kiowa, Comanche, Apache, Sioux, Crow, and Arapaho—best to appoint former military officers, who by training possessed a nose for trouble and the skills to end it. Because the Indian Bureau thought the Utes "savage" yet peaceful, agents nominated by the Unitarians stood an equal chance of appointment alongside ex-military officers.

Once appointed, an agent took his orders from the Indian Bureau, which approved all major expenditures and any deviation from policy. An agent's responsibilities varied little from one agency or tribe to the next. The first and most important job, collectively, for all agents, was to keep peace in almost half of the entire nation. To insure that their Indian wards remained at peace with the Great White Father in Washington, agents were required to distribute food rations and clothing on a timely and equitable basis and to look after their general health; if the Indians had any specific complaints about the quantity or quality of the rations and annuities, they directed their grievances through the agent who, if he so chose, passed on their complaints with his own recommendation to the Indian Bureau. Frequent requests for additional rations often received little attention in Washington, given the budgetary restriction imposed on the Indian Bureau by Congress. A Ute agent in New Mexico complained to Washington, after repeated requests for additional rations, of not having the means to care properly for his Indians. "I regret that I am cursed and overrun by a daily increasing throng of filthy, lousy, naked, and starving Indians crying for food themselves and their little ones, [and I am] without the authority or the ability to alleviate their suffering. I regret that I am compelled to submit to such torture [and make a martyr of myself] simply because the Department has not sufficient confidence in my integrity and judgment."[16]

As government representatives, agents also were charged with protecting Indians against unauthorized whites coming onto the reservation and, in addition, investigating white complaints of Indian depredations off the reservation. The former responsibility came with no power of enforcement. The agent could report such incursions to the Indian Bureau, along with a request for army assistance if serious, while he awaited the always-slow response. The army, however, could not move against any Indians unless requested to do so by the secretary of interior. Agents spent an inordinate amount of time off the reservation investigating charges of Indian thefts and murders. More often than not, the events proved to be crimes committed by whites but blamed on the Indians.[17]

The agent also supervised other agency workers—white farmers, millers, blacksmiths, and teachers—all government employees responsible for providing the Indians with instruction. Most agents had no access to medical doctors or to medicine. The occasional doctor who served at an agency received $1,200, a salary not designed to attract the best of the profession. Married agents were encouraged to take their families to the reservation, where a spouse might serve as a teacher and supplement the agent's $1,500 annual income. But because of the meager salaries, the tenure of agents and workers tended to be short—usually about two years—and finding qualified replacements was a constant distraction to the agent and the bureau. One well-respected agent with the Sioux complained that he "was expected and required to keep his wards at peace, feed and cloth them in health, see that they received proper medical attention while sick, encourage them in habits of industry, especially farming and cattle-raising, prepare all sorts of accounts for ... [the Indian] bureau, and in ... moments of leisure instruct the aborigines in the Catechism and Testament." Raise salaries to "a standard that the position will be an inducement for first-class men to consider," the agent suggested, "and there will not be so much trouble in getting an honest administration ... "[18]

Agents gained over the years a well-deserved reputation for corruption. They often engaged in profitable arrangements with contractors to receive kickbacks in cash or supplies intended for the Indians. The most common practice was for an agent to inflate the number of Indians under his charge and order food and supplies accordingly. The surplus items would be sold or traded off the reservation or used as a payoff to an Indian for a favor, such as a bundle of hides. In 1865, one agent for the southern Utes, Lafayette Head, personally profited by accepting ransom money from non-Ute Indians in return for handing over Indian servants enslaved in the homes of Spanish settlers in Conejos and Costilla. Head was exposed for "fraud and dishonesty," but his reputation was not so tarnished as to prevent his election to the office of Lieutenant Governor in Colorado some years later.[19] Suppliers and contractors, sometimes with the connivance of agents, swindled the government with over-charges and providing the Indians with poor quality food and supplies. A military officer at the Los Piños Ute Agency noted that on one visit he "found quite a number of Indian agents, interpreters and lobbyists, contractors, etc.

all eager in the prosecution of their individual schemes." He noted the presence of an agent from an English company who wanted to lease or buy the Ute reservation.[20]

Agents also came under criticism from white settlers immediately outside of the reservations. Desiring to see the Indians removed and reservation land opened for settlement, settlers often complained to Washington about agents who became too supportive of their wards or who tried to close down the settlers' illicit trade with the Indians—usually guns, ammunition, and liquor. The usual accusations received in Washington were that the agent suffered from alcohol (a "broken down minister"), that he did not understand the Indians, or that he was too naive or too old for the job. "What we need are Westerners, not eastern ministers," said the *Laramie Times*, agents "who will act on behalf of what whites want in the West." The "eastern philanthropists" seem not to understand "that western men are the bitter enemies of the Indians."[21]

Regardless of the background or training of agents, they found it impossible to control whites entering and, in many cases, settling upon the reservations. On the Ute reservation, almost immediately after the signing of the Treaty of 1868, miners discovered rich deposits of gold and silver in the heart of the San Juan Mountains. To the Utes, digging into the earth by miners violated the Indians' respect for the land they revered. The shacks of the miners and their mine tailings dotted the mountainsides in and around the present towns of Silverton, Ouray, Lake City, and Rico along the Uncompahgre, Gunnison, and Animas Rivers and into the high country. The agent at Los Piños wrote to Washington to say he had no way to halt the flow of miners into the San Juans, nor could he convince them to leave. Indian Agent J. N. Trask wrote to the miners, telling them to "quit the reservation forthwith" or face prosecution. They neither moved nor faced legal action. One recipient of the agent's letter replied that he had met Chief Ouray, exchanged gifts with him in the mining district, and said the Indian leader had made no complaint about the presence of miners—a doubtful claim. Since the Utes did not wish to see them leave, the miner wrote back to the agent, it would require a great many "broken down preachers [agents] and carpetbaggers [other government officials] to dispossess us of our property."[22]

Ouray complained to the agent, but received neither a sympathetic ear nor any encouragement about measures he or the government might take to expel the miners. The Uncompahgre chief and his sub-chiefs immediately set off for Washington to express their displeasure to the Indian Bureau, reminding the government it had a treaty obligation to halt the migration and expel the miners. Grant, at Ouray's urging, sent a poorly trained and undermanned army detachment from eastern Colorado to the San Juan Mountains to remove the miners. Hindered by burdensome wagon trains traveling over steep, unfamiliar mountain passes, the troops arrived to find little forage for their exhausted horses and a crowd of angry and armed miners ready to defend their new home and investment.

Local and state politicians came to the defense of the miners settled in the San Juans. The Colorado legislature sent a plea to the president asking for the government to take possession of the San Juans. Newspapers across the territory supported the request and called for the Utes' removal from Colorado altogether. The *Boulder News* said that if the Utes refused to sell and remove themselves peacefully, the mining area should be settled "by force of arms."[23] The *Denver Tribune* exploded in anger at the army's attempt to remove the miners. How could the government support "a few straight-haired vagabonds against the property rights of a brave, energetic, intelligent class of white men"? In concluding its defense of the seven hundred "hearty pioneers," the paper said they were being "prodded out of the country by American bayonets in order that a small band of nomads can idly roam over 20 million acres of hunting ground." It was "an atrocity that no other government on the face of the earth but our own would be guilty of committing."[24] In a letter to the secretary of interior the San Juan Miners' Cooperative Union complained: "For three years we have occupied this country, unmolested; we have developed a greater wealth of mineral than has ever been seen upon this continent in so small a compass. Most of us have all our worldly possessions now invested in the country and to force us from it would be doing us an injustice and wrong."[25] The army detachment recognized that they had a fight on their hands, not against Indians but against whites, and with orders from Grant, the troops departed quietly for their barracks at Fort Garland.

Grant immediately appointed a special commission, headed by Felix Brunot, the chairman of the board of the Indian Commission, a steel magnate from Pittsburgh, friend and associate of Andrew Carnegie and founder of the American Church Missionary Society, to negotiate a purchase of the San Juans from the Utes. They met with Ouray, who continued to ask, Why can't Washington abide by the former treaty and expel the trespassing miners? Is the government not strong enough to enforce it? "We do not want to sell a foot of our land—this is the opinion of all. The government is obligated by its treaty [1868] to [protect] our people, and that is what we want. For some time we have seen whites coming in on our lands; we have not done anything ourselves [to stop the inflow], but we have waited for the government to fulfill its treaty." Further, Ouray argued that if they sold the land, they would have the white man living close to their own lodges, bothering their livestock, and trespassing on their land once again.[26]

In an attempt to placate the miners and their representatives, Ouray offered to let them enter the region during the summer months, work the mines, and then leave via agreed-upon roads. Ouray told the Brunot delegation that "the whites can go take the gold and [then] come out again." No permanent homes, he declared. Impossible, said the commissioners: too difficult to police and a surveying nightmare.[27] Instead the government countered by offering to purchase the entire San Juan district and pay the Utes $25,000 in additional annuities above and beyond those guaranteed under the Treaty of 1868. Ouray pointed out to the commissioners that some of the rations given to his band under the former treaty included rot and mold; the "gentle" cattle proved so wild they vanished into the Rocky Mountains; and too many agents were either corrupt or unfriendly, and usually both. Commissioner Brunot promised amends, but Ouray stood his ground. One commissioner, Edward McCook, the territorial governor and friend of President Grant's who was once charged with making fraudulent contracts with the Utes, tried to embarrass the chiefs. Why don't you work at agricultural endeavors, he asked? Ouray replied that their work was hunting. Another member of the commission tried intimidation. If you don't sell now, he explained, the Democrats might soon elect "bad men [to] Congress [and] stop your annuities and rations." Sell now and it would be binding on the new Congress.

Ouray claimed not to understand the machinations of American politics. Brunot then suggested that maybe the Utes would like good teachers "so that your children could compete with white children." No, Ouray replied, we'd rather teach them ourselves. Ouray had let it be known at the outset of his meetings with the commissioners that he would be more amenable to their requests if the government would find and return his son, whom the Arapaho captured ten years earlier during a hunting trip to eastern Colorado. Government agents located his son, so they told Ouray, but the young brave said he did not want to return to the Utes, that he was now an Arapaho. Ouray refused to believe the report, telling a newspaper the government "could make the Arapaho give me back my son, but they do not want to make the Arapaho mad. That is not right and I will not forgive that."[28]

Still Ouray recognized that without going to war he and his band of Uncompahgres could not prevent miners from coming onto the reservation. Ouray, ever the realist, recognized the futility of such an action against a larger, better-armed force. Throughout the negotiations, Ouray gave orders to his band to stay clear of the white miners coming onto the reservation and to avoid trouble. The Utes, their agent at Los Piños reported, are "good neighbors to the whites," and on occasion the Utes have fed and sheltered miners, engineer surveying parties and prospectors "in time of need." They want peace, said the agent, and "confidence may be placed in their word," especially that of Ouray.[29]

At a critical juncture in the negotiations with Ouray, Brunot asked for the assistance of Otto Mears, a civilian contractor to the Los Piños Agency and friend to Ouray. Over the years, Mears, a Russian immigrant, had profited handsomely from government contracts, first as a mail carrier, then as a provider of food and supplies to the Los Piños Agency, later as a builder of mountain toll roads and railroads. He spoke Ute fluently and had ingratiated himself with Ouray through gifts and advice, always designed to profit Mears personally. To break the impasse in the negotiations, Mears suggested to Brunot that Ouray might be amenable to a "gift," say $1,000 a year for ten years, as an inducement to sign the treaty. Brunot responded that neither he nor his commission would be party to a "bribe." It was not a "bribe," responded Mears, but a "salary."[30]

Before Ouray and eight other chiefs agreed to the treaty, they accepted an invitation to meet with the Great White Father in Washington. Ouray and his party attended a White House reception in their honor and then were forced to endure a lecture from Grant about the benefits of farming. When asked by a newspaper correspondent what he had discussed with the president, Piah, a Ute sub-chief, answered, "White father at Washington said Indian must make potato, cabbage and work. I tell white father no make potato, no cabbage no work; Indian hunt and fish. ... Me great warrior. Warriors no plow. ... Grant great warrior. He no work. Me see ... Grant's squaw. She no work, either. Great warriors no work."[31] The reporter did not record President Grant's response. Nor did anyone think to ask the Utes, after a visit to New York's

Chief Ouray and his advisor, Otto Mears. Mears played an important role in obtaining Ouray's approval of two treaties with the U.S. government. (Courtesy of the Denver Public Library, Western History Collection, #WHJ-10219)

Carl Schurz, secretary of interior from 1877 to 1881. Schurz was an advocate for reforms in the Indian Bureau and defender of the Utes against those wishing to "exterminate" the tribe. (Courtesy of the Library of Congress, #LC-USZ62-15582)

"Conquer by Kindness"

Central Park, what they thought of the caged buffalo, elk, deer, and bear. The royal treatment given to the delegation and the special attention paid to Ouray helped cement the "agreement."[32]

The Utes agreed to sell the San Juan mining district, almost 4 million acres—including what are today the counties of San Miguel, Ouray, San Juan, Montezuma, La Plata, Archetelta, and Hinsdale. The cession shrank the reservation by a quarter. The Utes kept a long strip of land fifteen miles wide and a hundred miles long along the Colorado–New Mexico border and another strip twenty miles wide and eighty miles long, along the Colorado-Utah border. The Utes would continue to have hunting rights on the ceded lands (mining district) as well as the hunting rights in Middle and North Parks, as allowed in the Treaty of 1868. The Los Piños Agency would be moved from its location east of Gunnison to a warmer and more convenient site close to Ouray's farm on the Uncompahgre River; the southern Utes (Muaches, Capotes, and Weeminuches) would be provided with an agency of their own in southern Colorado to replace the defunct agencies at Abiquiú and Cimarron, New Mexico. In return, the Utes would receive an annual payment of $25,000 to be dispersed not by the Indians but "at the discretion of the President ... for the use and benefit of the Ute Indians annually forever."[33] Ouray was to receive $1,000 a year for ten years "so long as he shall remain head of the Utes, and at peace with the people of the United States." Other provisions of the Treaty of 1868 carried forward.[34]

Almost immediately after the signing, the Utes became suspicious of the agreement and of the government's intentions. Ouray had been led to believe that the sale included no part of a rich 15,000-acre valley (Uncompahgre Park and its sacred hot springs adjacent to present-day Ridgway) close to his headquarters, where the Utes grazed 6,000 head of cattle, sheep, and horses. But when white farmers and ranchers began to settle in the park, Ouray charged the government with deceit. The government asked the squatters to vacate the park and sent in a small army detachment to oversee their removal. But when they refused to move and offered armed resistance, Grant ordered the army to back off. To avoid further trouble, Washington offered to purchase the property for $10,000. Ouray had to remind the Indian Bureau, however, the semantic and important difference between "four square miles" (Washington's offer) and "four miles square," the park's definition in the 1873 treaty. Besides, said Ouray, "we have no land to sell to people who have not paid for what they bought before."[35]

The Utes believed they would receive their additional annuity immediately upon signing the treaty. No one informed them that it would be a year before the U.S. Treasury bonds, set aside to provide for the additional annuities, had accrued the necessary $25,000 in interest. Nor did the Utes understand that Washington, and not the chiefs, decided how, when, and where the funds were to be spent. With 3,734 Utes enrolled on the annuity rolls at the time of the agreement, and with rations calculated for 1,867 heads of family, the government budgeted $.12 a day for each family (half of what it spent on a soldier). Congress only appropriated $60,000 to fund the provisions of both the 1868 and 1873 agreements. The agreement also further antagonized the southern Utes. Ignacio, their leader, protested three years later that the southern bands had not received payment for lands ceded in the 1868 treaty and "that any business done by or through Ouray for him and his country [in the San Juan district]" would never be recognized.[36]

Ouray may have believed the Utes could survive on a smaller reservation, and with the payment of additional rations and annuities, they might even thrive. The tribe would not be put at risk by selling off mostly mountainous terrain that most Utes believed to be noncritical hunting lands. The remaining 12 million-acre reservation possessed ample game for the 3,800-member tribe, and the tribe would still be allowed to hunt on former lands. Ouray also recognized the attractive provision whereby the government promised to keep whites, particularly illegal squatters, off the reservation.[37] Remembering his experience of growing up within the Hispano-Indian culture of northern New Mexico, Ouray may also have believed that whites and Indians could peacefully coexist adjacent to each other in Colorado. Finally, Ouray firmly believed the Utes could and should learn the agricultural skills necessary to provide crops for their own use, plus a surplus for the lucrative trade with the nearby miners. Ouray's own farm, deeded to him by the government under the provisions of the 1868 treaty, had proven the likelihood of both possibilities.

The Indian Bureau thought Ouray and his 160-acre farm a model for the Utes. The farm grew grains, fruit, potatoes, and onions, all skillfully tended by Mexican servants. A large band of sheep and a select herd of horses grazed nearby. Ouray lived much like a white frontier middle-class merchant in a twenty-by-forty-foot adobe house built with the assistance of the government and furnished with kerosene lamps, window shades, a brass bed, oak furniture, and an iron cook stove. Outbuildings included tenant houses, a mess hall, warehouse, carriage house, tool shed, horse barn, and vegetable cellars.[38] At work, Ouray wore his traditional buckskins. But for meeting with whites, he dressed in a beaded vest and polished black boots. On more formal occasions, he dressed in a black broadcloth suit adorned with a gold chain and pocket watch. Only his long braided hair, often topped by a derby, suggested his Indian heritage. When he entertained white guests, Mexican servants prepared the meals while his attractive wife, Chipeta, played her guitar. Ouray's critics claimed he dishonored his heritage for the sake of friendship with whites.[39] Behind his back, his enemies called him an "apple" Indian, red on the outside and white on the inside. An employee at Los Piños who claimed to know Ouray said of him, "Everyone lauds him ... but I do not think him above lending his influence to schemers, to seekers after the office of agent, or after opportunities to make money out of Agency business ... "[40]

Ouray's non-Indian lifestyle and his cozy relationship with white authorities both within Colorado and in Washington caused considerable resentment among his Uncompahgres and, especially, among other Ute bands. Renaming the local mining town after Ouray did nothing to improve his standing with his fellow Utes. Nor did the constant attention given to him by white dignitaries and photographers enhance the chief's standing with some jealous sub-chiefs. William Henry Jackson, the famous western photographer, claimed to know Ouray well. He observed that Ouray was vain and loved to be photographed, "always ready to pose ... he was probably the most photographed man in the Rockies."[41] One of Ouray's many southern Ute enemies, Suckett, traveled to the Uncompahgre "to make trouble" with Ouray. Suckett received a bullet to the head for his challenge to the chief. Over the next year, Ouray killed four more challengers to his leadership. One frequent visitor at Ouray's headquarters observed that the chief's "summary methods of disposing of his enemies is probably without a parallel in the annals of the American Indian."[42] Within Ouray's own band, Shavano, his brother-in-law and a sub-chief with a reputation among the whites as "a great drunkard and gambler and easily influenced by either whiskey or money," tried on occasion to replace his leader, but always without success.[43]

If a number of the Utes thought Ouray too conciliatory toward the whites, Ouray himself had long recognized that the future of the Utes could be secured only by peaceful negotiation. He understood well the power of the white world surrounding his tribe. The Utes could not match up against the U.S.

Army and its firepower. Better to live peacefully on a guaranteed reservation with the promise of no white intruders than to constantly be moved about at the whim of the ever-changing politicians in Denver and Washington. Ouray explained his reasons for accepting the 1873 agreement to a friend some years later:

> I have resigned myself to submission to the United States government, and I have persuaded many of my chiefs to think as I do. We see that you white men submit yourselves to your government too. But we must be left alone in the possession of our lands and this free life we are leading. It is very hard for me to keep the young men of the tribe quiet now. They are restless, and I know they have fights with the hunters and the prospectors who come on the reservation without right. Some day some of these troublesome Utes may do something that may bring the troops down on us, and we will be destroyed. We are only ten thousand and there are two times that many troops. If the government would guarantee to let us alone[,] we would not even want the agency rations because we have on the reservation game that we can trade for flour and bacon and coffee, and besides we have much gold that we tell no one about. We know where it is—no one else does.[44]

Ouray maintained control of the Uncompahgre band, but not all bands possessed leaders of Ouray's caliber. Far to the north, at the White River Agency, "troublesome Utes" would soon react violently to the strict discipline of a patronizing agent and, as Ouray prophesied, bring "the troops down on us."

It is difficult to believe the Indian Bureau had the best interests of its wards and its agents in mind when it selected the site for the White River Agency. It benefited the Utes only because of its isolation from white settlements in southern Wyoming. Placed in a cold river valley that drained the high snowy peaks on the western edge of the Rockies, the agency served the three small bands of the northern Utes who had for over two centuries congregated on the Yampa, Grand, and White Rivers. The Yampas, who had lost their traditional river-valley home in the Treaty of 1868, sought refuge with the White River band to the south. The Grand River (Colorado) band, many of whom had intermarried with the two other northern bands, had also moved into the White River area, enticed in part by the annuities offered at the new agency. But the agency's isolation—a three- to four-day journey from the nearest white settlement through high mountain country, often blocked by snowdrifts or flooded rivers between November and May—made it one of the country's most remote and isolated Indian agencies. The Indians called the river the "Smoking Earth River." White visitors to the agency called it "the rat hole."

The post required agents to be accustomed to a rough frontier life and capable of living comfortably (often with their families) and securely with "savages" without complaint, far distant from any military protection in the event of an "Indian problem." To maintain peace among the Indians, the agent had to disperse the promised rations and annuities on a timely and equitable basis. Best also if he recognized and appreciated the cultural habits of his wards, including their ceremonies, language, political and social structure, dietary needs, and familial arrangements. Off the reservation, the agent often needed the negotiating skills of a diplomat to convince the whites that the Indians meant no harm as they passed by the white homesteads on their way to traditional hunting grounds. He would implore settlers not to trade liquor and arms for hides, but was powerless to stop the trade. When called up to investigate Indian thefts of livestock, he learned of government contractors who stole for their own accounts. One agent discovered Indian Bureau cattle (branded USIB) in a rancher's herd at the railhead in Rawlins, Wyoming, ready to be shipped east to Chicago. He told another settler he could not come onto the reservation looking for a missing horse and causing trouble. Where diplomatic skills and the knowledge of Indian culture were required, the Indian Bureau appointed agents who ranged from political hacks ready to accept contractor kickbacks to experienced and honest men who knew Indian ways and the tribal language. Later, in conformance with Grant's "Peace Policy," the Indian Bureau sent out well-meaning reformers to the Utes, including a few Unitarian ministers, whose entire frontier Indian training consisted of a theological degree from Harvard.

One such agent, the Rev. Jabez Nelson Trask, a graduate of Phillips Exeter Academy, Harvard College (1862), and its Unitarian Divinity School (1866), came to Los Piños from a brief stint as minister in New Salem, Massachusetts. Despite his passion to reform the Utes, or maybe because of it, he immediately antagonized the Utes under his care. Trask complained about the cold weather, the difficulty of getting supplies to the agency, and how the postmaster at the nearest town, Saguache, intercepted and read his mail. Lacking a survey or maps, no one—not the Indians, the agent, or local whites— knew the location of the reservation boundary. The Utes, he reported, had a "repugnance" to both reading and writing and, given their "nomadic way of life," they could not be kept on the reservation. The local whites, particularly miners, constantly trespassed and were "always looking to make a profit off of the agency and its business."[45]

Trask walked about the agency in a dark-blue swallowtail coat, skin-tight trousers and, to protect himself from the sun, an old-fashioned floppy beaver hat with broad brim, and a set of green eye goggles. To the modern observer he might resemble Kermit the Frog. But to a nineteenth-century Ute, he looked more like an evil spirit. Though a man of "sterling honesty and guileless simplicity," and a "deadly enemy to the 'grafter,'" a coworker at Los Piños Agency said his "supreme hobby" was to "civilize and Christianize the Utes all in one day." In the end, Reverend Trask proved to be "a needless crank," "tactless and incompetent," and no more fit an Indian agent than would be "the devil ... placed in charge of a powder house."[46]

Another observer noted, "I don't believe Mr. Trask is a sane man. ... [his] eccentricities unfit him for an agent."[47] Trask did, however, remind his Unitarian colleagues back in Cambridge that his Indians wanted bread not as a sacrament but as a defense against starvation. Within a year of his appointment, Trask was replaced.

To the north, the White River Utes fared somewhat better under their agents, at least in the short term. In the early days at White River, agents worked effectively alongside the Utes, patiently demonstrating what might be gained by learning agricultural skills. One agent, Charles Adams, worked effortlessly and with some success to convince young Indians to learn white man's agriculture. By 1871, he reported some thirty lodges, or two hundred Indians, had broken ground for crops under the direction of Chief Douglass. "Douglas[s]'s authority is unquestioned and he is a good man and has a great deal of common sense. I have managed without much trouble," Adams reported in a letter to Colorado's territorial governor, Edward McCook. "Douglass has repeatedly assured me of his lasting friendship towards the American people" and "is completely satisfied with the designs of the Government towards his people. ... I have had some experience amongst different tribes and [I] can honestly say that these Utes are the best behaved of all I have come in contact with."[48] Exaggerated stories in the press about the Utes wanting war were false, Adams reported. The Utes "take an interest in the mechanical arts and the English language, [and] are well behaved and willing to learn."[49]

A subsequent agent at White River, J. S. Littlefield, also expressed his pleasure with the agricultural progress of the Utes. "The Indians are more peaceful and inclined to farm than [I] expected." Agency personnel, with Indian assistance, had constructed nine log buildings, a sawmill, and a stable. For lack of fencing, the 1,600 horses, 150 goats, and 440 head of cattle had, unfortunately, grazed off the grain crop of wheat and oats. But the potatoes and garden vegetables, plus fifty tons of hay, had survived the invasion. The Indians complained, Littlefield reported, about the cold valley and expressed a strong desire to have the agency moved to the wider and more temperate climate of the Yampa River. They also asked for a schoolhouse for forty students since "some Indians have expressed interest in learning." The agency needed a physician, more plows and seed, and an irrigation system; the Indians could use guns and ammunition for hunting. "If the Department gives these articles to any tribe, it should be to the Utes as they have only a few rifles for hunting and have to subsist half the time on their own. ... [They] have been well behaved and [the] chiefs are doing their best to comply with the treaty stipulations. Little lawlessness and no acts of violence. [Chief] Douglas[s] has been very helpful."[50]

The Indian Bureau in Washington failed to understand the agent's slow progress with the Utes' agricultural training. Quite aside from the Utes' reluctance to give up hunting for farming, Washington's miserly expenditures for seeds and tools only added to the problems faced by the agency's employees in training Utes to plant and harvest vegetables and grains. But the biggest obstacle remained the natural environment. Situated at elevations at or above 6,500 feet, the agencies at Los Piños and White River could count on a growing season of no longer than seventy to eighty days. The agent at Los Piños reported that in the year 1873–74 hardly a day passed without frost, with frequent droughts between mid-June and late August. All summer crops in the semi-arid climate required irrigation, and even then they struggled in the face of mountain winds and grasshoppers.

The Indians thought the agency's location was too high and cold for agriculture and stock raising, a reason why the Uncompahgres and the southern bands, with their "dread of snow," remained in the vicinity of the agency only during the summer months. With a plentiful supply of game, in addition to the provisions supplied by the government, there were no incentives, agents reported, for the Utes to learn agriculture. They worked hard at what they knew and liked, such as hunting, but not so hard at unfamiliar activities such as formal schooling and agriculture. The band at White River, for example, failed to understand why they needed to grow summer crops for winter consumption when they followed the game migration in the late fall to green grass at lower elevations west along the Colorado River toward Utah. In the winter at White River, agents found the place a lonely and harsh environment.[51]

In fact, agents faced more problems with whites immediately outside the reservation than they did with their wards. Agents reported that too often whites "stirred up trouble" in the hope the army would be called in. On those occasions when a small army detachment appeared, its presence only managed to further aggravate the Indians, thereby providing an excuse to kill the Indians. The press encouraged the conflicts with exaggerated reports of Indian depredations. Agent Adams reported that "ambitious newspaper correspondents try their utmost to make excitement worse" with the Utes.[52] Another agent complained to Washington that the biggest problem he faced involved whites trading whiskey to the Indians for hides at a trading post on the Yampa. The Indians, particularly Ute Jack (as he was known to the agents) and some young braves under his influence, returned to the reservation and wanted to "stir up trouble." Chief Douglass, the agent reported, "will do what he can to keep them in order," but it was difficult to put a stop to the practice. "If the white men who come in contact with the Indians behave as well as the Utes, there will be no trouble," he concluded.[53]

Whites continually complained to territorial politicians and Washington about Indian hunting parties passing by their homesteads in Middle and North Parks on their way to traditional hunting grounds. The farmers and ranchers wanted the Indians removed and returned to their White River reservation either by persuasion or, if necessary, by military force. The Treaty of 1868 had, of course, guaranteed the Utes access to these hunting grounds as long as the lands remained unoccupied, the game lasted, and the Indians kept the peace. The agents at White River generally supported the Indian off-reservation hunts so long as they did not bother white settlements. Local whites persisted, however, in their calls for a halt to the hunting and for the creation of a nearby army post. A special investigator for the Indian Bureau, James P. Thompson, reported to Washington that the Utes had not violated either the 1868 or 1873 agreements and remained peaceful—unlike the openly hostile Kiowa, Arapaho, and Comanche. If troops were to be used, Thompson suggested, they should be placed in eastern Colorado to protect against the attacks of Plains tribes, not in western Colorado against the Utes. "I assert ...

that there is no more use for a military post or the services of a cavalry company [adjacent to the Ute reservation] at this time, so far as the Utes are concerned, than there is for the establishment of a Government ice house on the top of Pike's Peak." The cause of any trouble resulted from "the wantonness and brutality of the [whites] and through the giving of whiskey to Indians." The Utes, Thompson went on to report, had been misrepresented by the false and exaggerated reports emanating from the press. Thompson's replacement, in a letter to Washington, offered a similar message about white settlers to the north of the reservation. Settlers on the Yampa and Snake Rivers, he said, fabricated reports about Indian depredations so as to make the case for a permanent military post on the Yampa. There was no need for a post and if placed there, it would "do more harm than good."[54]

If neighboring whites and the threat of the army's presence in the area antagonized the Utes, no entity—least of all the Indian Bureau—could anticipate the problems brought on by incompetent leadership of the agent at the White River Agency. The Rev. Edward Danforth, a Unitarian from Boston appointed by President Grant at the end of his second term in 1876, proved to be a poor administrator in the judgment of Washington and an uncaring agent in the eyes of the Utes. During the harsh winter of 1877–78, grain rations never arrived at the agency. The railroad, awaiting payment of the freight bill, refused to release the grain from its Rawlins depot. Danforth said the contractor was responsible for the payment. But when the agent failed to force the payment, and as the rations sat rotting in the Rawlins warehouse throughout the winter, the Indian Bureau blamed Danforth. In addition, the bureau charged the Boston minister with allowing "his Indians to scatter and wander off the reservation" in violation of a recent Indian Bureau regulation requiring Indians to have a military guard if they wished to leave the reservation. The Utes, in turn, personally blamed Danforth for the new regulation, while Washington condemned him for nondelivery of rations and for his constant complaints about the agency's isolated, cold location.

Nor did the Indian Bureau wish to hear Danforth's continual grumbling about his Indians leaving the reservation. They left, he reported, because of the bureau's regulation that prohibited white traders from entering the reservation to sell arms and ammunition to the Indians. The foolish regulation only encouraged the Indians to go off the reservation in search of weapons they needed for hunting, an activity critical to their survival given the government's stingy ration allotments. And to add to his problems, local whites railed against his efforts to halt the profitable off-reservation liquor trade. Danforth, like so many Indian agents, found himself in an untenable position. Because Congress failed to appropriate adequate funds for the Indian Bureau, often as a result of the connivance of western politicians, agents found themselves unable to supply the basic needs of the Indians under their care. When the agents defended the Indians, their treaty rights, and their general welfare by criticizing Washington and its politics, they faced the overt threat of dismissal. But if agents followed to the letter the dictates and regulations of the Indian Bureau, they threatened their own lives and those of their agency coworkers. In the end, Washington no doubt saved Danforth's life when the head of the Indian Bureau wrote to the secretary of interior, "[Danforth] is generally inefficient" and "needs to be replaced."[55]

With the election of a new president, Rutherford Hayes, in 1876, and the appointment of a new secretary of the interior—both of whom opposed incompetent but well-meaning religious appointees in the Indian Bureau— Danforth became both an embarrassment to the bureau and a political liability to the president. Carl Schurz, the newly appointed secretary of the interior, believed the Utes needed a man of the soil rather than one of the cloth.

Schurz, who in the next few years would come to play a critical role in saving the Utes from virtual annihilation, came to the Department of Interior with a distinguished military and political background. Born in 1829 in Germany near Cologne, he fought as a student leader in the German revolutionary movement of 1848–49 before seeking political refuge in England to avoid arrest. In 1852, he immigrated to Philadelphia, where he settled for three years in a German colony, involving himself in abolitionist politics. He then moved to Watertown, Wisconsin, gained admittance to the Wisconsin bar, and helped build the new Republican Party. He campaigned for John Fremont in his unsuccessful presidential campaign of 1856, supported Abraham Lincoln in 1858 in his unsuccessful run against Stephen Douglas for the Senate, all the while gaining a national reputation as a staunch abolitionist. In 1860 he helped Lincoln with the Republican nomination for president. The press called him "the foremost among the Republican orators of the nation." After his election, Lincoln appointed Schurz as U.S. Minister to Spain, but within six months he resigned to accept, as general, the command of a Union division that fought at the Second Battle of Bull Run, Chancellorsville, and Gettysburg.

After the war, he undertook an inspection tour of the South for President Andrew Johnson, worked briefly for Horace Greeley's *New York Tribune*, served as editor of the *Detroit Daily Post*, and then moved to Saint Louis to become editor and part-owner of the German-language newspaper *Westliche Post*.

Never one to avoid a presidential campaign or a political battle, Schurz worked hard to support Grant's election in 1868, the same year the Missouri senate recognized his political skills and influence and elected him to the U.S. Senate. However, he quickly became disenchanted with the corruption rampant throughout the Grant administration and after vicious personal attacks against Grant, decided not to seek reelection. Schurz returned to journalism, campaigning effectively and tirelessly in the East and Midwest on behalf of the Republican nominee for president, Rutherford B. Hayes, the governor of Ohio. Schurz's critics, of whom he had many in both parties, called him the "Dutch Viper," as much for his acid criticisms of incompetent politicians as for his blistering attacks against corruption in Washington, particularly the Indian Bureau. He gained a reputation as a political maverick, a strong advocate of civil service reform, but something of a "bookish doctrinaire." On the campaign trail for Hayes, he drew large audiences and delivered critical votes to help elect the Ohio governor president over New York Governor Samuel Tilden in the highly controversial election of 1876. In return for his support and as a signal to the party's Old Guard that he would clean Washington of its corruption, Hayes in 1877 appointed Schurz to head the Department of Interior, targeted by the press as a scandalous den of crooked contractors, all in profitable partnership with incompetent Indian agents. Schurz's appointment met with favor among northern Republican reformers and moderate Democrats, who looked favorably upon Schurz's support for local government in the South and an end to the bitterness of Reconstruction.[56]

Schurz quickly set about to change the image of the Department of Interior from a dumping ground for political appointees to a model of good administration. While Grant's church-related Indian agents may not have fallen into the category of political appointees, for Schurz they proved to be ineffective, even if well-meaning, guardians of the nation's wards. They did not possess those critical agricultural skills necessary to prepare Indians for inclusion into white civilization. Religious conversion was important, Schurz believed, but more than anything, Indians needed to become agriculturalists and skilled craftsmen before their conversion to Christianity. To this end, Schurz opened the Carlisle

Indian School in Pennsylvania where young Indians, separated from the influences of their "savage home surroundings," might learn the components of American citizenship, including important mechanical trades. Schurz also advocated a policy of "allotments in severalty," an idea put forth by eastern reformers that would give to each Indian family 160 acres of reservation land. Individual ownership rather than communal ownership, the reformers believed, would encourage individual initiative among the Indians, while simultaneously weakening tribal ties. Lands remaining after the allotments could then be sold off to the highest bidder, even though the "surplus" lands might consist of more than half the reservation.

Schurz outlined his policy for the nation's 252,000 Indians and the seventy-one established agencies under his responsibility: (1) put Indians to work as agriculturalists. "Industrial habits" would encourage individual initiative; (2) educate the youth in schools, on and off the reservation; (3) allot parcels in severalty where and when possible and dispose of lands not used by, or deeded to, Indians; 4) when all of the above is accomplished, treat Indians like other inhabitants of the United States. There must be, Schurz emphasized, "a better fate than extermination." It may have been a "great mistake" to have made treaties with the Indians as distinct nations, but they were "entitled to respect." While Schurz called for "respect" for past commitments, he was also mindful of political realities, including the specific problem surrounding the Utes. "Many treaty reservations turned out to be of far greater [value] in agricultural and mineral resources than they were [originally] thought to be, and are eagerly coveted by the white population surrounding them ... a fact which ... must be taken into account in shaping Indian policy." Schurz summed up his report with the observation that all Indians "have been savages and that many of them are savages now is true, but ... many tribes have risen to a promising degree of civilization ... and the rest, if wisely guided, will be found capable of following their example."[57]

While Schurz's policies reflected much of the reform agenda of the old abolitionist wing of his party, he remained mindful of how westerners looked upon their Indian neighbors. The loss of the Seventh U.S. Cavalry and the death of their national hero, Gen. George Armstrong Custer, at the hands of the Crow only emphasized for westerners, and many easterners as well, the magnitude of the "Indian problem." Western newspapers called for the immediate eradication of all western tribes, regardless of their involvement at the Battle of the Little Big Horn. Denver papers headlined: THE UTES MUST GO. Grant's "Peace Policy" proved to be a dismal failure. "Who slew Custer?" asked the *New York Herald*. Its answer: "The celebrated peace policy of General Grant, which feeds, clothes, and takes care of their [Indian] noncombatant force while the men are killing our troops ... [and] the Indian Bureau, with its thieving agents ... and its mock humanity and pretense at piety—that is what killed Custer."[58]

Among all of the many requests Schurz faced at the Department of Interior to speak before veteran, literary, and political groups, and the constant attention paid to the special pleadings before Interior's Land Office, the minor problems faced by a single Indian agency in Colorado did not command his immediate attention. But when his commissioner of Indian affairs, Edward A. Hayt, passed to him the application of Nathan Meeker, a Colorado resident, for appointment as Indian agent at the White River Agency, he took immediate interest. Meeker's son Ralph a reporter for the *New York Tribune* had, more than anyone, brought to light the corruption in the Indian Bureau prior to the critical election of 1876. His series of articles detailed instances of fraud, theft, and mismanagement on reservations and in Washington's Interior and War Departments.[59] Schurz also knew of Nathan Meeker from his agricultural articles, which had appeared over the past five years in Horace Greeley's *New York Tribune*. Greeley himself, a national Republican leader whom Schurz had backed for the presidency at the party convention in 1876, spoke highly of his former correspondent, the founder and leader of a new and exciting agricultural community: Greeley, Colorado. What Schurz didn't know, however, was the background of the man he was about to ask the president to nominate as Indian agent at the White River Agency.

THREE | *"Father Meeker"*

Millard Fillmore does not rank high in the pantheon of American presidents. During his two-year tenure, he is best remembered for signing into law the Compromise of 1850, a major cause of the Civil War, and for introducing into the White House its first bathtub. This second-rate politician may also be the only president to have a third-rate novel dedicated to him.

The novel's author, Nathan Meeker, hoped the dedication might elevate both the book's sales and his own literary reputation. It did neither. Copies of *The Life and Adventures of Captain Jacob Armstrong* languished unread in a publisher's stockroom, while another author, Herman Melville, drawing from similar material, awaited the fate of *Moby Dick* published a year earlier. Meeker never attained the literary stature of Melville, but his own bizarre novel foretold the actions of an arrogant and stubborn man soon to be appointed agent among the Ute Indians of Colorado.

Nathan Meeker, the third of five children born to Enoch and Lurana, spent a happy and work-filled youth on his family's hardscrabble farm along the shores of Lake Erie in Euclid, Ohio. Born in 1814, young Meeker and his family had moved into Ohio's Western Reserve immediately after the British vacated the area, following their defeat in the War of 1812. The Meeker family traced its roots back to the New Haven colony where descendants had migrated in 1637 from East Anglia. The Congregational colony's strict blue laws quickly pushed the family to Elizabeth, New Jersey, where they obtained a small freehold from the Dutch crown. The Meekers proudly claimed eighteen members who had served in the Continental Army, and when George Washington with his troops had retreated before the British from Manhattan Island to New Jersey, the general made his headquarters at the farm of Josiah Meeker (Nathan's great-uncle) outside of Elizabeth. Nathan Meeker's mother, Lurana Hulbert, came from a distinguished family in Northampton, Massachusetts, descendants of whom included John Elliot, an early Indian missionary in New England.

With only a grade school education, Meeker decided early in his life that he wanted to be a writer. At age seventeen, absent any desire to learn his father's shoemaking trade or to help on the family's small farm, Nathan headed to New Orleans. He worked briefly as a copy boy for the *Times Picayune*, which ran a few of his romantic poems, while at the same time writing short essays for the *Louisville Courier* and the *Cleveland Plaindealer*. Within the year, with his savings spent and insufficient income, he returned to Euclid.[1] He worked briefly for his father, taught grade school, and, with a year's savings, set off again to seek his fame, if not his fortune, as a serious writer. He moved to New York's Lower East Side and hired on as a cub reporter with the New York Mirror. When not reporting local events, he devoted all of his free time to composing flowery poems, corresponding with friends and family, and reading books and newspapers. He kept an extensive diary filled with philosophical jottings, hieroglyphic notations, and ideas for future essays. He read extensively in the classics (Plato, Aristotle and Cicero, Demosthenes), the Old and New Testaments, contemporary political theory (Locke, Jefferson, Webster, Clay, Bacon, Carlyle, Pitt), English romantic poets (Byron and Shelley), and contemporary novelists (Dickens and Richardson). His political philosophy, such as it was, Meeker summed up in his diary, "I do not believe in war, resistance, injustice nor capital punishment."[2] From his reading in the works of Emerson and Thoreau, he learned about the new utopian community at Brook Farm. He studied other utopian experiments—the Millerites, the Campbellites, the Shaker and Oneida communities. Never one to tire of his self-educational efforts, Meeker reflected in his diary, "Thank God that no amount of learning can hurt a man. Yes, I do thank Him that I think so."[3]

Meeker enthusiastically shared the romantic optimism of the utopian writers of his day. Progress was possible if one paid attention not only to the laws of nature and reason but also to one's intuition. As Emerson had written in "The American Scholar," to find truth, man must first "learn to detect and watch that gleam of light which flashes across his mind from within." With this new emphasis upon emotional revelation and intuitive knowledge, Emerson added the importance of the individual and "self reliance," believing that man released from the constraints of the past was capable of unlimited potential. Man was no longer a helpless and passive sinner before the eyes of a strict Calvinist God, but a self-reliant, free-willed individual, capable of making choices not only for his own personal benefit but also for others less fortunate. Social reformers of the 1830s and 1840s, in conjunction with sympathetic theologians, carried forth the message that human progress was inherent in God's plan for mankind, because, in the words of the Boston preacher Theodore Parker, "from the infinite perfection of God there follows unavoidably the relative perfection of all that He creates." Reformers envisioned few impediments to a radically improved society. "No reform is now deemed impossible," said another Massachusetts's preacher, "no enterprise for human betterment impracticable. Everything may be made easier."[4]

Meeker, the aspiring writer-poet-reformer, filled his diary with reflections about the human condition and the measures needed to be taken to improve it. He tortured himself with thoughts that switched back and forth between the dark clouds of death, poverty, slavery, capital punishment, and rape to romantic notions that expressed sweet sentiments of pure love in a reformed world. After leaving New York in the early 1840s and returning penniless to Ohio, Meeker wrote in his diary, "I can not think of happiness without some mixture of anxiety, or misery." Influenced by contemporary reformers, Meeker believed American society must stop giving "blind admiration" to God "without knowing why or wherefore," reason enough for him to question traditional religions and their vain, uninformed preachers. The Bible, for Meeker, did not explain the modern world. If citizens accepted every word of it, as contemporary religion urged, they would become passive, unintelligent slaves incapable of reforming man. Original sin was a falsehood; man could be reformed. True Christianity, Meeker believed, taught that man's miserable condition could be avoided and eventually changed. Because we live "under such regulations as are calculated to make [us] dishonest," the solution for Meeker was simple enough: find, develop, and then practice the "right principles."[5] To those principles Meeker devoted his life.

To prepare himself for the life of a reformer and writer, Meeker continued to read the classics and contemporary philosophers. In his diary he corresponded with Gabriel in Heaven, argued with Plato and Locke, and contemplated the causes of poverty, a condition he lived in fear of. To avoid the latter condition, and to illustrate his reform ideals, Meeker commenced writing a novel. The writing, he admitted in his diary, flowed best when encouraged by opium. The drug "is glorious stuff ... except for the terrible consequences. My morning opium is the most delightful of all things, the most horrible of all horrors. I detest it. I adore it," he wrote his friend Chester. He went on to acknowledge his one bad habit—chewing tobacco—defending his candor with the observation that while tobacco "will get a man in trouble, a sure way to hell according to the church," honesty is the best path. As he reflected on his "undistinguished life," Meeker exhorted himself to "do something of significance before I die." Expecting to die at age sixty, he meticulously calculated he had before him but 8,124 days to put his mark on the world.[6]

Meeker's personal finances, however, did not allow him the luxury of writing without an income. In 1844 he moved to New Jersey to accept a teaching position, a job which clearly failed to excite him or fulfill his ambitions. He made no entries in his diary to suggest any enthusiasm for the profession, observing only, "Such a fool I am for teaching at $5 per month when I could be a salesman for $3000 a year."[7] After a year in New Jersey, Meeker returned to Euclid.

Meeker promptly courted a childhood friend, Arvilla Smith. In Meeker's frequent absences from Euclid, he and Arvilla conducted a friendly, but by no means romantic, correspondence. Arvilla cheerfully shared news about mutual friends and family in Ohio, while Meeker wrote back to burden her with the misery of the human condition, including agonizing confessions about his bad personal habits (but not his opium dependency), and his efforts toward self-improvement. For someone given to romantic flourishes in his writings and frequent displays of affections with other friends, his correspondence with Arvilla remained cool and detached, almost as if he were writing to an editor about a prospective job. Their marriage, however, was to be strong and mutually supportive.[8]

Meeker continued to occupy himself with utopian writers. One in particular caught his attention. At a lecture in Cleveland, he learned from local reformers that they planned to bring into Ohio the cooperative agricultural communities envisioned by the French socialist philosopher Charles Fourier. Meeker had read of Fourier's theories in a series of articles published in Horace Greeley's

Hon. N. C. Meeker

Nathan Meeker, agent at the
White River Agency, 1878–79.
(Courtesy of the City of Greeley
Museums, Permanent Collection)

Arvilla Meeker, wife of Nathan Meeker.
(Courtesy of the City of Greeley Museums,
Permanent Collection)

New York Tribune, which speculated that cooperative agriculture could be, with the proper group discipline, far more productive and personally satisfying than traditional (individual) farming endeavors. The Frenchman's ideas commanded a small but loyal following among eastern reformers in the late 1830s and early 1840s. Nathaniel Hawthorne and Ralph Waldo Emerson, both associated with the utopian community at Brook Farm in Concord, Massachusetts, and Horace Greeley all touted Fourier's agricultural socialism. Each community, or "phalanx" as Fourier called them, would be composed of a thousand residents owning in common four thousand to five thousand acres. The phalanxes were designed to be both self-supportive and profitable. They were also designed to replace competitive capitalism and the sins that derived from it (misery, vice, poverty) with cooperative enterprise. With the profits distributed to workers according to their talents, communal and individual happiness would result. By the mid-1840s twenty-five phalanxes had sprung up in upstate New York, with another cluster near Cincinnati and others spread across the Midwest into Iowa.

Meeker quickly and enthusiastically joined the movement, sharing as he did with the reformers the idea that in "association" men and women "can do jointly what they can not do singly." The phalanxes will, Meeker wrote in his diary, "make man love his neighbor as himself." After addressing one Fourier meeting in the summer of 1843, he bragged, "[I am] the prime mover of a social reform. Hundreds of men look to me as a means of lifting them."[9] Within the year, Meeker and his new bride, filled with enthusiasm for the socialist experiment, committed to joining the Trumbull Phalanx, a new Fourier community on Eagle Creek in Braceville, Ohio. Here, Meeker believed, he could finally earn an ample income and, at the same time, participate in a model cooperative community. The "right principles" would demonstrate to the disbelievers not only a near-perfect, harmonious society but also a respectable profit!

At the Trumbull Phalanx, everyone lived in community housing in a common village where they shared meals in a common dining hall and worked side by side in the field. The phalanx included a common school and library, orchards, vegetable and grain fields. Under its constitution, a twelve-member elected board of directors made all operational and marketing decisions. Profits from the sale of grains and animals were divided into twelfths: five-twelfths to laborers, four-twelfths to those "capitalists" who had invested in the common ownership of the land, and the remainder to those possessing "talent." The latter category included the community leaders and the small administrative staff. Laborers received their compensation based on the principle that the highest reward went to "the most repulsive and laborious occupations, and the lowest to those that are easy and attractive." "Labor performed by females," according to the bylaws, "shall be paid as high, in proportion to its productiveness, as that done by males."[10]

Almost from the beginning Trumbull fell on hard times. An unusually dry summer hurt crop production, and members complained about their work loads and inequitable salaries. Meeker, the auditor, reported in May of 1845, almost a year after the Trumbull commenced operation, that the twenty-two member-owners remained $10,000 in debt with a payment of $1,200 due a local bank in six months. "We are all very much pinches," Meeker wrote to a friend, "living on johnny cake & potatoes & veal & milk till we get out of debt."[11] For another year, the phalanx struggled to survive poor crops and an outbreak of a unspecified disease among the 112 members. In the spring of 1847, bitterly disappointed and with little to show for his efforts, Meeker quit the Trumbull experiment. "My labor is not rewarded," he wrote. "I don't go to the meetings of the Society anymore. I haven't been since last fall. I don't choose to unite with people who threaten me with violence if I express honest views." He summed up his experience, "I learned [at Trumbull] how much cooperation people would bear."[12]

Disillusioned and without his uncollected credit of $56.04, Meeker and his family returned to Euclid where, with his brothers, he operated a small store for three years. To supplement his income and to support his growing family—he and Arvilla had two sons by then—Meeker worked a small fruit and vegetable farm on shares. But he still found himself in debt and displeased with his life. "I have produced more babies than books," he noted in his diary, a reference to his failure to find a publisher for the novel he had started in New York.[13] Somehow he managed to locate enough money, probably from Arvilla, to open a country store in Hiram, Ohio, a small village east of Cleveland. That the store profited handsomely from liquor sales seemed not to have caused Meeker, a temperance man, the slightest discomfort. But when Meeker applied to the Hiram church (Disciples of Christ) for membership, a gesture designed to placate Arvilla, the local deacons insisted Meeker halt his liquor sales. For someone who wrote and preached about the evils of liquor, and who would continue to do so throughout his life, Meeker recognized no moral inconsistency in selling whisky. The evil was to drink it. But Meeker would have no more of organized religion. This time, regardless of Arvilla's pleadings, he would leave it forever. Meeker and his family immediately departed Hiram.

Despite his problems with the local religious authorities, Meeker did accomplish two major goals. He finished his novel and found a publisher for it. Meeker considered the novel his most outstanding accomplishment—as important to him as his marriage or his family—a work of literary merit that would stand, he believed, with the best of Swift, Melville, and Hawthorne. While working on it in New York, a diary entry provided a hint as to the novel's main character and thematic content. "Here I am all alone again, Saturday night. No letters, no papers ... I have nothing to do but wade along with Capt. Strong. I am making a character of him, perhaps rather an exuberant one ... who tells his story in an offhand mad mind style—A Puritan scholar, a prejudiced moralist, a sensible fool. Time will show his true nature."[14]

The Life and Adventures of Captain Jacob Armstrong, written in the form of a personal journal, centered on a stern New England Calvinist who, after two years at Yale College and employment as a ship's mate, captained a vessel (*Romeo*) bound from New York City in 1838 to the Sandwich Islands. Accompanying the captain and crew are missionary families, a cargo of Bibles, a printing press, weapons and ammunition, large amounts of liquor, a billiard table, medicine, Sunday school books, and two hundred pounds of opium. After four months at sea, the *Romeo* sails onto some coral reefs and the ship sinks. Captain Armstrong and four crewmembers manage to abandon ship, and after four days adrift, land safely on an isolated island paradise laden with fruits and happy natives. The natives, "a lower race of mankind," live peacefully in a condition of eternal bliss and equality where everyone shares the rich, natural bounty of their small island.

The first order of business for Captain Armstrong, of course, is to address the natives' need for Christianity and the construction of a church. Soon the natives are introduced to some of capitalism's finest institutions—a bank and paper money and private property. Real estate sales soar along with theft, bribery, inflation, and robbery. New laws are introduced and with them, inevitably, lawyers. Equality yields to inequality. The new constitution encourages political parties (including the dictates of majority rule) and, naturally, political dissension. Sexual discrimination gradually appears alongside alcoholism, suicide, and usury. Come the inevitable revolution, Captain Armstrong abdicates the presidency, saying, "I had believed in depravity, but I thought it a shallow stream. I had not calculated upon its depth. Hereafter, let no one felicitate himself upon reforming mankind, when they think they are reformed already."[15] For reasons unclear, though maybe as a ploy to boost its sales, Meeker dedicated the novel to President Millard Fillmore.

In the event the reader may have missed Meeker's undisguised satire, he outlined the novel's intent in his diary nine years earlier. "Strong [later changed to Armstrong] will civilize these simple and gentle people. The natives will quit [their communal living] and live in isolated dwellings, clothe themselves, feed themselves, and even get a bank in operation and be a Christian people. They will be converted. Then they will want religion. But they will be changed. They get drunk, fight, steal, ... and become honest in every sense, and so much so the Capt. lays it to their natural depravity. What room for satire. What an engine for disassociation. At last the people get mad. They discard the Capt. & return to their former way of living. He, in despair, fits up a vessel & leaves them forever. I hope I shall not be under the charge of copying Swift or More."[16]

After completing the manuscript, Meeker faced the more difficult task of finding a publisher. So intent to see *Captain Armstrong* in print, he wrote in his diary, "I am going to steal money from my business to publish it on my own account." If it failed, he noted, it would be because it was poorly written, not for its story.[17] He wrote his friend J. L. Chester in Philadelphia to search out a publisher. Earlier he also penned a letter to Nathaniel Hawthorne, to whom Meeker was unknown, asking Hawthorne to review an unspecified manuscript. Hawthorne replied, "I write to request you forward on this 'thing'—be it book, pamphlet, or brief article—which you entertain having published."[18] It is not known if Meeker sent the "thing" to Hawthorne, but there is no record of further communication from the famous author.

Horace Greeley, who admired Meeker's agricultural essays in the *Cleveland Plaindealer*, suggested he try a minor publishing house rather than approach one of the bigger houses. "A small house would try and sell your book. A large one would never think of it," Greeley advised. He also said it would take $200 of Meeker's own money to see the book through to publication.[19] Meeker traveled immediately to New York to oversee the preparation and publication of his book. In March 1853, with high hopes for the book's reception and sales, he wrote in his diary, "I think it will succeed," and be read "by two classes," one for its story and the other because of its "occult and suggestive matter." But it seems neither "class" read it. It failed to attract attention, not even a single review. "I almost despair of printing any more books," Meeker wrote. "Dark clouds hang over my literary prospects. But I promise myself ... I shall pay off my debts ... I will write again and again. ... "[20]

While Meeker waited impatiently for income to accrue from book sales, he moved in 1854 with his family to a small farm at Dongala, in southern Illinois, far distant from the harassing deacons of Hiram. To pay for the farm, Meeker borrowed money from his brother, and achieving immediate success with the farm, he purchased a nearby orchard. Within a year he had repaid his debts. For the first time in years, Meeker admitted to better spirits. Arvilla ran the small store connected with the orchard while Meeker attended to the planting and harvest. Their relative prosperity was short lived, however. The economic panic of 1856–57 hurt their small business and, to supplement his income, Meeker once again returned to writing. He penned long, detailed agricultural essays for the *Cleveland Plaindealer* and, at the request of his friend Horace Greeley, similar pieces for the *New York Tribune*. Only the small income from his essays allowed Meeker's growing family to survive the hard times of the late 1850s.[21]

Horace Greeley respected Meeker's reportorial skills, and in 1861, after the outbreak of the Civil War, he hired Meeker as the *Tribune*'s war correspondent in the southern Illinois district. Meeker covered Gen. John Pope's victories at New Madrid and Island # 10, developing a friendship with the general that Meeker would later exploit in Colorado. In the meantime, Meeker's glowing reports of Pope's leadership enhanced the general's reputation with Lincoln, who appointed him head of the Army of Virginia. With income from the *Tribune* and other agricultural publications, Meeker found himself with some cash savings. He wrote a family member in 1864 that "we ... have several hundred dollars on hand to meet expenses and to educate the children [Ralph is attending Normal University in Indiana]. Besides I am making money all the time with my pen. You cannot think how glad we are to be out of debt. In a year or so we hope to have a surplus sufficiently large to enable us to enjoy more."[22] With the war coming to an end, Meeker finished a collection of agricultural essays for publication: *Life in the West, or Stories of the Mississippi*

Valley. Unlike *Captain Armstrong*, Meeker's second book sold moderately well to a limited audience. The essay collection so impressed Greeley that after the war he invited Meeker to move to New York to become the *Tribune's* agricultural editor. He would be paid $50 a week.

Meeker sold part of the Dongola farm and moved with his family to New Jersey, close to the old Meeker homestead. Besides his column, he spent considerable time corresponding with friends and relatives about books to read, matrimony, personal health, religious precepts, visions of heaven, and a good deal more about hell. In one letter to his mother, Meeker informed her of his new two-story house close to the railroad station, and how with a $1,200 debt on the house, he could use a small loan ($100) to help with payments. "I expect the value to double when fixed up with shrubbery," he noted. Times were so tight that he had to decline his mother's request for a copy of his new book. "I could have sent you a copy ... but it would do me a great deal more good to have you buy it and help make a demand. Several hundred copies have been given to the press."[23]

Horace Greeley kept his agricultural editor busy on the road. He sent him on assignments throughout New England, the Midwest, and the South, gathering material for essays ranging from old Virginia buildings to cheese production in North Carolina, the cattle industry on the Great Plains, and the reform efforts of the New York Insane Asylum. It was the West, Meeker's next assignment, that most interested the editor of the *New York Tribune*.

The pink-faced bewhiskered Greeley shared Jefferson's belief in farming as the vanguard of American democracy. Aided by new rail transportation, the West, Greeley believed, needed to be developed and settled by yeoman farmers who could, with proper irrigation and conservation practices—tree belts, crop diversification, soil analysis, and flood control—make the prairie bloom and the region prosper. In addition, the empty but fertile West should host new agricultural experiments combined with social reform, including rural colonization projects, where farmers might practice the new scientific techniques in a cooperative climate of Christian temperance.

But cooperation for Greeley stopped short of including Indians, for whom he demonstrated little sympathy and mostly contempt. Forget the idealized view of the Indian as portrayed by Cooper and Longfellow, Greeley wrote, "the average Indian does little credit to human nature—a slave of appetite and sloth, never emancipated from the tyranny of one animal passion save by the more ravenous demands of another. ... These people must die out—there is no help for them. God has given this earth to those who will subdue and cultivate it, and it is vain to struggle against His righteous decree."[24] It made little sense to Greeley that good prairie land sat idle while Indians did "nothing" but hunt and accept government annuities. On his trip across the continent in 1859, he passed through the Sac and Fox reserve (then the Potawatomi and Delaware) and observed, "I give the good-for-nothing rascals credit for admirable judgment in selecting their land." But, Greeley advised his readers, if the "aborigines" were to survive, and it was unlikely they would, they needed to learn the useful agricultural skills of the white man.[25]

In 1869 Greeley sent his agricultural editor to the West, a destination the New York editor constantly recommended for young Americans, but a region he romanticized and misunderstood throughout his career. Greeley assigned Meeker to write a series of articles on the West and, while in the region, seek out new agricultural opportunities that the newspaper might highlight and encourage. On the train westward, Meeker encountered Gen. William Jackson Palmer, a Civil War hero and wealthy Philadelphian who headed the Kansas Pacific Railroad. The general explained to Meeker how he planned to build lines north and south from Denver to link with other railroads connecting to the West Coast. The line north from Denver to Cheyenne would link with the Union Pacific, he went on to explain, and the land through which the railroad would soon pass, and serve, was both breathtaking in its beauty and fertile in its composition. On the train Palmer introduced Meeker to William N. Byers, the first editor of the *Rocky Mountain News*, who also served as a land agent for Palmer's railroads. As one of Colorado's first real-estate evangelists, Byers encouraged Meeker to look at available agricultural land north of Denver. Colorado Territory, thought Meeker, with its new railroads, fertile soils, and mild climate would be a perfect location for a new cooperative agricultural community, one that might serve as a model for the West, if not the rest of the nation.

Meeker returned to New York, extolling Colorado to Greeley as a suitable place for people of temperance, monogamous morality, religion, tolerance, and high educational standards to live and thrive. Meeker mentioned other planned agricultural cooperatives in Colorado—the Chicago Colorado Colony at Longmont, the Saint Louis–Western Colony at Evans, Colorado, as well as the economically successful, though "immoral," Mormon experiment in Utah. Greeley responded enthusiastically to Meeker's idea and, together back in

New York, they drafted the charter for the Union Colony. Meeker was to serve as the in-residence president of the colony while Greeley presided as treasurer in the colony's *New York Tribune* office.

To promote the new farm colony and organize and finance it through subscriptions, Greeley called a meeting at the Cooper Union in New York in December of 1869. Meeker explained the idea of the Union Colony: a cooperative agricultural community of seventy thousand acres (fifty thousand to be purchased from Palmer's railroad and twenty thousand to be acquired by pre-emption and the Homestead Act) founded on the "doctrine of association." An initial subscription of $155 allowed individual members to purchase from the colony a residential lot and 160 acres. The colony's remaining farm and grazing land, owned in common by the members, would be sold off as needed in order to finance irrigation systems, schools, churches, a town hall and library, and the purchase of a cattle herd and dairy cows.

To avoid the pitfalls of the Trumbull Phalanx, there would be neither communal living nor any requirement for individuals to contribute to a common fund. Instead, the two founders advertised the benefits of personal profits for "temperance men of good character" willing to put individual initiative and skills to work in a family-centered community. In addition to the banning of liquor and saloons, there would be no gambling, billiard halls, or fences—all fairly common structures throughout the West. Finally, the sale of colony land was designed for "the general good" and "the benefit of all the people, and not for the schemers and speculators."[26] The Union Colony would promote "happiness, wealth, and the glory of the ... family, pure in all its relations, and to labor ... to make the home comfortable ... attractive and loved."

The news articles touting the new colony in the *Tribune*, a widely read paper throughout the North and Midwest, were designed to attract small farmers, tradesmen, and professionals looking for a new opportunity, particularly cheaper land. More than eight hundred initial inquiries arrived at the *Tribune's* office from throughout the United States and Europe. Most said they wanted to farm, others expressed a desire to pursue their trades. Others, such as widows and older bachelors, sought a new life in a healthy climate. One man wrote from Pittsburgh to say he sought "my Utopia." Another correspondent expressed a common ideal of many respondents, "I want to associate with good, sober, church-loving people."[27]

To finance the project, Meeker reported to General Palmer he knew of

three hundred individuals who wished to join the colony, a majority willing
to invest $1,000 each, and another twenty or thirty men worth $10,000 to
$30,000. "The great work is now to get this first colony on its feet," Meeker
wrote to Palmer. "I never was more ambitious than I am to demonstrate 'how
to do it.' I am devoting every moment of my time. It is a glorious thing that I
have Mr. Greeley and the *Tribune* to back me. ... I thought when I commenced
this enterprise that I was too old," but not so, the fifty-five-year-old Meeker
added.[28] Despite the *Tribune's* enthusiastic articles and advertisements about
the new Union Colony, Greeley had collected only $90,000, enough to allow
for the first land purchase and some improvements, but far less than Meeker
had expected. Wealthy investors, except for Greeley and the circus entrepreneur
P. T. Barnum, never materialized. Almost all enlisters were struggling small
farmers and marginally employed tradesmen.

As head of the "location committee," Meeker departed for Colorado to
select the colony's site. Accompanied and guided by the ever-present Byers,
Meeker looked at land around Colorado Springs, some seventy miles south of
Denver (too dry) and another site farther south at La Veta (too isolated). He
finally settled on a location four miles above the junction of the Cache la
Poudre and the South Platte River, forty-five miles northeast of Denver. Meeker
reported back to Greeley that the location was well watered with streams and
springs, had excellent soil, the land dotted with trees in the shadow of majestic
mountains, and was close to an excellent source of coal. With Greeley's
approval, Meeker paid the inflated price of $5 per acre for 12,000 acres,
most of it (9,300) purchased sight unseen from the Denver Pacific Railroad
via Byers, with the rest, including some primitive improvements, bought at
high prices from local homesteaders.

In the first wave of settlers, most found the location dry, windy, treeless,
the hardpan soil difficult to plow. And there was too little work for too many
people. Some colonists complained about the inflated cost of land ($30 per
acre), while others lamented the wasteful expenditures of their leaders. One
early critic observed, "The chosen ground was unbroken for miles; the wind
of centuries had blown off the light soil leaving gravel. Fifty to hundred persons
arrived daily, without enough blankets or provisions, and in the whole town
there was but one well. Some seem to forget that it was the work of a colony
to create a city; they expected to see one already built. They remained to curse
only so long as the next train east delayed [their] going."[29] Yet all the negative

reports failed to halt the migration to the new colony. By the fall of 1870, an estimated one thousand men, women, and children lived and worked at the colony, an indication of Greeley's influence and that of his newspaper and Nathan Meeker's growing reputation as a progressive agricultural entrepreneur.

"Father" Meeker, as he came to be known by the settlers, promised improvements: lumber for houses, an irrigation system for the dry fields, a schoolhouse, and a meeting house to serve as a church, lyceum, and home for a dramatic society. To boost the colony's reputation across the country, Meeker renamed it in honor of his mentor, a clever strategy that attracted new recruits and needed cash. But it became apparent to those early settlers that Meeker, like his mentor in New York, lacked the financial and management skills necessary to lead a successful colony. And as luck would have it, a major drought and grasshopper infestation hit the community in the midst of the first growing season.

Meeker's promised irrigation system put more water into town basements than it delivered to surrounding fields. It also drowned the experiment in debt. The first of four planned irrigation ditches cost $20,000 to carry water three miles to two hundred acres. For lack of water, vegetable gardens blew away, 1,400 newly planted trees died, and cattle, unimpeded by fences, devoured what remained of the parched grain crop. The farmers blamed the stockmen and the stockmen demanded that the farmers build their own fences. By the end of 1870, the colony carried a debt of $10,000, with little prospect for raising additional money from the residents, absentee owners, or new members.

More and more settlers became disenchanted with the town of Greeley and its reform-minded leader, quitting the colony and leaving behind their depreciated investment. One new member who returned home to Genesco, Illinois, after a short stay at the colony, reported that the colony "is a delusion, a snare, a cheat, a swindle, ... a graveyard in which are buried heaps of bright hopes and joyous aspirations." Four hundred of the original colonists, he continued, "have looked, got disgusted and [are] gone, and the balance will ditto as soon as their friends send them money enough to do so." "There is no capital, there are no crops, except prickly pears, no wood, no coal, no lumber nor anything else but disappointed men and weeping women." The disillusioned colonist advised his readers: if you can't stay where you are but have the itch to go somewhere else, "don't dream of such a wild and foolish thing as striking out for the great colony of Greeley, Colorado Territory."[30] Of the 442 original colony investors, virtually all from the North and Midwest, fewer than half (195) ever appeared at the colony.[31] Within a year, more than half of the original members asked for a refund. Greeley told Meeker to buy out the malcontents. If that didn't work, "let us devise *some* way to stop the mouths of grumblers. They can never help the colony except by leaving it."[32] Many took Greeley's advice and departed.

Despite the disheartening news from Colorado, Horace Greeley continued to take an active interest in his land investment and the welfare of his town. His letters of advice to Meeker from two thousand miles away arrived weekly. "Don't let my trees go to ruin," he wrote, and be certain to "irrigate them [the two small plots] in the winter as well as the summer," expand the irrigation system; plant new trees (he was partial to hickory, locust, and white pine) at three-foot intervals; and plant more grain: "I want to hear of 10,000 acres in crops next year [1872]." "Your running too much [irrigation] water in the streets is the cause of your fevers," he wrote in another letter. He criticized Meeker for buying a water-powered gristmill rather than a steam-powered one. And as for the colony's rising financial problems, "keep out of debt," do not borrow money in New York (high interest rates), but sell more small lots through additional advertisements in Denver, Cheyenne, and Omaha newspapers. Greeley added in another letter, "I rejoice that our folks have resolved to *dig out* of [their financial difficulties] rather than *borrow* out. Borrowing out is only getting deeper in." If the colony needed money, Greeley said, "I'll buy more land for $1,000 ... a good investment for my children."[33] Above all else, Greeley constantly reminded Meeker, "have no fences and no rum."[34]

The colony's debts worsened, as did Meeker's. As president, he received only a small salary for the considerable time he devoted to meetings and correspondence. Meeker did receive small compensation from a few absentee owners, including Greeley, for overseeing their land and crops.[35] But to cover the cost of his property purchases and the construction of a new six-room, adobe-brick house for Arvilla and his four children, Meeker found himself once again in debt. As in the past when in debt, he looked to increase his income from writing. Meeker continued to author occasional articles for the *Tribune*, where he never missed any opportunity to exaggerate, if not misrepresent, the wonders of the new colony. "A Farmer can get rich here [in Greeley] for the taking," he wrote in one article, "where the fertile soil produces an abundance of vegetables, fruits, hay and livestock on land selling between $6–19 depending if it is tilled."[36] Meeker also earned fees from various agricultural journals, including *American Agriculturalist* and *Hearth and Homemember* on subjects such as wheat cultivation, hog cholera, and "cattle plague"—subjects on which he considered himself an expert.

But for his ultimate financial salvation, Meeker looked to the paper he founded at the colony—the *Greeley Tribune*. The paper, he hoped, would not only promote the colony but also provide the new editor and publisher with profits to pay off debts and allow him to invest in additional land at the colony. With two start-up loans totaling $1,500 from Greeley, Meeker devoted almost all of his attention for the next seven years to his new paper—a venture that managed to antagonize its readers, increase Meeker's debt, and eventually force him into the mountains of Colorado as an Indian agent.

As the colony's problems multiplied, Greeley continued to write letters of advice to Meeker, all the while trying to lift his declining spirits. Remember the "trials of Moses," Greeley wrote in one letter, "as his stiff-necked followers cried out, 'make us Gods like those of the Egyptians. Why have you brought us out into the Wilderness to perish, etc.' Let no one think of being a reformer till after he shall have read the book of Exodus carefully at least three times through."[37] Greeley advised Meeker to think about giving up his "official duties at the colony," so that he might "govern the colony through the paper." "You must frighten the people into plowing and planting this year all through April and May. Keep yelling at them till they are frightened out of the village [and into the fields] at all events."[38]

While the colony's crop yields improved somewhat in 1872, the Greeley newspaper occupied more and more of Meeker's time and limited resources. Meeker's paper reflected its editor's ideas for a reformed society—for which the Union Colony stood as a prime example. Forget about man's fall from grace and personal guilt, he reminded his readers; instead, work on God's behalf to build a strong, moral community. His editorials, like his decisions as the colony's president, were unyielding and uncompromising. In politics as a Greeley Republican, Meeker flailed away at Grant's corrupt regime in Washington, while simultaneously attacking the coercive tactics of Radical Republicans for continuing the "politics of vengeance" toward the South. In local matters, "Father" Meeker did not deign to give long explanations for saying no, nor did he hesitate to add long moral messages to his speeches and editorials.

On the platform and in the paper, he continued to be incensed by new evidence of liquor in the colony, while taking up the causes of vegetarianism, the annexation of Canada, the abolition of both children's profanity and dancing among adults. He also railed against fishing, which he thought cruel, and the picking wildflowers, which he considered a childish waste of time. To women's suffrage, he gave his overwhelming support. One admirer noted Meeker's honesty and integrity, calling him a selfless visionary, not an obstinate man "except when it was a case of moral principle as clear to him as the multiplication table. ... he had no art of sugar-coating unpalatable truths."[39] But for all of his eccentricities and moral strictures, few doubted Meeker's generosity or his love for family and the colony. He could be brusque, stubborn, tactless, frequently overbearing, and "a good hater," but no one accused him, as he accused others, of being a slacker or dishonest.[40]

His opponents, growing monthly, started a rival newspaper, the *Colorado Sun*, which only added to the financial problems of Meeker's *Tribune*. Greeley wrote from New York, with outstanding loans to Meeker no doubt in mind, to suggest that maybe Meeker should give up the paper, "I do hope you are selling out your paper. One man cannot do everything. You are growing old [at 58], like me [61], and ought to take the world more easily. Just sell out, and then you will no longer be harassed in money matters or otherwise."[41] As for himself, Greeley said in another communication, he wanted to come to Colorado to live "after my trees get a start." "You see," he explained, "I don't want four more years of Grant. I will not stand it if there is any reasonable alternative—and that may drive me out of politics and newspapers. I feel my trade is a menace, because it compels me to think other men's thoughts. ... I prefer my own," Greeley concluded.[42]

Greeley's plans changed radically and, by extension, so also did Meeker's life. In the summer of 1872 the New York editor accepted the joint nomination of the Democrats and the Liberal Democrats to run for president against Grant. Meeker's paper, of course, became the mouthpiece for Greeley's presidential campaign in Colorado, attacking Grant personally and the corruption within his administration. In the midst of the presidential campaign, Greeley continued to monitor the colony named in his honor. A week before the election, Greeley found time to write and remind Meeker once again to look after his trees. Meeker's enthusiasm for his mentor and his trees failed, however, to prevent Colorado or the nation from reelecting Grant by an overwhelming margin. Days after his defeat and saddened by his wife's death only a week before the election, Greeley, in failing health, wrote Meeker about the colony's precarious financial condition and his own personal debts. "We [the colony] are in no condition to make new contracts today, nor ... can we soon. Our luck is very bad. Not many of us [can] buy land; I would very much rather SELL mine at any price. If there is a chance to sell either piece [two forty-acre parcels], let me hear of it. But we can make no contracts which incur obligations at present."[43] Two weeks later, Greeley died.

Upon Greeley's death, Meeker's $1,000 unpaid debt to his mentor transferred into his estate and ultimately to Greeley's two daughters. The estate's executor immediately requested payment of the debt, or, if Meeker was unable to pay, that he sign a note collateralized by fifty acres of Union Colony property. Short of cash, Meeker signed a note. To add to Meeker's problems, the new owner of the *New York Tribune*, Whitelaw Reid, no longer accepted Meeker's articles. At the colony, a fence to enclose its thirty-thousand acres cost twice the estimate, while grasshoppers once again infested the crops. The Panic of 1873 soon pushed Colorado and the rest of the nation into an economic depression.

The personal debt to the Greeley estate remained uppermost in Meeker's thoughts. He had over the years worked off the loan interest by looking after Greeley's real estate lots and trees, but he still owed $1,170, an amount that far exceeded Meeker's capacity to repay. Almost a year after Greeley's death, in a letter to Greeley's executor, Charles Storrs, Meeker said he couldn't settle the debt "at the present time" in part because he had not been "paid for the work he had put into the colony."[44] To improve his finances, Meeker left the colony briefly for New York to take up free-lance writing and then returned to Colorado in 1874 to run for the territorial legislature. He failed in both endeavors. Pressure from Greeley's estate mounted. To protect his assets against possible foreclosure, Meeker transferred to his wife the title to his house, three farm lots (ten acres), and six town blocks. The newspaper he signed over to his son Ralph, his daughter Rozane (Rosie), and assistant editor E. J. Carver.[45] With no improvement in his personal finances in sight and his reputation at the colony coming under increasing criticism, Meeker accepted the position of heading the Colorado exhibit at the Centennial Exposition in Philadelphia. At the state's exhibit and dressed in buckskins, Meeker took up residence in a faux mountain man's cabin where he explained to fawning easterners the

benefits of Greeley, Colorado—the "Damascus of the West"—and the
romance of frontier life. He missed his family back in Greeley and wrote often
to Arvilla whose "prophetic confidence" he cherished. "I am still courting
you," he wrote in one letter and assured her that his debts, which he admitted
had hurt their marriage, would soon be paid off.[46]

The romance and pleasure of the West had dissipated for Meeker. Awaiting
him upon his return to Colorado was a letter from the Greeley estate lawyer.
"We have no option other than to send your claim forward for collection,"
Charles Storrs wrote to Meeker. Further, "we think you would do well to call
upon our attorneys and act in harmony with them" by putting up security for
the outstanding loan and "avoiding further legal action."[47] At about the same
time, a clandestine brewery at the colony burned; Meeker's son Ralph became
the major suspect. New and expensive irrigation ditches sunk the colony into
further debt.[48] And the death of Meeker's son George, who had suffered from
tuberculosis for years, only added to Meeker's depression and disillusionment
with the colony.

By the fall of 1877, Meeker began to believe he could no longer serve the
colony as president or pay off his debt to the Greeley girls. He let his friends
in Denver know he'd be interested in a postmastership. To Washington, he
submitted his name for appointment as the American Agricultural Commissioner to the upcoming Paris Exposition. Neither inquiry received a response.
He looked into the position of U.S. Indian Commissioner until he discovered
the job paid no salary. And finally he inquired of Colorado's senator, Henry
Teller, about the possibility of an appointment as Indian agent to the Utes at
White River. The salaried position, Meeker believed, would allow him to pay
off his debts and preserve his and the family's reputation. Equally significant,
the agency appointment would be an opportunity to serve humanity, a
supremely important obligation in Meeker's mind. Had the Lord not put
Nathan Meeker through three failures to test his courage and prepare him for
his final trial, and success, with the Utes? Like the fictional Captain Armstrong
in the Pacific, Meeker believed he could, with his agricultural knowledge and
reform ideas, teach the savages how to become civilized Christian human
beings. In so doing "Father" Meeker would gain, as a dedicated and committed
reformer, the recognition of a grateful president and nation.

For the remainder of his life, Meeker would devote his energies to the
Utes, the same tribe he encountered nine years earlier in Denver on his first

visit to Colorado. He said of the Utes then, "The extension of the fine nervous organization [of the whites] is impossible in the Indian, because he is without brain to originate and support it."[49] But these children of nature, unspoiled by the temptations and vices of white society, did possess, for Meeker, the capacity to learn. And he, "Father" Meeker, who had learned his lessons from the failed Trumbull, Hiram, and Greeley experiences, would teach and guide them toward a new "civilized" life—not in the autocratic manner of Captain Armstrong, but with an intelligent combination of firm discipline and paternal understanding.

FOUR | "*They Deserve a Lesson*"

Nathan Meeker recognized the difficult task before him. It was May of 1878, and as the sixty-four-year-old editor-turned-Indian agent put it in a letter to U.S. Senator Henry Teller of Colorado, Meeker's White River Agency faced imminent danger. Rations were short, there had been no annuities for almost two years, and Agent Edward Danforth, his predecessor, not only lacked knowledge of agriculture or understanding of Indian ways, but he had left the agency wholly disorganized. "I doubt whether they [the Utes] understand what is their fate," Meeker wrote, "to be overthrown by prospectors and others. ... It seems to me ... that this agency ... should be placed on a self-sustaining position as soon as possible, preparing for the evil day."[1]

Meeker's fatalism was at odds with his earlier convictions about how the Utes could be reformed in the ways of civilization. The Indian, Meeker believed, needed only the firm guidance of someone trained in agriculture and, within a generation, he would be delivered from his "savage" existence. It was a belief shared by Interior Secretary Carl Schurz, whom President Rutherford B. Hayes had appointed following the contentious election of 1876. The appointment surprised and angered western politicians; the president, however, believed Schurz, a former senator from Missouri, could shore up badly needed support from the reform wing of the Republican Party.

Schurz entered office pledging to clean up the Interior Department's Indian Bureau. In the wake of the scandals unearthed by Ralph Meeker (Nathan's son) for the *New York Herald*, he promised to make the department a model for honest and efficient administration.[2] As editor and senator, Schurz had advocated a policy put forth by Indian reformers as early as the 1850s allowing Indians to take title to individual land parcels. With proper training and instruction, Indians could learn to forego their hunting culture for sedentary agriculture and thereby come to appreciate the attendant values of individual initiative and responsibility. Ultimately, the reformers believed, Indians possessed the capacity to become self-sufficient members of American society. However, the reformers preached that first Indians must be taught to think "I" instead of "we"—"this property is mine," not "this land is ours." The policy, known as "allotments in severalty," gained increasing popularity among reformers beginning after the Civil War. However, the key to success for the reformers and particularly for Schurz involved the appointment of skilled and dedicated Indian agents. He opposed the government relationship with the religious denominations instituted under Grant's Peace Policy, believing most of the church agents to be incompetent and unfit. Nor did they possess the necessary political support after Custer's defeat. The Indians required a military thrashing, Congress believed, not religious coddling. Better, thought Schurz and Hayes, to return appointments to the political process and allow congressmen a degree of patronage than to have to fight Congress for desperately needed funds for the Indian Bureau.

Meeker learned of the new policy and, in January of 1878, sent off his letter of application to the head of the Indian Bureau, Edward A. Hayt. Meeker emphasized both his experience and honest character, "I have been laboring for seven years in a philanthropic way in organizing these people [in Greeley] and protecting them ... during which time I have dispersed of their money about a quarter million dollars without the loss of a dollar and without compensation or salary." Never one to question his own abilities, Meeker closed by adding, "I have some definite ideas on the best methods for making the Indians, to some degree, self-supportive."[3]

The letter gained the secretary's immediate attention. Though they had never met, Schurz knew of Meeker from his writing in the *New York Tribune*, the paper of choice for Republican reformers. Still, Schurz had his reservations. He thought Meeker to be something of a political liability, maybe even personally unstable given the secondhand reports he had heard from Colorado. Schurz recognized that Meeker's appointment would raise considerable political opposition within the party, particularly among Colorado's hard-liners. Through friends, the secretary advised Meeker to secure the support of Senators Teller and Chaffee and other Republican allies.

Lining up the support of both Colorado's Republican senators for his confirmation proved a difficult task for the liberal editor of the Greeley *Tribune*. When in 1872 Meeker had supported the liberal Horace Greeley against the Grant wing of the Republican Party, including Colorado's Senators Teller and Chaffee, his standing with Colorado's congressional delegation suffered a serious setback. Meeker first went to Senator Henry Teller, a Grant Republican and leader of the state party. Republicans controlled the nation's newest state, and Teller controlled all federal appointments in Colorado. A New York native who had moved to Colorado Territory in 1861, Teller had made his reputation as a lawyer defending Colorado's powerful mining interests. In the 1870s, the state's politics revolved less around issues on which both parties agreed than on personalities. Democrats and Republicans agreed on three basic principles for the new state: (1) transfer all public lands in Colorado as soon as possible to new settlers; (2) increase federal expenditures for transportation to and through Colorado; and (3) remove, by force if necessary, all Indian tribes in Colorado within a decade. In the meantime, the Utes should be cared for by Washington to keep them at peace. Meeker faced in Teller a senator inherently suspicious of all liberal reformers, particularly Carl Schurz. To all western politicians, the German immigrant reputedly was a friend of the Indians and an enemy of land policies designed to assist Colorado miners and farmers.

Teller and the state's mining interests shared a close working relationship with Frederick Pitkin, the state's first elected governor. Born in 1837 in Connecticut, where he graduated from Wesleyan in Middletown, Connecticut, Pitkin came to Colorado in the early 1870s after two years of painful attacks of consumption. He regained his health in the San Juan mining district where, in addition to making a small fortune practicing law and investing in mine stocks, he befriended Otto Mears, the confidant of Chief Ouray and an influential Democrat who assisted Pitkin in his election as governor. Pitkin and Teller shared the commonly held attitude of their constituents toward Indians. In an address before the state legislature in 1876, Pitkin suggested that the Utes' presence in Colorado scared off new settlers and acted as an "obstacle to the advancement" of Colorado's business interests and reputation.

He reminded the new state's lawmakers that the Ute reservation, all 12 million acres of it, contained nearly one-third of Colorado's arable land, a tract three times the size of Massachusetts (a bit exaggerated), rich in minerals and under-utilized by the Utes. "If the land was divided up between individual members of the tribe," the governor pointed out, "it would give to each man, woman, and child a homestead of between three and four thousand acres. ... I believe that one able-bodied white settler would cultivate more land than the whole tribe of Utes [estimated by Pitkin at two hundred acres]. These Indians are fed by the government, are allowed ponies without number, and except when engaged in an occasional hunt, their most serious employment is horse racing. If this reservation could be extinguished, and the land thrown open to settlers, it will furnish homes to thousands of people of the state who desire homes."[4]

Teller had no immediate plan to remove the Utes, but he did want to ensure that the Indians at White River remained at peace with white settlers adjacent to the reservation. He had received reports about the agent at White River, Rev. Edward Danforth, who had lost the confidence of the Indian Bureau and angered the Utes. The Indian Bureau told Teller that Danforth was a sloppy administrator who could no longer be counted upon to control his charges. The Utes complained that the agent failed to provide them with adequate rations or annuities for almost two years, a breach of a treaty obligation.[5] "They despise him," a friend wrote to Teller. What the Indians needed was not an eastern minister "without knowledge of the Indians" but a "sensible westerner."[6] That Danforth became a scapegoat for the Indian Bureau's mismanagement surely occurred to Teller. A new agent, a Coloradan, one who could advance Teller's political career by carrying out his plan vis-à-vis the Utes, looked more attractive to the senator.

He first needed to know Meeker's views on the Indians. Meeker sent along a recent article he had written for the *Springfield Republican,* "Indians and Farmers." The Indians, Meeker wrote, must learn to farm with irrigation, but they would always remain inferior to "the common white laborer" because of their "small hands," "underdeveloped shoulder muscles," and "small brain." Those deficiencies made them "radically different in the qualities which make a civilized man."[7] On this the senator agreed. Meeker and Teller also shared an enthusiasm for temperance and the importance of agriculture for the Indians. In the end, and with more letters demanding Danforth's dismissal, Teller supported Meeker. Danforth would be fired, the senator confided. "He knows nothing of irrigation or farming in the West." Besides, Teller wrote Meeker, "the Indians can be taught to raise cattle and ... you are the man to do it." Recognizing Meeker's financial problems, Teller reiterated the benefits, "[the position] will pay you $1,500 a year and you would have a house to live in free, a garden, and so forth. So I think you can save something. It is only 100 miles from the railroad and quite easy."[8]

Meeker encountered more difficulty lining up the endorsement of Colorado's other senator, Jerome Chaffee, a Denver banker and mining-stock speculator. A few years earlier Meeker had antagonized Chaffee when he opposed the senator's choice of Golden instead of Greeley for the location of the Colorado School of Mines. Chaffee wrote Meeker to say "I do not feel called upon to favor your appointment."[9] Teller, however, neutralized Chaffee's mild opposition. Meeker also won support from Colorado's sole congressman, James Belford, and F. V. Hayden, the renowned government geologist. And to neutralize any potential eastern opposition, Meeker asked acquaintances and friends, including Henry Ward Beecher, the New York preacher/abolitionist, to write Schurz on his behalf.

Meeker was not without his detractors or competitors. The superintendent of instruction in Colorado, in a letter to Teller, characterized Meeker as "one of the wildest inflationists [exaggerators] in Colorado."[10] In an attempt to neutralize any opposition and advance his own candidacy, Meeker contacted two influential reporters for the *New York Tribune*. Of James Cooper, whom Teller had befriended for his criticism of the senator's favorite targets—striking miners, railroad rates, and the presence of Chinese and Indians in mining areas—he asked assistance.[11] Cooper wrote Teller, urging his support of Meeker. The second *Tribune* reporter wrote to Meeker to say he would try and help but he could not be very encouraging. "Not one applicant in a hundred is successful," in part, he explained, because the new administration now wished to avoid political appointments.[12] Meeker also asked his son Ralph to contact his friend, Schurz's private secretary, to put in a good word for his father's appointment.

Meeker's appointment was delayed through the winter and spring of 1878. As Schurz considered his options, Danforth had already submitted his resignation, citing bad health, but said he would stay on until his replacement was appointed. To the Unitarian Association, Danforth expressed his frustration with the job. He had learned that Meeker and two others were under consideration as his replacement, but thought them all "unfit for the position." "By all means," Danforth advised Unitarian headquarters, "I should appoint an eastern man and never one who seeks [the job] ... The way in which Indian matters now stand, and what we have reason to expect in [the] future, does not promise much success to our efforts. We [including Danforth's wife] are pretty thoroughly tired out."[13] When Danforth, some months later, read in a Denver newspaper that Meeker's appointment "augurs well for the settlers in Colorado," Danforth wrote the Unitarian Association in Boston, "I trust it will be well for the Indians also."[14] So did Schurz.

An article Meeker had only recently published in the *American Antiquarian* convinced Schurz that the Greeley reformer had done his homework and was indeed the right man for the post. In "The Utes of Colorado," Meeker wrote of the Utes, "they are savages, having no written language, no traditional history, no poetry, no literature ... [and] their constructive and investigative faculties have never been exercised." They are not, he wrote, "a powerful people, nor are they war-like ... they are friendly with the whites." But to remind the reader of their "savage" condition, Meeker added that they remained "a race without ambition, and also a race deficient in the inherent elements of progress. ... vermin abound on their persons." It might not be too late to reform and Christianize them, but past efforts had failed from "want of a strong and wise government, and second, from a defect in the character of the teachers or missionaries."[15]

Schurz recognized in Meeker a man with the appropriate agricultural background, a loyal "reform" Republican and a strong-willed Christian reformer who, under Schurz's direction, could change the wandering, hunting culture of the Utes. He also knew Meeker to be a foe of communal lands arrangements, such as practiced by Indian tribes, and an advocate of individual ownership—a reform principle important to the new secretary. In addition, Meeker's appointment would serve as a signal to political opponents that the secretary, and the president, wished to distance themselves from the religious denominations and their incompetent nominees.

President Hayes appointed and the Senate confirmed Meeker in March of 1878. Meeker, of course, delighted in the appointment for both the opportunity to reform the Indians and pay off his debt to the Greeley estate. Both goals, he believed, could be achieved in two years, at which time he and his family would return to Greeley with his reputation intact, if not enhanced.

The debt to the Greeley girls remained a matter of honor for Meeker. A letter Arvilla Meeker wrote to her son Ralph six months after the appointment explained her husband's motivation to leave Greeley for White River. "It would be an everlasting blot on your father's name to die a penniless man because it would appear that he was nothing more than a fraud. For how could a man plant a colony if he had not the ability to take care of himself and his family. ... we are likely to come out all right. If we do! N.C.M. [Nathan Meeker] will look a great deal better in their [the citizens of Greeley] estimation."[16]

While Meeker carried with him to White River the burden of debt and its repayment, he recognized his primary focus must be on his new employer and the policies set forth by the interior secretary. Schurz had made clear to all seventy-one agents (whose responsibility included the 252,000 Indians under the department's jurisdiction) that they must first and foremost put their Indians to work as agriculturalists with "industrial habits" to encourage individual initiative, that Indian youths must be educated in agency schools, and where and when possible, that they should be allotted individual land parcels. There must be for the Indians, Schurz wrote in his annual report, "a better fate than extermination," and all U.S. treaties with the Indians "are entitled to respect." That many reservations turned out to possess far greater agricultural and mineral resources than originally thought, "and are eagerly coveted by the white population surrounding them," was a situation that "must be taken into account in shaping Indian policy." Schurz summed up his report with the observation that all Indians "have been savages and that many of them are savages now is true, but ... many tribes [referring to the five "civilized" tribes of the Indian Territory] have risen to a promising degree of civilization ... and the rest, if wisely guided, will be found capable of following their example."[17] Meeker intended with all his energy to provide the guidance.

He departed immediately for White River, leaving his family temporarily in Greeley. Before his departure, Meeker read Danforth's final report to the Indian Bureau. Danforth counted 650 Indians, plus another 250 who moved from one agency to another to visit relatives, hunt and trade, or, as the agents charged the "bummers," to collect rations and annuities at more than one agency. The Utes "are disposed to be friendly with white settlers in this neighborhood," Danforth wrote, while the local whites exaggerated troubles to "precipitate trouble" as an excuse to bring in the army. "I am afraid ... trouble cannot be prevented in the future without the presence of a military force devoted as much to the interests of the Indians as to those of the whites." Danforth, like the agents before him, recommended the establishment of a military post on Bear Creek, to the north just off the reservation.

Supplying annuities to the Utes at White River had remained the biggest headache for Danforth. Only about half of the Indians' needs were provided for. "No clothing, blankets, tents, implements of any kind have been issued at this agency for nearly two years, no flour, except once, fifteen pounds to a family since last year. For over nine months flour has sat in a Rawlins [Wyoming] depot. Because of Indian Bureau regulations [prohibiting the sale of arms and ammunition on the reservation], the Indians are forced to go off the reservation." As for the Indians' "progress towards civilization," Danforth noted "very little advancement." They had refused to care for the agency cattle herd (1,250), and the fourteen families who cultivated fourteen acres (potatoes, corn, garden vegetables, and oats) received "nothing for their labor" due to drought and grasshoppers. The agency did manage to harvest sixty-five tons of hay. There was "no active opposition to school" with six boys in attendance who made "considerable progress." The buildings (six small log buildings with dirt roofs) were in poor condition and the irrigation system remained inadequate. If the government continued to prevent the Indians with the means (arms and ammunition) to hunt, "then it must provide [a larger irrigation system] and additional and experienced help to instruct the Indians in this method of farming ... peculiar to this country or it will render them destitute."[18] The report's summary implicitly questioned the government's commitment to the Indians, a charge Danforth made far more explicitly and forcefully in his two-year correspondence with the Unitarian Association.[19]

Yet for all of Danforth's complaints, the agency, under the direction of its two previous agents and the friendly cooperation of the local headmen, had made some progress toward self-sufficient agriculture. In 1871, two years after the establishment of the White River Agency, Agent Charles Adams reported that Chief Douglass had been particularly helpful in the "agricultural experiment" and had repeatedly assured him of his "lasting friendship towards the American people." Agent Littlefield, Adams's successor, reported Douglass to be "a man of good judgment and is anxious for the civilization and education of his people." By the time Danforth arrived, small plots of grain (oats, wheat, and corn) had been planted and harvested, and a fence constructed to protect the crops. An ample hay crop helped sustain the large herd of horses through the winter, and an irrigation ditch was completed.[20]

One major problem Meeker recognized immediately: the agency's present site in a narrow, shaded portion of the White River valley. Though it was a country rich in deer, elk, wild turkey, grouse, quail, bear, and fish, two previous agents had criticized the agency's location for its poor soils and cold climate. Meeker selected a new location twelve miles downstream in a large, open valley with better soils and excellent pasture. It was the area where explorer John Wesley Powell, the one-armed Civil War veteran, had spent the winter of 1868–69 prior to his trip down the Colorado River. He found the Utes to be friendly, with nineteen families engaged in agriculture under the supervision of the agent. The other Utes, Powell noted, held "superstitious prejudices against the performance of manual labor." The Indians should be forced into agriculture for their own good, Powell suggested. "The sooner this country is entered by white people and the game destroyed so that the Indians will be compelled to gain subsistence by some other means than hunting, the better it will be for them."[21]

The Utes called it "the valley of the one-armed man." White cartographers named it "Powell Park" and later "Agency Park." The new site with its milder climate was at an elevation five hundred feet lower than the former location, on an expansive meadow and adjacent to the White River. There Meeker would build the new agency—complete with an irrigation system, blacksmith shop, gristmill, and a new storage building—the perfect location "for growing all kinds of vegetables and grains" and commencing his reforms. He requested and received $20,000 to move the agency, construct new buildings, and hire additional help at the new site.[22] Meeker fired off to Washington request after request for harrows, plows, a gristmill, a corn planter, blasting powder, seeds, saddles, and harnesses. The requests were approved in Washington but not without complaints about the agent's constant requests. The Indian Bureau advised him to "condense your correspondence as much as possible" in the future.

The agent found that the reports and the accompanying correspondence required by Washington to be extremely time consuming. In a letter to Josephine, his daughter back in Greeley, he wrote, "There is a great deal of writing to do, probably half of one's time—so you can be employed, but it will be in the name of teacher. Salary will be $750 a year."[23] By midsummer of 1878, Meeker expressed pleasure with the Indians' progress and the physical improvement of the agency. To Ralph, his son in Greeley, Meeker wrote, "I like the Indians pretty well." Dealing with the government (Indian Bureau),

| *"They Deserve a Lesson"*

however, "is perplexing and difficult, but I do have a good clerk."[24] In his annual report to the Indian Bureau, Meeker noted construction of a new bunkhouse and corrals, the clearing of sage brush on potential farm ground, and the relocation of usable agency buildings to Agency Park. The new irrigation ditch was progressing as planned, in part because of the "double rations" he paid as an incentive to twenty-five Indian laborers. He also noted that a few Indians had planted some crops but had, upon leaving for a hunting expedition, left the crop care and harvest to agency personnel. "Of course," Meeker reported, "this style of Indian farming has, under my administration, come to an end." Though in Meeker's eyes the Utes made no educational progress and possessed poor health standards, he reported his Indians to be "peaceful, respecters of the right of property and, with few exceptions, amiable and prepossessing in appearance. There are no quarrelsome outbreaks, no robberies ... The marriage relation is strictly enforced. ... On the whole this agent is impressed with the idea that if the proper methods can be hit upon, they can be made to develop many useful and manly qualities and be elevated to a state of absolute independence."[25]

What Meeker failed to acknowledge, of course, was that the Utes had experienced "absolute independence" for centuries—long before the Spaniards, the Mexicans, the Anglos, or the U.S. Indian Bureau representatives appeared on the scene. For not all Utes shared Meeker's enthusiasm for the agency's move or his plans to make farmers out of hunters. The move not only challenged the Indians' exclusive use of the valley as a grazing ground for two thousand horses, but it also threatened to disrupt the traditional social and living arrangements within the White River band. Before the arrival of the Indian agency in 1869, the White River Utes had traditionally arranged themselves by lodge groupings, each occupying a specific area within the valley and each with its own headman or chief. While all the White River Utes often gathered on ceremonial and other social occasions, each group preferred to hunt separately, led by its chief, on their own favorite hunting grounds. Some were in Utah or Wyoming, others on Colorado lands ceded by treaties.

The White River Utes recognized no single leader. The Indian Bureau and the agents before Meeker, however, designated Quinkent, the oldest of the chiefs, the nominal head of the White River band. One agent nicknamed him Douglass—reportedly because he looked like Frederick Douglass, the black leader. The designation as head chief, the agents believed, made for easier administration by establishing a hierarchy of command within the band. After fighting against the Mormon occupation, Douglass had left the Uintahs for the White River in 1867 to join his brother. He and his followers often returned to Utah to hunt and visit friends and relatives. On one visit in 1872, Douglass, the agent at the Uintah Agency reported, "succeeded in persuading our Indians, who had to [this] time intended to farm, to give it up and let the white man [agency employees] farm for the Indians, telling them that Washington did not intend that they should work." Douglass, the agent said, ridiculed "those that farmed, calling them squaws, and finally succeeded ... in inducing our Indians to leave with him. ... Thus it has occurred that all the farming operations have been performed by the employees."[26]

Douglass gained his status not by growing crops but by raising horses and, in his opinion, Powell Park provided the best horse pasture in the entire area. In a culture that measured wealth by the number of horses one owned, Douglass, with one hundred ponies, was considered a wealthy Ute. His designation as chief and his coveted horse herd caused, however, considerable animosity and envy among the White River band. At age sixty-one and with only twenty lodges (including forty-five to fifty men) under his leadership, his influence had waned in recent years as he lost followers to a younger chief.

In his late thirties, Nicaagat ("one with earring") had earned his reputation as a respected warrior, most recently as a scout for fifteen months with General Crook in his 1876–77 campaign against the Sioux. Captain Jack, as Nicaagat came to be known by the whites, had grown up orphaned as a mixed-blood Apache-Ute in Utah and was later enslaved by a Mormon family. From them, he learned to speak English and hate whites before escaping to the White River. Danforth had frequently used Jack as his interpreter for English and, when necessary, for Spanish. Jack wore with considerable pride the peace medal given to him by President Johnson on the occasion when he accompanied Chief Ouray to Washington for the treaty negotiations in 1868. The captain and his followers—more than one hundred lodges including two hundred men, many well armed with rifles supplied to them by General Crook—lived off by themselves at the old agency upstream of Powell Park. Their favorite hunting ground was North Park off the reservation to the east.

Other sub-chiefs included Johnson, a muscular and, at six feet, an unusually tall Ute. In his mid-thirties, he was known as a good council listener and easily recognized by his ever-present .50 caliber Sharp's buffalo rifle. Johnson

Chief Douglass of the Ute White River band. (Courtesy of the Colorado Historical Society, #F-49874)

Chief Colorow, sub-chief of
the Ute White River band.
(Courtesy of the Smithsonian Institution,
National Anthropological Archives,
James Taylor Album, #46,785-C)

Captain Jack, war chief of the
Ute White River band. Captain
Jack led the fight in 1879 at the
Battle of Milk Creek.
(Courtesy of the Smithsonian Institution,
National Anthropological Archives,
James Taylor Album, #1571)

and his small band kept to themselves close to Powell Park, but separate from Douglass's lodges. He had close ties to the Uncompahgre band though his wife Susan, the sister of Chief Ouray. Colorow, the third sub-chief, a quick-tempered, sad-faced southern Ute from the Muache band, earned for himself a reputation from various agents as something of an outlaw and loner, and was fond of whiskey. He had only recently arrived at White River with a small group of southern Utes who had collected their rations in Denver before the city's Indian agency closed. Colorow and his lodges tended to isolate themselves from the other White River Utes.

Meeker never understood nor accepted the separate lodge arrangements among the White River Utes. Like most whites, he looked upon a tribe (the Utes) and a band (White River) as a single, unified organization. He failed to understand that the Utes at White River arranged themselves around lodges, each with its own distinct and separate leadership. Nor did Meeker recognize that each group of lodges had separated themselves over time and space because of divided loyalties based on somewhat different backgrounds, experiences, work habits, skills, and cultural attitudes. When, for example, Meeker moved the agency with Johnson's blessing, he failed to understand why other lodges—particularly those under Jack's leadership—not only refused to move, but also wanted no part of Meeker's plans for expanding the agency's agricultural activities.

Chief Johnson's initial support for both the agency's move and Meeker's plans for more agricultural productivity had given him hope that the other chiefs might catch Johnson's enthusiasm. For Meeker, Johnson was the "good Indian"—a family man willing to engage in agriculture, an Indian "well on his way to civilization. ... Johnson is one of those men who lead from the savage to the barbaric life on the way to civilization. He is not quite as far advanced as Cedric the Saxon, master of Garth, in Scott's *Ivanhoe*, but he is probably equal to the best among the British chiefs ... " To show his appreciation for Johnson's support, Meeker ordered the agency crew to build a new log house for the respected chief and his wife.[27]

The other chiefs, however, failed to share Johnson's cooperative spirit with and mutual respect for Meeker. They had heard too many Meeker lectures about how they needed to change their ways, spend less time with their horses and more time attending to crops. If they did, Meeker advised them, they would be "self-sufficient" in food and rich with money to purchase necessary items (such as bridles, saddles, and coffee) from the agency trader, a position Meeker promised for the agency. The White River chiefs had only to look at Chief Ouray, Chief Johnson's brother-in-law down on the Uncompahgre, Meeker suggested, as an example of a Ute leader who farmed successfully and lived in a well-furnished house like a well-behaved white man. The agent's lectures were met with cold stares.

For the White River Utes, the problem centered on Meeker's commands, delivered through long lectures, to remain on the reservation. They also knew that the agent and his predecessors had requested off-reservation traders on the Yampa and Little Snake Rivers to refrain from selling weapons to the Utes. Lastly, the Indians had no concept of the complex notion of money. To them it was an abstraction, a piece of paper or metal, worthless except maybe as a decorative object. Hides, meat, even bones they understood, items they had traded through a commission agent, often an Indian agent, for guns and ammunition—the very items needed to provide their own food. A young Ute gained status with his peers and lodge chief by bringing into camp a three hundred-pound dressed-out bull elk, not a three-bushel harvest of grain. To forego horses for farming was to injure, if not halt, a habitual barter arrangement that had, for decades, provided the Utes their sustenance, status, and work. Meeker's explanations and assurances about a self-sufficient economy based on something as abstract as agriculture—the planting and harvesting of grains with names many of which didn't begin to translate into their language—sounded not only foolish but also risky. Instead, they believed they should keep with raising horses and supply hides to the traders in return for those items required for their own survival and enjoyment.

Within three months of his arrival, Meeker understood that in order for him to succeed in moving the Utes toward "civilization," he needed to break, if not destroy, the one major obstacle in his path: the Utes' horse culture. In a letter after his first summer at the agency, Meeker wrote to Hayt, the commissioner of Indian affairs in Washington, that the Utes wasted their time and the agency's resources (primarily grass) with their constant attention to their horses. They were always "horse racing, and consequently gambling, their main pursuits for nine months of the year," Meeker complained to Washington, "and the Indian who has not a horse to run is nobody." Even his ally, Johnson, raced horses, and "only those [few] young men who have no horses will work. ... they would rather give up the cattle than the horses." With the agency divided between those who performed field work (about twenty-five and mostly women, according to Meeker) and "the vast majority" who refuse "squaw work," Meeker concluded, "this horse business is a powerful obstacle to progress."[28]

Besides being blind to the different gender roles accepted within the tribe, the agent also failed to understand the importance of the horse as the Indian's sole mode of transportation to distant hunting grounds. Ute boys and men gave careful attention and time to the training of their mounts, horses prized for their stamina and speed by other Indian tribes and neighboring whites. That some whites came onto the reservation, often with liquor, to trade for and race against the Ute ponies only added to Meeker's displeasure with the entire "horse business."[29]

As for the agency cattle, supplied to the Utes to encourage "self-sufficiency" and to develop the skills of animal husbandry (and as an inducement to halt hunting wild game), the Indians paid them little attention, except when the cattle moved in on their horse pastures. Meeker and the Utes thought the Mexican and Texas cattle a collection of uncontrollable wild beasts that wandered far and wide on and off the reservation. They needed to be herded and cared for close to the agency, in Powell Park if necessary, Meeker told the Utes. Against his orders and throughout the dry summers of 1877–79, the Utes continued to allow the cattle to graze unattended on marginal lands far distant from Powell Park. In response, Meeker offered to provide the materials for the Utes to build a wire fence to enclose their horses. The chiefs immediately vetoed the idea, which to them looked too much like a small reservation, a concept they thought as inappropriate for their horses as it was for themselves.[30]

Through the severe winter of 1878–79, about half the lodges departed the agency with their horses for a milder climate. Josephine (Josie) Meeker, the family's oldest daughter, reopened the log schoolhouse started by Danforth, but only three or four students circulated in and out. By the end of the winter, only one student remained. For Meeker, the winter allowed him time to out-line plans for the upcoming planting season, file official reports, and attend to business and personal correspondence.

From Ida Greeley, Horace's oldest daughter, Meeker received a letter requesting attention to his debt to her and her sister. She expressed the hope that "times are better with you than formerly" and that she stood "willing to accept a settlement which I trust you will make as liberal as possible. Please make me an offer also for the real estate we own in Greeley. ... I am prepared to close out my Colorado interests at great sacrifice." In a postscript, she said she wished to act independently of her father's executors, who had not consulted her in the "management of the business [the estate's] settlement."[31] Meeker responded to say he hadn't forgotten his obligation and that he planned to make a cash payment later in the spring. From his $1,500 annual salary, paid quarterly from Washington, Meeker put away $50 a month toward the loan payment.[32]

To his son in Greeley, Meeker wrote how he continued, despite his personal problems, to have the support of the Indian Bureau. "The Dept. seems to have confidence in me, grant all the money I ask & even more." But, Meeker added, he had "trouble with insubordinate employees [hired by Danforth] & shipped them [off] & will have none who do not do as they are told and mind their own affairs." Meeker located six new boys from Greeley, at a salary of $500 a year, whom he knew to be "first rate."[33] To the Unitarians, who continued to take an interest in the welfare of the Utes, Meeker wrote that he had made some progress with his nine hundred Utes over the past summer. With some ground under cultivation, "I am doing what I can to civilize these Indians." As for their religious training, however, he had made no progress. Meeker likely experienced the same reaction to his religious teachings as the Ute agent in Utah who reported "our services are little understood and of comparatively little value to them."[34] The Indians understood enough about Christianity, no doubt, to conclude that white man's religion disconnected them from their natural world. Meeker asked the Unitarians to deploy a "religious teacher" with the "practical skills" of carpentry.[35]

Meeker kept Senator Teller abreast of his progress—the move to Powell Park and his plans for planting wheat and plowing up one hundred acres for corn, potatoes, peas, and other vegetables. The Utes had "only a vague idea what it is to engage in farming" and "protested any change," Meeker reported, adding a prediction that when the new irrigation ditch was completed in the spring to farm one thousand acres, "they will want to work." The $3,000 cost of the system, Meeker admitted, he charged against their annuity account without the Utes' approval or knowledge. The major hindrance to progress, Meeker continued, were the two Indian factions: one led by Douglass who were willing work, the other led by Jack who refused to have anything to do with agricultural endeavors. Meeker reported he paid Douglass's people $15 a month cash and double rations as an inducement to farm. Meeker also advised Teller, who at the time supported the call for transferring responsibility for the Indians back to the War Department (the army), against using army officers as agents. For Meeker, the army was made up of "desolate men" from "a class that drinks" and therefore poor role models for Indians. Besides, they knew nothing of farming or small fruit culture, possessed no knowledge of "neighborhood organization," and their presence at White River would only provoke trouble. It would be "cruel and unwise," Meeker said, "to bring soldiers here and break up what seems so happily begun." These Utes, Meeker explained, were different from the wild Indians of the Plains where "the taste of military rule for a few years would do them some good." Expressing increasing impatience with his Utes, Meeker led the senator to understand that with discipline, something never imposed by the former agent, the Indians would be reformed and "civilized." They "had better be making up their minds pretty quick whether they are going to work or whether they propose to continue to be paupers. When I get around to it, in a year or so if I stay as long, I shall propose to cut every Indian to bare starvation point if he will not work. The 'getting around to it' means to have plenty of tilled ground, plenty of work to do, and to have labor organized so that whoever will/shall be able to earn his bread."[36]

If Meeker had little use for the army as agents on the reservation, he did want to remain in touch with the military in the event he needed their assistance. Meeker contacted Maj. Thomas Thornburgh, the commanding officer at Fort Fred Steele in southern Wyoming, the nearest post to the agency, to be on the lookout for some armed Utes he suspected might be headed north to assist the Sioux on the upper Missouri. "These [Utes] belong to the adverse faction that will not work." Yet, Meeker noted, "we are making good progress" and within a year "I hope the fruits of industry will be such as to keep all the Indians on the reservation."[37] But within two weeks, Meeker's mood had changed and with it came a call for tougher military action against his "strays." He wrote Thornburgh with the unfounded allegation that his Indians had bought arms and ammunition at trading posts on the Bear (Yampa) and Little Snake Rivers and had traded the items to the dreaded Sioux, a charge Meeker knew would attract the immediate attention of the army officer. These Utes "need to be arrested" and either held or returned to the reservation, Meeker informed the major, concluding, "They deserve a lesson."[38]

To Commissioner Hayt, Meeker reported the same message. As soon as the Indians collected their annuities, Meeker wrote, they wandered off to trade at off-reservation stores for more guns, ammunition, and liquor. "If I can provide them work for cash," he continued, they would have no need to leave. What was needed was a reservation store. Meeker, however, continued to hold out hope that his agricultural plan would keep the Indians at home. In another communication to Hayt, Meeker expressed optimism for the coming planting season. With the new shipment of implements and seeds, "I think I can promise you that we shall raise a great abundance of all kinds of vegetables, which will diminish the demand for both groceries and meat."[39] As for the Indians leaving the reservation, Hayt wrote back and told Meeker to "use stringent measures ... to prevent [Indians] from going beyond the limits of the reservation for any purpose ... " Hayt failed to mention what measures should be taken.[40]

The tone of Meeker's letters and reports swung between high optimism and dark despair. Throughout his life, he had exhibited the characteristics of a manic-depressive. At the Philadelphia Exposition, for example, where two years earlier he had taken the position to pay off his debts, he wrote Arvilla how excited he was to represent Colorado, how much he appreciated her "prophetic confidence," and the depth of his love for her. "I am still courting you," he wrote in one letter. Two days later, with no explanation, he wrote, "It is possible that these letters I am writing you are among the last I shall write to you in this world."[41] Meeker suffered the disillusionment that came from the belief that hard, honest work deserved its rewards, both personal and financial. He had received neither. Most people who had worked with Meeker over his career marched to a different, less optimistic, drumbeat. He would neither tolerate nor could he accept a slower pace in the march toward a reformed and better world. On those occasions when "Father" Meeker turned around to discover "stragglers" and "quitters" within the procession, he fell into long bouts of depression. The agent admitted to occasional bouts of "melancholy" (a nineteenth-century term for depression), which Emily Dickinson, whom Meeker much admired, said was like "a funeral in the brain."

After the severe winter of 1878–79, spring arrived late. Snowdrifts still lay on the north side of the agency buildings into early May, as Jack and his lodges and Johnson and his followers returned to the White River from their winter camps. Jack made it known immediately that he and his men would not assist the agency's white workers in any of their spring and summer work—building a new road, moving buildings, farming, or completing the irrigation system.

In fact, Jack and his band spent most of the unusually dry summer off the reservation hunting in Middle and North Parks. The Utes had lost these regions in the Treaty of 1868, but maintained hunting rights in both parks, a provision never accepted by white settlers throughout the regions. Throughout the summer, Meeker received reports from the settlers about horse thefts, the killing of game, and fires, all carried out by small Indian bands. He suspected it was the work of Jack's band. When Meeker reported the unconfirmed incidents to Washington, Hayt once again ordered the agent to have the Indians returned to the reservation. "I am powerless to do so," Meeker wired back.[42] Upon the authority of Hayt, the agent then wrote to Major Thornburgh at Fort Fred Steele "to cause said Indians to return to their Reservation."[43] Meeker received no immediate response. He also wrote Pitkin to seek his assistance. The governor suggested the agent contact U.S. military authorities in Washington for assistance, a strategy the governor said he would also pursue through his own channels. He first contacted the sheriff of North Park's Grand County, ordering him to arrest the Indians responsible for the fires. "Were it not for the expense [to Colorado] ... I should send troops in myself," Pitkin explained. Immediately thereafter, the governor wired Hayt, "I respectfully request of you to have [a] telegraphic order sent to troops at the nearest military post to remove Indians [the northern Utes] to their reservation." Pitkin further informed Washington that if "the General Government does not act promptly, the State must [act]. ... Immense forests are burning throughout Southwestern Colorado. ... I am satisfied that there is an organized effort on the part of the Indians to destroy the timber of Colorado." "These savages," referring to those in southwestern Colorado, "should be removed to the Indian Territory or New Mexico where they can no longer destroy the finest forest in the state."[44] Two days later, with additional reports of fires from Meeker, the governor wired Hayt again to say the agent's appeal to Major Thornburgh went unheeded. "The Utes have burned more timber these past two weeks than the White settlers have cut in twenty years." The same day (July 8, 1879) Schurz telegraphed the secretary of war to inform him that Meeker had received "no attention to his repeated requests [to Thornburgh] to keep the Indians where they belong."[45]

Impatient with the lack of attention to his letters and wires to civil and military authorities, Meeker traveled to Denver by way of Greeley to hire two new agency employees, Wilmer Eskridge (a sawyer) and George Eaton (a laborer), to replace workers who had quit. In Denver, he met with General John Pope, whom Meeker had befriended during his brief time as a Civil War correspondent in southern Ohio. He learned from Pope that the general had dispatched a company of black troops from the Ninth Cavalry out of Pagosa Springs to investigate the fires in Middle Park and North Park and to arrest two Indians of Jack's band, Bennett and Chinaman, whom local whites charged with burning the house of a former Indian agent, John Thompson. On Meeker's return by rail from Denver via Cheyenne, he encountered Major Thornburgh, the commanding officer at Fort Fred Steele in southern Wyoming. Meeker asked why the major had not "corralled his wayward Utes," to which Thornburgh replied he had not received orders from his head-quarters to do so. If he wanted troops, the major advised, Meeker should write the Indian Bureau and have them contact the War Department. As for the agent's complaints that his Indians had attacked white settlers and started fires, Thornburgh had made his own investigation in southern Wyoming. The army major reported to his superiors and to Meeker that one settler found the Utes to be "peaceful and polite and did not commit any depredations, or show any hostility towards any of the settlers in this part of the territory." Yes, they had slaughtered game, Thornburgh reported, but the fires were caused, most likely, by the "carelessness" of white settlers, in particular the railroad workers in the "tie camps."[46]

To Thornburgh, Meeker looked tired and spoke very slowly. "I could not help but feel sorry for him. Devoting his life to an attempt to civilize these savages [who] did not want to be civilized [,] I was sure ... he realized his cause was fruitless. His efforts to motivate the Utes to stay on the reservation and farm had failed; now he was seeking relief for his failure by saying the Indians' roaming was the cause. What he could not achieve through his moti-vational attempts ... must now be accomplished by force. If they did not wish to farm, then take away from them all things they wanted to do [hunt] and keep them penned on the reservation like other tribes in the Indian Territory." As Meeker departed the train at Rawlins, Thornburgh noted, the sixty-two-year-old agent walked to his wagon proud, unbending, aloof, stubborn, and with a hobbling stride.[47] During the long three-day ride back to the agency from the rail stop at Rawlins, the wagon turned over on the agent, severely injuring his shoulder. The injury would nag him the rest of his life.[48]

Thornburgh had likely judged both Meeker's character and mood correctly. By August, the agent clearly had lost control of his Utes. "These savages will not stay home," Meeker complained once again to Hayt, "a few, say 20 or 30, I have under my control and I have great hopes for them; but the rest, fully 700, will not stay here. It is useless for anybody to tell me to keep them at home while there is no obstacle to their going away." Off the reservation, the Indians were "intimately associated with the ruffians, renegades and cattle thieves," in addition to the white traders who sold them weapons and liquor and taught them "all kinds of inequities." To assist in bringing the Indians under his control, Meeker suggested the Indian Bureau "have the military break up the selling of ammunition and [liquor] and the [trading] of annuity goods at these stores. Then as the Indians could not hunt, they would work to get money ... and a store would be established here; of course the military must keep them on the reservation and the white man off. When these things shall be done, the Indians will consider the question of sending their children to school and they will open farms. Now they will not. Already they are making their plans for going north after they get their annuity goods to hunt for buffaloes."[49]

Hayt's bureaucratic response to Meeker put the disciplinary burden back on the agent. Because of reports of Utes illegally hunting and setting fires in Middle and North Parks, Hayt directed Meeker to "adopt, without delay, decisive measures to put a stop to these roaming habits of your Indians." If Indians were found off the reservation without passes (as per departmental circular December 23, 1878), they "should be treated as hostiles and liable for arrest. ... You should also give them to understand that their annuities will be withheld from them if they do not comply with the requirements of this office."[50]

Meeker lacked the force and the facilities to make arrests either on or off the reservation. Nor did the Indians pay any attention to the requirement for off-reservation passes. In an attempt to discipline his Indians and halt the exodus, Meeker used the only two weak weapons available to him: threats and rations. He withheld the monthly rations from the families of the missing men or their substitutes and, as an inducement for the rest of the adult males to remain on the reservation, he issued them double rations every two weeks.

"The only discipline exercised in this agency," Meeker wrote Hayt, "is when I get men to work day after day; and this on the penalty of withholding extra rations. This, in fact, is the equivalent to 'compulsory education,' and it is the only power that can be made to operate ... with plenty of coffee and sugar and dried peaches I can lead them forward to civilization." And, again, horses remained "the greatest obstacle." "Those who work have either few or no horses," but a Ute with horses "will not work, nor will he sell any of his stock. ... He is an obstacle to all progress."[51]

Meeker also used threats in an attempt to intimidate the Indians. He warned them that the army would arrest any Indian found off the reservation. If the Indians continued to violate Indian Bureau regulations, he'd have them all arrested and removed from "government land." Jack angrily reminded "Father" Meeker the reservation belonged by treaty to the Utes and not to the Great White Father in Washington or his friends.

Jack had only recently returned from an unannounced visit to Governor Pitkin's office in Denver. Jack and two young braves had marched into the governor's private office and demanded a meeting. He told Pitkin that Meeker had spread lies about the Utes in Denver newspapers. He said Meeker had also withheld rations guaranteed by treaty. The governor read to Jack a recent letter from Meeker charging the Utes with the fires and that two of Jack's band, Chinaman and Bennett, had burned the house of a former Indian agent (Thompson) on the Bear River. Jack replied they had set no fires, and the agent's house "was not burned." He had seen it on his way to Denver. Meeker had lied, Jack insisted, and he needed to be replaced. The governor said he'd investigate the matters and then ordered Jack back to the reservation. Pitkin refused to rescind his order to the Grand County sheriff to arrest Chapman (often miscalled Chinaman) and Bennett (known as "Glass Eye") and once again called for military intervention from Washington to both assist the county sheriff with the arrests, if called upon, and to accompany the Indians back onto the White River Reservation, by force if necessary.[52] For Governor Pitkin, the final solution was the complete removal of the Utes from Colorado. And to further inflame public opinion against the Ute presence, Pitkin turned to his friend, William Vickers, the editor of the *Denver Tribune*.

"The Utes Must Go," Vickers editorialized. "The Utes are actual, practical Communists and the Government should be ashamed to foster and encourage them in their idleness and wanton waste of property. Living off the bounty of a paternal but idiotic Indian Bureau, they actually become too lazy to draw their rations ... but insist on taking what they want wherever they find it. Removed to Indian Territory, the Utes could be fed and clothed for about half what it now costs the Government. ... the broader truism [is] that only truly good Indians are dead ones."[53]

While Meeker may not have shared Vickers's sentiments about the fate of the Utes, at least not yet, his attitude toward his wards had become, over the span of one year, decidedly more unfavorable, if not cynical. In his 1878 annual report to the Indian Bureau, he described the Utes as "peaceful" and "amiable" and, with his gentle guidance, making slow but steady progress toward "civilization." A year later, in August of 1879, Meeker had radically changed his opinion. He now found them to be "weak, both in mind and body," deceitful "savages" who wasted their time "racing [horses], gambling and begging," when not off the reservation trading for the latest-model rifle, ammunition, liquor, and a set of field glasses. Even with stricter disciplinary measures, Meeker complained, "how difficult, if not hopeless, is the task of civilizing these Utes." Only a few Utes had gained a higher "pastoral" level and none of them had attained the "enlightened, scientific and religious" stage of development. If the "savages" were stripped of their horses, they'd be without the means to leave the reservation and then, and only then, could they be induced to farm and tend to cattle and "learn a profitable industry." But to permit "any class of human being to do as they please, and at the same time be supplied with food, inevitably leads to demoralization." Meeker concluded with his scheme. "After I get hold [control] of the Indians," suggesting tougher disciplinary measures in the future, "I can tell a great deal better what can be made of them." To control the Utes, I have no choice but to "take away their horses, then give the word that if they [do] not work they should have no rations."[54]

Meeker possessed neither the means nor the authority to strip the Indians of their horses. He did, however, devise one strategy to force the Indians to cut down on their horse numbers by limiting their pasture. He would bring this "horse business" under control. In early September, he informed Chiefs Douglass, Johnson, and Jack he planned to have a fifty-acre portion of Powell Park plowed up for farm ground. The eighty acres already under cultivation would not yield enough crops for the entire agency. The parcel Meeker selected, prime horse pasture, lay close to the river and the lodges of Chiefs Johnson and Douglass. Jack, playing the other chiefs against the agent, suggested a smaller parcel, much to the annoyance of Johnson and Douglass, who said they didn't want the big curved knife cutting into and tearing up any part of their horse pasture. Douglass also reminded Meeker that only recently the agent, in a gesture of appreciation for the senior chief's loyal support and assistance, had reserved a portion of the fifty-acre parcel for his lodges. Johnson also opposed the plowing on the site adjacent to his new, agency-built house. The chiefs suggested that instead the agent should look to plow some unused slough ground some distance away. Meeker answered he would have the horse corrals moved and a new well dug, and he'd see to it Johnson's people would receive a stove for the winter. But the plowing would proceed as planned. The next day, as the agency plowman made his cuts, an unidentified Ute fired over the head of the white worker. Meeker halted the plowing and immediately requested a council with the chiefs. Jack refused to attend. Meeker informed the other chiefs that the plowing would continue, that neither he nor his workers would be intimidated, and that the land was not theirs but the government's. He threatened them with arrest and imprisonment by the army if they attempted again to halt the plowing.

That evening, September 8, Meeker reported the incident to Hayt and informed the commissioner that the Indians "know the danger of opposing me." He assured Hayt the "plowing will proceed, but whether unmolested I cannot say. This is a bad lot of Indians. They have had free rations so long and have been flattered and petted so much, that they think of themselves as lord of all."[55]

The plowing proceeded two days later. At midday, Chief Johnson approached Meeker outside his office and once again demanded a halt to the plowing. They exchanged angry words. When Meeker threatened Johnson with prison for responsibility in the shooting and for insubordination, Johnson told Meeker "that it would be better for another agent to come, who was a good man, and not talking such things." Johnson, in testimony a year later, went on to explain, "I then took the agent by the shoulder and told him it was better that he should go. Without ... striking him or anything else ... I went to my house." Meeker's account of the incident differed. He charged Johnson with dragging him out of his office, throwing him to the ground, and reinjuring his shoulder. Only by the intervention of two agency workers, Meeker exaggerated in his claim, was his life saved.[56]

Shaken and stunned, Meeker sent a messenger to Rawlins with a telegram to Washington. "I have been assaulted by a leading Chief, Johnson, forced out of my house and injured badly but was rescued by employees. It is now revealed that Johnson originated all the trouble stated in letter [of two days ago]. His son shot at the plowman and the opposition to plowing is wide. Plowing stops. Life of self, family, and employees not safe; want protection immediately; have asked Governor Pitkin to confer with General Pope."[57]

In the heat of the moment, and in pain from his reinjury, Meeker had distorted the threat to his life and those of his family. Even Jack, no friend of the agent's, remained calm after Meeker informed Jack that troops had been summoned onto the reservation. "I told him again," Jack later testified under oath, "that the trouble between him and Johnson was a very small matter and he had better let it drop and not make such a fuss about it."[58] But Meeker would not let the matter drop. The presence of troops on the reservation, Meeker recognized, would enhance his authority, although he knew the troops might antagonize the Utes. As a band, and even as a tribe, they had never, as far as he knew, demonstrated a willingness, much less the capacity, to tangle with the army. They needed, he reasoned, a short, quick disciplinary lesson.

To guarantee that his request not be lost or disregarded within the administrative layers of the Indian Bureau, Meeker turned to Governor Pitkin for political reinforcement. He informed the governor that he had been "assaulted in my own house, while my wife was present ... and considerably injured" by the ungrateful Johnson, for whom he had built a house, "given him a wagon and harness, and fed him at my table many, many times." The trouble with Johnson, Meeker explained to Pitkin, was that "he had 150 horses, and wants the land for pasturage. ... Is it not enough I must suffer at the hands of Johnson, but now the chiefs and headman of the tribe ... laugh at my being forced out of my house." And to ensure that Pitkin understood the racial overtones and the danger of the situation, Meeker added, "and I feel none of the white people are safe." He then asked the governor to confer with General Pope (commanding officer for the military district), Commissioner Hayt, and Senator Teller and requested the immediate dispatch of "at least 100 soldiers" for protection. He concluded his telegram with the warning, "Don't let this application get in the papers, for I know the Indians will hear of it in a few days. Of course what the Indians have done is a matter of news."[59]

That same evening, Meeker wrote his old friend from whom he had purchased land for the Union Colony, William Byers, who had become Denver's postmaster, to lobby on his behalf before Pitkin. "Johnson attacked me violently," he wrote, "and I am considerably hurt. I have dispatched to Washington that I want protection, and [have] written to Pitkin and Senator Teller to confer with General Pope. I think they [the Utes] will submit to nothing but force. How many are rebellious, I do not know; but if only a few are, and the rest laugh at their outrages, as they do, and think nothing of it, all are implicated. I didn't come here to be kicked and hustled out of my own house by savages, and if the government cannot protect me, let somebody else try it. You know the Indians and understand the situation. Please see Governor Pitkin, etc. I don't want anything but the bare facts of their hostility to get into the papers. Future movement [of the army], if printed, will reach the Indians in four days. This I know."[60]

By the day after the claimed attack on Meeker, Pitkin, who did not yet know of the incident, had already requested the assistance of the U.S. Army, less to protect Meeker directly than to arrest Bennett and Chinaman, a task not accomplished by the Grand County sheriff and his two deputies. In a letter to General Pope, Pitkin asked him to order the Ninth Cavalry to arrest the two Indian outlaws who, Meeker warned, would not submit readily. "It would require at least fifty men to make the arrest." Pitkin went on to report that the Utes continued their fires, "depredations," and "indignities" to which Colorado settlers "are constantly subjected." The Utes, Pitkin insisted, had to be "speedily removed from the State." They occupied valuable mineral and agricultural ground while "they claim immunity from the laws of the State when off the reservation." "May I ask you in the interest of peace, and in the name of the people of the State, both for the welfare of the Indians and the white people," Pitkin concluded, "to use your good offices to secure the speedy transfer of the tribe beyond the boundaries of the State."[61]

Meeker's telegram to Washington, sent from the nearest telegraph office at Rawlins, a four-day ride from the agency, received immediate attention, though not from Schurz or Hayt.[62] With Hayt in Chicago and Schurz already on his way to Denver to confer with Pitkin about the Meeker incident, Acting Commissioner E. J. Brooks forwarded (presumably with Schurz's approval) Meeker's request: send "a sufficient [military] guard for the arrest of such Indians as may be found implicated in the disturbance and, that the ring leaders be held as prisoners until the matter has been thoroughly investigated."[63]

With no immediate response to his request, Meeker again wired Hayt to insist that when the troops arrived, they "must REMAIN." There existed, the agent reported, "an insubordinate spirit" among the Indians, the result, Meeker failed to mention, of his call for troops and the certainty of arrests. That same day, now five days after Meeker's incident with Johnson, General Sherman wired his western commander, Philip Sheridan, "Secretary of War approves request of Interior Department, just received, and General of the Army directs that necessary orders be given the nearest military commander to the agency to detail a sufficient number of troops to arrest such Indian chiefs as are insubordinate, and enforce obedience to the agent ... also that the ring leaders be held prisoners until investigation can be had." Acting Commissioner Brooks telegraphed Meeker, "War Department requested commanding officer nearest post to send troops for your protection immediately. On their arrival cause arrest of leaders in late disturbance and have them held until further orders from this office. Report full particulars as soon as possible."[64]

Anxious about how the Utes might respond to the troops' arrival but satisfied he had made the right decision, Meeker sat at his desk the same day (September 22, 1879) and wrote a check to the Greeley estate to pay down a major portion of his debt to his mentor's daughters. He had not yet reformed the Utes, but he would save his honor, as he suggested in a letter to David Boyd, an executive at the Union Colony. "By the close of the year, I shall have all my debts paid up." After that, and with some money saved, Meeker expressed an interest in buying that portion of the colony reserved for a college. "How long I shall stay here [at White River] I do not know, but I want to stay here long enough to have something [saved] ahead. I have trouble with the Indians. They cannot stand it to see progressive movements, and they rebel; but there are soldiers coming in and we shall see. By the way, the soldiers are Negroes, and it is sufficient that this race, once so despised, shall compel ... the civilization of Indians."[65]

On September 16, six days after Meeker's encounter with Chief Johnson, Maj. Thomas Thornburgh at Fort Fred Steele in Wyoming received orders from army headquarters in Omaha to move as quickly as possible "with [a] sufficient number of troops" to assist the agent at White River Agency. When Meeker soon learned of a larger force of white troops headed his way from nearby Wyoming, he could only take comfort that he, his family, and his workers would be protected.

REPEATING RIFLES.

SAVAGE UTE:—"We want *no improvements* but this!"

Illustration in Puck, *15 October 1879.*
(Courtesy of the Library of Congress,
#LC-USZ62-105272)

FIVE | *A Battle and a Massacre*

When in September of 1879 Maj. Thomas Thornburgh received the order at Fort Fred Steele to come to the assistance of Agent Meeker, he knew nothing of the circumstances requiring army troops at the White River Agency. He knew only of the need to make arrests and of Meeker's stubborn, inflexible management of his Indians. He had learned over the summer to mistrust the agent's reports. Had the agent, to protect his authority with the Utes and his reputation with the government, exaggerated his trouble and lied again?

Thornburgh's cavalry and infantry troops had spent more time surviving the harsh environment of southern Wyoming than fighting Indians. Nestled in a semicircle of sand ridges adjacent to the North Platte River on thirty-six square miles of sand and dirt, the post provided no protection in the "wind corridor," which funneled hot and cold airstreams off the Red Desert directly to the west, nor did the soil, which grew some prairie grass, but mostly sage brush and salt-weed bushes, provide ample nutrition for the army's horses.

As part of its mission to protect white settlers, the army had built the small, temporary post in 1868 on the North Platte River adjacent to the Union Pacific, sixteen miles east of Rawlins. The railroad carried the vanguard of civilization, the "hearty pioneers," as Gen. Philip Sheridan referred to them, and the tracks into the West required protection. With the army's assistance, the railroad would open western lands "redeemed from idle waste [of the Indians] to become a home for millions of progressive Americans."[1] For the small detachment of troops at Fort Fred Steele, its specific mission was to guard the railroad construction crews and pioneers who followed in their path against any Indian interference. None had occurred in the vicinity, though to the east and north the army had only recently completed successful campaigns against the Sioux following Custer's defeat in 1876 at the Little Big Horn.

At army headquarters in Washington, General Sherman held no compassion for the Indian. Throughout his career, Sherman had wanted to pursue a policy of military extermination against the "savages," but he had come to accept the policy to remove them to out-of-the-way reservations where they could, for all he cared, starve to death. By 1879, he thought the "Indian problem" about over, maybe a few scattered and sporadic disturbances, but no serious battles or engagements. That summer he wrote to an old friend that "time is working so beautifully in our favor that it is folly to precipitate trouble with the Indian." And with the West's filling up with settlers that "soon we shall have no Buffalo, no Elk, or Bear, and may be no Indians. I think our new Museum (The Smithsonian in Washington) will have to collect samples of them for preservation to show our children."[2]

With the slow expiration of the "Indian problem," the army targeted a number of small western outposts for closure, including Fort Fred Steele. As at most isolated frontier installations in the late 1870s, Fort Fred Steele's troops fought boredom more often than they engaged Indians. That the army ultimately called upon the troops at Fort Fred Steele to assist Agent Meeker in Colorado had less to do with the troops' capacity or experience in handling an Indian police action than it did with its proximity to the White River Agency. Two hundred miles distant and a hard five-day ride over rough, unmapped terrain, the agency's location created a major challenge to any military officer, especially Thornburgh, who lacked experience in Indian ways and who commanded a poorly trained and severely undermanned troop contingent.

Thornburgh had in his command at Fort Fred Steele in the fall of 1879 a cavalry company and an infantry company (both under-strength by about 25 percent) for a total of 143 enlisted men and six officers. After the Civil War, Congress, to guard against President Grant's use of the army as a Republican weapon against a defeated South, had slashed the army's size. As for the "Indian problem," congressional Democrats thought it to be exaggerated by the president and the army, an excuse for a larger budget. Even after Custer's defeat, Congress's allowance for a 2,500-man increase lasted only six months.

Major Thomas "Tip" Thornburgh, commanding officer at Fort Fred Steele, Wyoming Territory, who led a combined infantry-cavalry detachment at the Battle of Milk Creek.
(Courtesy of the Smithsonian Institution, National Anthropological Archives, James Taylor Album, #77-13323)

Soldiers with their pet elk at Fort Fred Steele, Wyoming Territory, circa 1878. The fort provided protection to the Union Pacific Railroad and white settlers and sent troops to the Ute White River Band Indian Agency to protect Agent Nathan Meeker.
("Fort Fred Steele, Soldiers with Pet Elk."
Courtesy Frank J. Meyers Collection (#5195), American Heritage Center, University of Wyoming)

By 1879, the army ranks included only 24,262 enlisted men and 2,187 officers (including eleven generals). Aside from its considerable responsibilities in the East, the army's western forces responsible for keeping watch over a quarter-million Indians found themselves stretched out over 1.6 million square miles. General Sheridan, who headed the western forces, commanded 15,500 soldiers, plus 300 Indian scouts, organized into nineteen regiments—seven infantry, eight cavalry (including two black units, "the blacks in blue") and four artillery regiments—scattered about at almost 100 forts, posts, and canton-ments. With poor pay and low morale, soldiers reenlisted at about the same rate they deserted. Officers and soldiers alike complained of shoddy living conditions; shortages of equipment, ammunition, and horses; and virtually no opportunities for advancement.[3]

Garrison life at Fort Fred Steele, as at all frontier posts, centered on field training, an occasional scouting patrol, but mostly the constant care and maintenance of equipment and the post's hastily constructed, poorly heated buildings. Horses required daily attention, particularly training, if not as much as the raw human recruits. Company sergeants conducted classes in riding techniques, march procedures, battle formations, horse care, and marksmanship. Army fare consisted of boiled range beef, bread, and whatever fresh fruits and vegetables grasshoppers had left standing in the post garden. On maneuvers or routine patrols, it was the same diet but in dried form, except maybe for wild fruit and game the troops managed to forage. When given a rare and short furlough, never long enough to return to their homes, the troops rode into Rawlins or Cheyenne. They purchased items not available at Fort Fred Steele's sutler's store—especially liquor, which was banned from all military installations—and patronized the towns' various "hog ranches." With their paychecks demolished, those who did not desert returned to the fort.[4] For more healthful recreation at the post, soldiers engaged in baseball, soccer, horse races, hunting, and fishing. Mrs. Thornburgh and the few other women at the post organized social events—a birthday party or a musical if the talent allowed—and provided whatever culinary treats they could create from the limited supplies of the fort's quartermaster or sutler's store.[5] The Thornburghs brought a new energy and spirit to the soldiers at this isolated outpost where the wind never died and the dust never settled. And they did so in the face of a sudden tragedy when, in their first and only winter at the fort, they buried their two-year-old son, who died of pneumonia.

As a career officer, Maj. Thomas "Tip" Thornburgh brought to his assignment at Fort Fred Steele considerable military experience. Born in 1843 to the son of an antislavery state legislator in eastern Tennessee, "Tip" Thornburgh ran away from home after his father's imprisonment (and death by starvation) at the Andersonville prison. He enlisted as a private in 1861 in the Sixth Tennessee Regiment, a Union infantry unit under General Sherman's command. Thornburgh participated in the Battle of Stone River, rose through the ranks to sergeant major, and in 1863, with his enlistment completed, received an appointment to West Point with the assistance of his brother, a Tennessee legislator. He did not fare particularly well at West Point, finishing in the bottom half of his class. But he compensated for his academic short-comings by marrying well. In 1870, he married the daughter of an influential army officer in the Paymaster Corps. Five years later, his father-in-law, assisted by his brother's friendship with President Grant, arranged for the first lieutenant's promotion to major and his appointment to fill a vacancy in the Paymaster Corps.

With the promotion, the army had jumped Thornburgh over 250 captains and 100 lieutenants with senior service; at age thirty-two, he became the youngest major on active duty. Stationed in Omaha, he began attending the Omaha Gun Club, where his marksmanship skills impressed the headquarters commander, Gen. George Crook, the famed Indian fighter. Crook had inaugurated the Indian scout service into the army and introduced the mule pack train as a replacement for the slower oxen- and horse-drawn trains. The general took such a liking to the young major and his shooting skills that he appointed Thornburgh to his personal staff. As a fellow avid sportsman, he frequently invited his aide to accompany him on hunting trips into Wyoming's prime hunting grounds, now accessible with the westward extension of the Union Pacific rail line.

For Thornburgh, the friendship resulted in another important assignment. In the spring of 1878, he received orders to command Fort Fred Steele. Thornburgh knew the fort to be a decrepit outpost that had, with the completion of the railroad, outlasted its usefulness, except to house three companies of troops. Crook had already planned to abandon it, but suggested the command to Thornburgh for the short duration before its closure. For Thornburgh, it meant a troop command and a far better path to higher rank—a colonel or even with luck a general's star—than through his present staff position. Fort Fred Steele also presented the exciting opportunity to hunt and fish—his passions in life. He knew the post commander's house to be adequate for his wife and new child, and Crook promised he would be back in the comforts of Omaha within eighteen months.

Upon arrival, Thornburgh busied himself with the usual duties of a post commander—overseeing the preparation of monthly reports to headquarters in Omaha and directing the troop's preparedness. To his dismay, he spent an inordinate amount of time on disciplinary matters—drinking, gambling, and desertion—while wasting valuable manpower in the search for and transport of deserters under guard back east to Fort Leavenworth in Kansas. In the winter, he worried about outbreaks of pneumonia and scurvy and, throughout the year, the ever-present dysentery and venereal diseases. He received constant reports and complaints from his company commanders and adjutant, the post quartermaster, the post physician, the head teamster and blacksmith (usually civilian contractors), and the sergeant major (the enlisted men's chief spokesman). When in the field, Thornburgh led the cavalry's traditional drills and formations, changed not at all from his instruction at West Point. Within six months of taking command, Thornburgh, with the aide of his wife, had improved the troops' morale. But for lack of congressional funding, his command continued undermanned, underequipped, and unprepared for an engagement with the Utes.

Thornburgh's frontier inexperience and that of his troops was evident when, in the fall of spring of 1879, General Crook ordered Thornburgh, a skilled horseman, and his small combined force of infantry and cavalry to move into Nebraska Territory to intercept two small bands of Northern Cheyenne under Dull Knife and Little Wolf, moving north from Indian Territory to join up with the Sioux. Thornburgh transported his small force by train to Ogallala, Nebraska, and then headed north into the unmapped territory where, lacking proper scouts and a mobile pack train, the supply wagons mired themselves in the region's notoriously sandy soils. Once extracted, Thornburgh and his troops marched and rode more than 250 miles in the sandhills. In search of water for their horses, they lost their way, only to be rescued by a detachment of the Third Cavalry Regiment, which guided Thornburgh's troops back to their embarkation point.

That Thornburgh was not relieved of his command was due, no doubt, to his mentor's friendship and to General Crook's belief he would not have occasion to call upon Thornburgh and his troops prior to the fort's abandonment within the year. Thornburgh returned to Fort Fred Steele embarrassed. His Nebraska experience had taught him, however, that whatever task he and his small command might be ordered to carry out in the future, he must have under his command a sufficient number of troops to accomplish the mission. When a year earlier Meeker had requested Thornburgh's assistance to force the Utes back onto the reservation, Thornburgh reminded General Crook that he had few troops at hand to "force them to return without running the risk of war, for which [I] would be held accountable."[6] Crook never issued the order, nor did Crook send reinforcements to Thornburgh. Forever cautious after the inglorious humiliation he suffered in Nebraska, Thornburgh remained determined, however, to make amends.

Thornburgh and his wife thoroughly enjoyed hosting civilian and military dignitaries passing through on inspection trips or, as was more common, coming to hunt and fish near Fort Fred Steele amidst the vast wilderness south along the Wyoming-Colorado border. Such visits brought news of current events and friends, some special foods and gifts, often a case of claret and a box of cigars, or a new sidesaddle for Mrs. Thornburgh. But most important of all for the major, the visitors brought a welcome break from the boredom of the post's routine. It was on one such trip, his first summer, that Thornburgh guided General Crook and Webb Hayes, the president's son, on a hunt into the mountains south of Fort Fred Steele. Crook had shot a trophy buck deer for the young Hayes, who asked if Thornburgh might have it mounted and sent to the president in Washington.[7] The president responded with a personal note of thanks to the major. A year later, in mid-September of 1879, Thornburgh was involved in another such pleasant diversion when, on the eve of a hunt with his older brother, ex-Congressman Jacob Thornburgh of Knoxville, and two Tennessee bankers, he received his orders to move quickly and without delay to the assistance of Agent Meeker at the White River Agency two hundred miles distant in Colorado.

A messenger from Fort Fred Steele bringing Crook's telegraphic order found Thornburgh and his companions making preparations for the hunting trip into the mountains south of Rawlins. Thornburgh hastily made preparations to gather a "sufficient number of troops" for the march to Meeker's assistance. He telegraphed Crook's headquarters to say he would move as soon as possible but added, "I don't believe it safe or prudent to go to White

River with troops [presently] at my disposal. I could not take more than eighty men and it is evident that the Utes mean mischief." In a telegram the next day Thornburgh added that if he had three cavalry companies he would face "little risk" with his mission.[8] Immediately two cavalry companies were dispatched by train from Fort Russell in Cheyenne to join Thornburgh's infantry and cavalry companies at Fort Fred Steele for the expedition to White River. After assembling enough wagons to carry the infantry, ammunition, and other supplies, Thornburgh had under his command about 175 cavalry and infantrymen, plus 25 or so civilian teamsters. He departed Fort Fred Steele on September 21, five days after receiving Crook's initial order, and by early evening made camp outside Rawlins. The major was quick to post guards that evening to insure no one slipped off to the nearby bars and "hog farms."

That evening Thornburgh hired a guide, Charles Rankin, a Rawlins livery stable operator whose company's supply trains carried provisions to Meeker's agency. He informed Thornburgh that four supply trains had only recently departed for White River: one transporting flour for the Utes; another larger ten-wagon train loaded with more flour, hardware, and flannel shirts; the third carrying china, a threshing machine, and a steam engine to power Meeker's newest agricultural experiment; and the fourth, only three days gone, a shipment of barbed wire and hardware to assist Meeker with the "horse problem." With his troops assembled, an experienced guide, and a new set of orders, Thornburgh and his combined infantry-cavalry force of 191 officers, enlisted men, and civilians departed the next morning on their journey toward White River.[9]

The assembled troops did not resemble a Hollywood rendition of a "spit and polished" cavalry unit riding quickly in close, orderly formation toward an Indian battle. Like all similar expeditions, it moved only as fast as allowed by the weather and the rough terrain, at best twenty to twenty-five miles a day. The cavalry unit's speed and maneuverability (and hence its effectiveness) depended as much on the health and condition of its horses, and the blacksmiths and farriers who kept them shod, as it did upon the riding and handling skills of the troopers and teamsters. The summer of 1879 was dry, and sufficient forage for the 370 head of mules and horses presented a daily challenge.

The slow-moving supply train of thirty-three six-mule teams set the limits of a day's march. Spread out along the rutted single-path road, the heavily loaded wagons lumbered along with thirty days of rations (barrels of fresh and died meat, hardtack, beans, flour, cornmeal, potatoes, and coffee). Added weight and bulk consisted of extra horse feed and ammunition; soldiers' packs with their bedrolls, tents, and spare clothing; equipment and supplies for the blacksmiths, farriers, cooks, and saddler; plus ropes, spades, horseshoes, axes, spare weapons, harnesses, and saddles. A cavvy of spare horses and mules, guided along by outriders, and the mule-drawn medical and sutler's wagons accompanied the main pack train. At streams or rivers, the teamsters sought out crossings no deeper than four feet and with a firm bottom. And as on all cavalry maneuvers, hourly stops to water and rest the horses, inspect their shoes, and adjust harness and saddles further slowed the column's progress toward White River.

As they departed from their camp on the outskirts of Rawlins at sunup, everyone believed that their mission—a relatively uncomplicated and simple police action—would allow for a pleasant, safe, and relatively short excursion to White River. The army contingent would then make the few necessary arrests at the agency and then make its leisurely and celebratory return to its respective posts. Thornburgh's adjutant, Lt. Samuel Cherry, class of 1875 at West Point, brought along his greyhound in the event a hunting opportunity presented itself. And Lt. Butler Price, the infantry company commander, kept an eye out for burrowing owls on behalf of the Smithsonian Institution. Thornburgh carried his trout rod and a handful of personal items: a solution to prevent diarrhea, a photo of his wife, witch hazel (for mosquitoes), a bottle of Holland gin and lemon extract, a box of Regina Victoria cigars, and a small leather-covered Bible his sister gave him upon graduation from West Point. He had taken the precaution of arranging for a medical doctor, Dr. Robert Grimes, to join his command, not because he believed his troops faced danger of an Indian engagement, but because his troops would require medical attention for injuries and sickness common on all extended field maneuvers.[10] That Thornburgh decided not to haul two weapons available to him—a mobile twelve-pound howitzer and a Hotchkiss "mountain gun," (a deadly two-pound weapon, mounted on a wheeled carriage, that fired a 1.65-inch exploding shell with accuracy up to four thousand yards)—indicated that he believed the mission to be easily accomplished with the "sufficient" force he had assembled and now commanded.

Once out of Rawlins, the troops followed the wagon road through the high and dry plateau country that defines much of northwest Colorado, a landscape of large, gently rounded hills covered with sage, oak brush, and some small piñon. Aspens gave way to spruce in the higher elevations off to the east and into the snowcapped mountain peaks of what is today the Flat Tops Wilderness Area. They passed by some of the sandstone outcroppings where the Utes displayed their rock art—pictorial representations of deer, elk, and bear common to the area. In the shallow valleys, large grassy meadows interspersed with patches of alkali spread out from the small stream beds, mostly all dry due to the unusually hot and rainless summer of 1879.

As Thornburgh's troops made their way south toward the agency, they did not lack for weapons or good spirits as much as for experience. Capt. J. Scott Payne, the ranking officer of the two Fort Russell cavalry companies, had fought in two small Indian campaigns, but his troops lacked any combat exposure. Lt. Butler Price and his company of Fourth Infantry troops had spent their short military careers absorbed in garrison duty and an occasional field-training exercise. Only Company E of the Third Cavalry, under the command of sixty-year-old Capt. Joseph Lawson, a veteran of the Civil War, had any prior exposure to an Indian engagement. He had fought in Indian engagements in Arizona, New Mexico, the Dakota Territory, and, with Crook, in the Sioux campaigns in 1876–77. Lawson reminded his unit that this was the second occasion on which they had been called to the assistance of Major Thornburgh. The year before, Lawson's Third Cavalry unit had assisted in the long and unpleasant mission of locating Thornburgh's lost column in the Nebraska sandhills. With his troops, Lawson, whose whiskers smelled of whiskey and tobacco, brought up the rear of the column as they sucked dust on the road to White River.

Cavalry troopers rode with a single-shot, breech-loading .45-caliber Springfield carbine slung across their left shoulder, with a canteen, a sheath knife, pistol, and one hundred rounds of ammunition attached to their newly issued "prairie belt." For a saddle, they rode the McClellan model, so poorly designed with its high candle both front and rear and open two-inch slot in the seat that soldiers referred to the small leather torture chamber as the "ball crusher." A saddlebag carried personal items, gloves, and turpentine to clean weapons. The standard army wool uniform, with its gold-braided piping and the cumbersome saber, they left behind at the barracks. For utilitarian comfort, the cavalry soldiers preferred a pair of canvas pants reinforced with thin buckskin in the crotch, seat, and legs, which they tucked into the tops of their high leather riding boots. A loose cotton blouse they found more comfortable than the trim, but stifling, five-button traditional tunic. And to replace the army's hot and useless felt hats, the soldiers preferred a wide assortment of cotton or straw wide-brimmed headgear of their own design. For warmth and protection, if needed, a mounted soldier tied a blanket to the front of his saddle and a wool coat and rain gear to the rear. Given the wide assortment of the troops' attire, it was difficult to distinguish a soldier's rank except for where he rode in the column and an occasional shoulder board insignia of the eight officers.

The troops' prior training consisted of marksmanship, when ammunition was available, and riding in traditional European formations designed for conventional frontal attacks. Despite former engagements with Indians, army commanders had been slow to adjust tactics to their guerrilla-type raids. As skilled horsemen and experienced wilderness tacticians, Indians selected the terrain and the appropriate time they wished to engage an enemy in a minor skirmish or larger battle. Extremely mobile, with well-trained mounts, and accustomed as they were to living off the land, the Plains and mountain Indians had learned how to outmaneuver the slow-moving U.S. Cavalry, which was constantly burdened by, if not locked to, their heavily-laden wagon trains. Thornburgh and his few experienced officers, however, understood Indian tactics well enough to recognize his troops' vulnerability to a more mobile Ute force in their home territory.

Four days out of Rawlins and about halfway to the White River, Thornburgh recognized the need to speed his journey. He made the decision to drop part of his main supply train at an easily defended position along Fortification Creek where, using the infantry company for protection, they made their temporary headquarters. Preparing to move with a more mobile force the next morning, Thornburgh received a new set of orders, which, though they did not alter his mission, did significantly clarify the earlier instructions he'd received at Fort Fred Steele from General Crook. With a report suggesting that possibly not all was peaceful amidst the White River Utes, Crook telegraphed Thornburgh and advised the major to "proceed with the utmost prudence and if you ... have not sufficient force [,] communicate at once by telegraph stating [the] number which you require. They will at once be sent to you." Lacking reliable information in Omaha, Crook told Thornburgh he was leaving "matters entirely to your discretion and good judgment."[11] Had he believed he faced even the possibility of a military action, Thornburgh, in consultation with battle-hardened Captain Lawson and Lieutenant Price, certainly would have requested more troops. Instead, he simply acknowledged receipt of the order. The major could not but fail to recognize and understand, however, the "discretion" allowed him—an important, though by no means unique, delegation of authority by a commanding general.

Before leaving Fortification Creek and his wagon train, Thornburgh sent a message to Meeker informing the agent of his progress and requested information about the state of affairs at White River. "I have heard nothing definite from your agency in ten days," Thornburgh wrote, and "don't know ... whether the Indians will leave at my approach or show resistance." Thornburgh asked for an immediate reply so "that I may know what course to pursue." "If practical," the message concluded, "meet me on the road at the very earliest moment."[12]

The next day as Thornburgh and his troops crossed the Yampa (Bear) River, Lieutenant Cherry and Rankin the guide rode to the local store to inquire about mail and the availability of ammunition. About the time the storekeeper informed Cherry that the Utes had recently purchased his entire inventory of ten thousand rounds, Captain Jack appeared from the store's back room and asked the officer the reason for the presence of army troops. Were they not headed south to the agency? Cherry suggested a meeting with Thornburgh. Thornburgh first offered Jack a cigar—Jack took the entire box—and then explained his orders to proceed to the agency and arrest the "troublemakers" and restore peace. Jack informed Thornburgh that Meeker had been the cause of all the trouble—the plowing of the horse pasture, the withholding of rations, the false charges against the Utes about setting the fires, and now the threat of arrests. In short, Jack counseled, he was "a bad agent" who needed to be replaced. If they were to come onto the reservation with troops in violation of the Treaty of 1868, Jack further warned, they could expect trouble. Instead, the chief suggested, Thornburgh should come to the agency with two or three of his soldiers and leave the rest of his troops behind. Thornburgh replied that as an officer of the government he and his troops had treaty authority to enter the reservation to enforce U.S. laws, including those relating to bodily injury to an Indian agent. But Thornburgh added that he liked Jack's idea about a meeting and would, with his officers, give it consideration. Thornburgh also recognized that Jack's appearance on the Yampa was no coincidence, that Jack and the sub-chiefs with him came north not to hunt, as Jack had explained, but to spy and count the troops. But neither had Jack threatened Thornburgh, except to warn him and his cavalry to stay off the reservation. A peaceful way could be arranged, Thornburgh believed at this time, to fulfill his police-action mission. He knew the very presence of troops close to the reservation served as a warning to the Utes that if they started trouble, Thornburgh would respond with an armed force. He would go to the agency alone with a small guard, talk with Meeker and the chiefs, insist upon the arrests, and then return with the prisoners to his main encampment just off the reservation. Thornburgh sent off a message to General Crook informing his commander of the meeting with Jack and his two sub-chiefs. "They seem friendly and promise to go with me to the agency. [They] say Utes don't understand why we have come. Have tried to explain satisfactorily. Do not anticipate trouble."[13] Jack rode off south toward White River rather than north to hunt.

The next day (September 27), Thornburgh received a message from Meeker in response to his inquiry about the situation at the agency. Meeker reported that "the Indians are greatly excited, and wish you to stop at some convenient camping place, and then you and five soldiers of your command come into the agency [for a talk]. ... The Indians seem to consider the advance of troops as a declaration of real war. In this I am laboring to undeceive them, and at the same time to convince them they cannot do whatever they please. The first object now is to allay apprehension."[14] Thornburgh replied that he planned to move his troops to Milk Creek and come to the agency with five men and a guide.

As the troops moved slowly and cautiously toward Milk Creek, they overtook the wagon train hauling the thrashing machine to the agency. The bullwhacker told Thornburgh he'd encountered Chief Colorow the day before, who'd warned that if the army crossed into the reservation, the Indians would fight. The bullwhacker then showed Thornburgh a drawing the Indians had planted on the wagon road—a picture of four army officers riddled with bullets. That evening, Colorow appeared in the army camp and confronted Thornburgh. He wanted to know the reason for the presence of troops. Thornburgh gave the same explanation to Colorow as he had to Jack. The troops would stop at Milk Creek, and he'd come to the agency with a few troops for a talk with Meeker and the chiefs.[15] The same evening, an agency courier arrived to report that, under Jack and Douglass's direction, all the Ute women and children at the agency had departed to a location south of the agency. For the past two nights, the messenger reported, the agency Indians had conducted a war dance. Had Meeker's efforts to "allay apprehension" failed or, as Thornburgh suspected, were the Indians up to their old tricks of trying to intimidate their agent? And if Meeker thought his life and those of his family and employees were at risk, certainly, Thornburgh believed, the agent by this time would have informed him of such danger and requested an escort party to assist in their evacuation. As far as Thornburgh knew, the Utes had never fought against U.S. troops, unlike the warring tribes of the plains. And they had no reason, he believed, to do so now. Thornburgh thought it unnecessary to send a message to Crook indicating any anticipated trouble or calling for extra troops.

The next day, the day before the final march to Milk Creek, where he planned to make camp before proceeding with his small guard detail to the agency, Thornburgh noticed smoke from fires ahead. He pressed on, and with scouts to his front and flanks, no Indians appeared. By early afternoon, the troops arrived at Deer Creek, eleven miles north of Milk Creek, where much of the grass had burned. As the soldiers made their night camp and watered and fed their tired horses, Thornburgh discussed with his officers his options on how best to proceed the next day upon his arrival at Milk Creek, the reservation boundary.

He could move forward with all his troops across Milk Creek so as to be closer to the agency, but would the move—as Jack had warned and Colorow confirmed—invite attack? Thornburgh had told both Jack and Colorow he would stop at Milk Creek. The Utes expected the troops to advance no farther south. The more attractive and safer alternative, Thornburgh believed, would be to hold his troops at Milk Creek while he, at Meeker's suggestion, proceeded twenty miles south to the agency for his parley with the agent and the chiefs. He could only guess at what Meeker had told the Indians at the agency, but the agent's recent message had indicated the Utes to be "friendly," and surely Meeker had addressed the Utes' anger by conveying the message the troops would not advance beyond Milk Creek. The secondhand report of a war dance did suggest that Meeker may not have, as promised, "undeceived them." Still he had little reason to believe Meeker had lost control of the agency and couldn't use his influence to calm the Utes' fears. And why, Thornburgh may have thought, would the Utes wish to engage in what was certain to be a suicidal defense of three troublesome Indians? They certainly recognized the overwhelming force he commanded. Might Jack be bluffing? After considering all the evidence, he accepted the assurances of a white agent, rather than submit to the threats of an Indian. And with his orders from Crook, didn't Thornburgh possess the authority to use his "discretion"? Thornburgh also considered his tarnished reputation that was in need of polishing.

The Utes, too, were weighing their options, trying to decipher the conflicting signals from Thornburgh (via Jack) and the little information gleaned from Meeker. If, as Meeker told them, the troops meant no harm and wished to avoid war, why had the agent called for the army and told Johnson, Bennett, and Chinaman they would be placed in manacles and handcuffs? Was the army so weak that it required 175 heavily armed soldiers to arrest three Utes? Hadn't the agent initiated the trouble, not Johnson? As for Bennett and Chinaman, the Utes believed that they had been falsely accused by unnamed, rumormongering white settlers, a governor, and an agent. They trusted neither Pitkin, who promised a new agent, nor Meeker, who lied to them, withheld rations, and now called in the army to enforce his lies. Could this be the prelude to another Sand Creek Massacre, the Ute chiefs may have asked themselves, where the white authorities promised peace and the army waged slaughter? If Thornburgh with a small guard wanted to come in and talk, they would listen and try to explain to him the problem with the agent. But if they spotted cavalry troops crossing Milk Creek onto the reservation, they would defend their land and their people. They had been warned and the Utes were prepared to do battle.

That evening the thirty-five-year-old Thornburgh conferred with his officers. Captain Payne told Thornburgh that if after making camp at Milk Creek the next day he proceeded with a small guard force to the agency and encountered trouble either on the way or more likely at the agency, the main force of troops would be too far away to render assistance. Payne suggested to Thornburgh a diversionary tactic. Go to the agency with five troops as the Utes expected, Payne advised, and the Ute braves would follow him, as agreed upon. Meanwhile, the main body of troops on Milk Creek would "go through all the forms of encampment for the night" and then at first light Payne would "take the cavalry column ... through the canyon [Coal Creek, where Thornburgh and his officers recognized the danger of an ambush] and place it near the agency." They could get through without trouble, Payne confidently assured his commander, and the troops would "be within supporting distance, and yet meet the requirements of the Indians not to go to the agency."[16]

Thornburgh liked the advice of his veteran captain for its tactical caution, though he would slightly modify Payne's plan the next day. The evening before the final march to Milk Creek, Thornburgh sent a messenger to Meeker informing him that "after due consideration" he had altered his plans. He planned to move his entire command to "within striking distance of your Agency," arriving the next day and then proceeding toward the agency with a guide and five soldiers. Thornburgh informed the agent that he had "carefully considered" whether to leave his troops behind "as desired by the Indians" but because "my orders ... require me to march this command to the agency," he was not "at liberty" to leave his troops behind "in case of trouble." He authorized Meeker to say on his behalf "that my course of conduct is entirely dependent on them. Our desire is to avoid trouble, and we have not come for war." Thornburgh also repeated his request of three days earlier to meet with Meeker on the road north of the agency with "such chiefs as may wish to accompany you."[17] That Thornburgh mischaracterized his orders, that in fact he was "at liberty" to use his own discretionary judgment, he failed to mention to Meeker. Thornburgh had learned in his military career the army did not take orders from civilian employees of the Indian Bureau. It had its own mission and Thornburgh would be the final arbiter of how and when he would proceed with his military mission.

At the agency that evening, Meeker and his workers witnessed a war dance but anticipated no trouble with the arrival of Thornburgh and his guards. Frank Dresser, a young laborer from Greeley, wrote to his mother late that evening to allay her fears, if not his own. "I must stand guard part of the night. Meeker is afraid they [the Indians] will fire the hay. As regards [the] danger, don't fret Mother. We are safe and sleep as soundly as if in your quiet town of Greeley." He assured her that the next day "the soldiers will be in and the plowing will go on, for Meeker must carry out orders or resign."[18]

Morning dawned clear and cool after an unusual skiff of snow the prior evening. Thornburgh departed early from Deer Creek for the two-hour march to Milk Creek, where he planned to make camp, meet Meeker or at least hear from him, and then prepare for his visit to the agency. By midmorning, as the troops approached the reservation boundary, they noticed that much of the surrounding grass had been burned. Scouts reported evidence of Indian campfires still smoldering and hoofprints, indicating the recent presence of an estimated fifty horsemen. Milk Creek had dried to stagnant pools.

Without adequate feed and water for his horses, Thornburgh faced a critical decision. He could either proceed alone to the agency with his small guard and have his main command return to its earlier, better-watered camp or move with his entire command onto the reservation, searching for water and feed on his way to the agency, the strategy agreed upon by Thornburgh and his officers the night before. After a brief conference with his officers and his civilian guide, Rankin, the commander chose the latter alternative. Rankin suggested that, after crossing Milk Creek, the troops take a cutoff trail from the main wagon toward a good water source at Beaver Springs five miles inside the reservation. Thornburgh agreed with Rankin that if the Utes ambushed, they would do so as the troops entered the confines of Coal Creek Canyon, ten miles ahead on the wagon road. Best to circle off the road, assess any Ute presence and their intentions, find some water, and then bring up the wagons into an overnight camp closer to the agency. From that camp, they would determine how and where to make contact with Meeker and the chiefs.

At about 11:00 A.M., Thornburgh ordered Lieutenant Cherry to take a small detachment of troops to scout the trail across Milk Creek. If they saw Indians, they should signal back, but not fire, Thornburgh ordered. The major followed about two miles behind, leaving the wagons on the other side of the creek on an unprotected grassy knoll. As Cherry, Rankin, and five troops moved up the trail, they spotted about fifty mounted Utes and an equal number of Utes dismounted and armed with rifles holding a position above them, partially hidden and protected in some brush and behind rocks. With all the troops across Milk Creek except the wagons, the Utes lay in wait. As the troops proceeded up the trail, the Utes recognized the maneuver as an aggressive attempt to bypass the road and trespass onto the reservation. And when Jack, from his lookout above the troops, witnessed a company of cavalry to the rear of Cherry's advanced guard dismount, hand over their horses to two guards, and take up a skirmish line, he knew from his service with Crook that they were preparing for battle. They had, as he hoped and expected they would not, invaded the reservation. Meeker had lied again.

Cherry waved his cap at the Indians, a signal both sides recognized as an invitation for a meeting. In another friendly gesture, the Indians waved their rifles. Jack, unarmed and dismounted, walked toward Cherry, who also had dismounted, an indication to Jack that he, too, wished to talk. Then, without warning, a gunshot broke the tense silence. In a conditioned response to the shot, both sides opened fire and battle commenced. As Meeker had predicted in a letter to Senator Teller more than a year earlier, the "evil day" had, indeed, arrived.[19]

From behind rocks and clumps of sage brush, the Utes, well-armed mostly with .44-caliber Winchesters and Henry repeating rifles, quickly picked off the horses at ranges of up to four hundred yards. Two soldiers also fell dead and another three were seriously wounded. Thornburgh recognized the Utes' attempt to flank the troops and attack the undermanned wagons. He ordered one cavalry company to defend the flank as he rode back to organize a defense of the wagons. Within five hundred yards of the wagons, he took a sharpshooter's bullet to the head behind his right ear and died instantly. Under constant and unrelenting rifle fire from the Utes above them, the two decimated cavalry companies retreated, most on foot and some by horse, carrying and dragging their wounded and dead comrades.

Three hours after the battle began at Milk Creek twenty miles to the north, Arvilla Meeker and her daughter Josie were at home cleaning up after the noon meal. Shadrach Price, the post farmer, and Frank Dresser, the young Greeley laborer, had returned to work on a new agency building nearby, where they were throwing dirt and sod onto the roof. Art Thompson, another employee, was spreading the dirt and covering it with the green slabs of new sod. Nathan Meeker had walked over to the storeroom to help William Post, the agency storekeeper and carpenter, complete a monthly inventory. Earlier in the morning, Meeker had sent off a message by courier to the Rawlins telegraph office informing the Indian Bureau in Washington of the army's presence fifty miles distant (actually fewer than thirty miles) and his plans to meet with Thornburgh. Meeker reported that the Indians "propose to fight if troops advance. ... Sales of guns and ammunition brisk for ten days past ... " The agent also reported that he had learned that Capt. Francis Dodge had only recently arrived with a company of the Ninth Cavalry (a regiment of black "buffalo soldiers") at Steamboat Springs, a four-day ride from Milk Creek, with orders to halt the sale of weapons and ammunition to the Utes. "When Captain Dodge commences to enforce the law, no living here without troops. Have sent for him to confer." After lunch, Meeker penned a message to Thornburgh: "I expect to leave in the morning, with Douglas[s] and Severick [a sub-chief], to meet you. Things are peaceful, and Douglas[s] flies the U.S. flag. If you have trouble in getting through the canyon today, let me know in (what) force. We have been on guard three nights, and shall be tonight, not because there is danger, but because there might be." He added, "I like your last programme, it is based on true military principles."[20] Meeker must certainly have recognized the danger he, his family, and employees faced if Thornburgh and his troops came onto the reservation. Yet Meeker never warned Thornburgh that the Utes "propose to fight if troops advance," an indication that the agent either did not take seriously the Ute threat or, if he did, he thought he could control the Utes by allaying their fears.

He clearly misjudged not only the Utes' resolve but also his own influence. Meeker had assured Chief Douglass earlier in the morning that the troops would not cross into the reservation. He suggested that Douglass should select his chiefs for the meeting with Thornburgh, an indication Meeker believed a meeting would take place either at or on the agency road, thus avoiding a military conflict. Whatever the reason for not cautioning Thornburgh, Meeker put Thornburgh and his troops at risk, not to mention his family and agency employees. He also misrepresented or lied to the Utes about what he knew to be Thornburgh's plan to come onto the reservation with all his troops. By withholding information from both sides, Meeker transformed himself from the protector of the Utes into their arrogant and stubborn enemy.

Meeker handed the message to his trusted employee, Wilmer Eskridge, and told him not to delay its delivery. Thornburgh never received the message. On the way to Thornburgh's camp, Eskridge's two Indian guides killed the messenger.

Just as Arvilla had finished her chores, she noticed an Indian gallop into the agency compound and confer with some Indians and Chief Douglass, who had finished dinner with the Meekers. Less than an hour later, twenty armed Indians stormed the new building and opened fire on the agency employees. The Indians may have selected Price, the agency farmer, as their first target because of his constant bragging about killing nine Indians on the plains a few years back. He took a close-range shot to the abdomen and collapsed. They fired at the laborer, Thompson, and he fell dead from the roof. Dresser, the young man from Greeley, suffered a leg wound. He stumbled toward Meeker's house, where he found Mrs. Flora Ellen Price, her two young children, and Arvilla. He located a rifle and began firing through the shattered glass windows of the dining room, killing Chief Johnson's brother. As the firing continued and the Indians started to break into the agency stores, the three women with the children and Dresser ran for cover in the agency's small milk house. They remained there all afternoon as they watched Meeker's house and other agency buildings burn. As for the whereabouts and safety of Nathan Meeker, they could only guess.

Josie Meeker, daughter of Nathan and Arvilla Meeker, and Mrs. Flora Ellen Price with her children, all taken captive by the Utes in 1879 at the White River Agency Massacre. (Courtesy of the City of Greeley Museums, Permanent Collection)

Late in the afternoon, Dresser and the women, with Mrs. Price carrying her children, broke from the milk house, fearing it, too, would be burned. As they ran from the small building, Dresser was gunned down at the north end of the agency compound. The Utes captured the three women and two children and held them. One Indian ordered Mrs. Meeker to go back to the agency office and return with the cash box. She ran to the office past her husband, who lay faceup, bleeding from the mouth, and dead. Stunned, she kissed his forehead. In the office, she quickly gathered up the small amount of cash and her treasured "Spirit Book," a heavy, leather-bound copy of *Pilgrim's Progress*. She ran, limping painfully from a hip wound, back to her captors, fearful of her own fate. The Indians placed Arvilla, Mrs. Price and one child, and Josephine with the other child on horses; in three separate parties, they rode off south from the agency to rendezvous with the Ute women and children who had been evacuated two days earlier. By evening, all the agency buildings, with the exception of Chief Johnson's new log home, lay smoldering. All but one of the eight male employees lay dead, their bodies stripped and, in some cases, hacked, scalped, mutilated, and burned. The survivor, Henry Dresser, Frank's brother, escaped with a severe wound, but soon died in the entrance of a small coal mine, where he had crawled seeking protection. Two other civilians also perished that day. The freighters with their two wagons carrying flour to the agency were murdered, their bodies hacked and disfigured, their cargo untouched.

The battle at Milk Creek raged on throughout the day and into early evening. After the initial late-morning encounter with the Ute warriors, the cavalry soldiers retreated to the isolated wagons on an exposed bluff two hundred yards from Milk Creek. One soldier recovered Thornburgh's body, which had been stripped of its uniform, riddled with bullets, and scalped. At the wagons, now arranged into a protective semicircle, the soldiers received unrelenting fire from the hills to their front and both flanks. In the midst of volleys of Indian bullets and the cries of wounded soldiers and horses, they hastily dug rifle pits for protection. Though outnumbered by about two to one, the Indians commanded the strategic high ground and from behind rocks and boulders they continued to fire down on the open defensive position of the army. To protect themselves as best they could, the soldiers piled dead horses and mules to their front and flanks to form protective breastwork, adding kegs, barrels, boxes, bedding, and sacks of flour and corn—and three dead comrades wrapped in canvas. The Indians picked off two soldiers who were attempting to make their way across the unprotected field for water at Milk Creek. As the Indians shot and killed more horses and mules, they set fire to the grass in front of the wagons in an attempt to burn the soldiers from their position. The troops, now under the command of Captain Payne, quickly set a backfire, only to have one of their wagons burn in the middle of their defensive position. The troops managed to drag it away from the breastwork, but not before suffering additional injuries. They captured what few animals had not been killed or seriously wounded. By nightfall, Thornburgh, ten soldiers, and three civilian teamsters lay dead, with another twenty-five wounded, including Payne and the surgeon. The Utes had lost twenty-three men in the day's battle, more than ten percent of their estimated fighting force, and made off with the runaway army mounts.

Unable to move without horses, surrounded by Indian snipers, injured himself, and having to attend to the wounded troops, Payne sent couriers for help. He sent one to Capt. Frances Dodge and his company of the Ninth Cavalry, known to be in the vicinity of Steamboat Springs, and another to the Rawlins telegraph office (by way of Fortification Creek and Lieutenant Price) with a message to General Crook calling for reinforcements. "This command [three cavalry companies] was met a mile south of Milk Creek by several hundred Ute Indians who attacked and drove us to wagon train ... with great loss. It [is] my painful duty to announce the death of Major Thornburgh, who fell in harness ... and [killing of] 10 enlisted men and a wagon master, with the wounding of about 25 men and teamsters. I am now corralled near water with three quarters of our animals killed after a desperate fight. ... We hold our position at this hour [8:30 P.M.]. I shall strengthen it during the night and believe we can hold out until reinforcements reach us if they are hurried through. Officers and men behaved with greatest gallantry. I am slightly wounded in two places."[21] Payne, too, could only guess at the fate of Meeker and his employees at the agency.

The messenger arrived at Fortification Creek to inform Price to stay put and await orders and then proceeded to Rawlins, arriving only twenty-five hours after leaving Payne's command at Milk Creek. The next day, on orders from Crook in Omaha, 200 cavalry troopers and 150 infantrymen, plus wagons and supplies, under the command of Col. Wesley Merritt, assembled at Rawlins and started on their forced march toward Milk Creek. The second courier, unable to locate Captain Dodge and his company of black cavalry, alerted white settlers to the battle. One settler left a message on a trail in the hope Dodge would encounter it. He did. It read, "Thornburgh killed. His men in peril. Rush to their assistance."[22] Picking up a guide on the Yampa, Dodge and his cavalry company of thirty-five soldiers and two officers endured a forced march of seventy miles. They rode quickly, past a burnt wagon train and two dead teamsters, their bodies hacked and mutilated, and on to Milk Creek where they arrived early the next day. The Utes, tired of battle, suffering casualties, and witnessing black troops for the first time, put up no resistance and retired temporarily from the battle to rest and regroup in preparation for battle the next day.

If not for the assistance of the "buffalo soldiers," Payne and his exhausted troops would certainly have met the same fate as Custer's troops at the Little Big Horn.[23] The black soldiers immediately took up positions within Payne's barricade, and together the troops displayed superb discipline and bravery as they held out for another four days awaiting the arrival of Colonel Merritt's larger relief force. Indian snipers, in their rifle pits close to the wagons and from behind rocks on the surrounding hills, continued to harass and punish the U.S. troops. Before Merritt arrived, now six days after the commencement of the battle and three days after the buffalo soldiers' arrival, the army troops would suffer another three deaths and nineteen wounded. Most of the animals were dead and rotting, either in the breastwork or in the nearby fields. Dodge reported to Omaha, "The stench from the dead animals and the distance from water are our greatest disadvantages."[24]

With almost 450 troops, some in wagons, Merritt moved quickly south from Rawlins to pick up Thornburgh's supply wagons and infantry guard at Fortification Creek and then proceeded on to Milk Creek in record time. Merritt's command traveled 170 miles in three days, the last seventy (including a night march) in twenty hours.[25] With Merritt's arrival at Milk Creek, the Utes withdrew from the battle. Chief Ouray, who at his headquarters on the Uncompahgre had received word of both the battle and massacre two days after hostilities commenced, dispatched an immediate message north to the White River chiefs, including Johnson, his brother-in-law. With little influence and even less authority over the White River band, he ordered them to "cease hostilities," to injure "no innocent persons [the white women and children]," and foresaw that further warfare "will ultimately end in disaster to all parties."[26]

Jack's decision to pull his warriors from the battle had less to do, however, with Ouray's order than with the fact that Jack and his men had halted the invasion, at least temporarily. He had, as he said later, inflicted enough casualties on the army, and with the arrival of Merritt's reinforcements, he saw no need to suffer additional losses. Thus ended one of the longest Indian battles in American history.[27]

Merritt and his troops rode into Milk Creek without opposition. They attended to the wounded, buried the dead on the Milk Creek battlefield, and proceeded to the burned, vacant agency. The bodies of agency employees lay scattered about the compound, bloated and, in one case, fed upon by wolves. They found Agent Meeker lying face up in front of his smoldering office, his body stripped of his pants and boots, a logging chain wrapped around his neck. The Utes had clubbed his skull with a blunt instrument before or after putting a bullet to his head. Through his partially open mouth, a Ute had pounded a metal stake into his throat and out the back of his skull. He would tell no more lies.

SIX | *A Peace and Removal*

Word of the battle and massacre spread quickly across the country from the incomplete reports filtering into Denver, Omaha, and Washington.

In Colorado, the more moderate newspapers renewed the cry for the Utes' removal from Colorado. The *Rocky Mountain News* editorialized that Colorado citizens could no longer look to Washington to solve the Indian problem and must now take matters into their own hands. The army would not remove Utes because, said the newspaper, they would lack an excuse for their "ineffective" presence in the state; and the Indian Bureau would not act because they continue to profit from "swindling contracts." The Colorado militia should at once force them out and "make the red devils hop." In another editorial, the Denver paper said, "We must assimilate, exterminate, or remove the Utes. The first remedy is unrealistic, the second is cruel, and, as for the third option, the Utes must be sent to the Indian Territory, New Mexico or Utah[;] one thing is settled—the Utes must go." As for the rumor opined by "humanitarians" that the Indian culture was advancing, the *News* squelched it: "the truth is they are as savage and untamable as when Columbus first arrived in San Salvador 300 years ago."[1]

The eastern press reported both the battle and the massacre, but generally withheld judgment as to the instigators, while reminding its readers of the Utes' treaty rights. Rozane Meeker, the agent's daughter, wrote the *New York Tribune* to ensure that eastern readers and politicians understood that "savages" had killed innocent whites, that had the army acted sooner, faster, and with a larger force as requested by her father, the agency workers and her father would still be alive. The life of a "common white man is worth more than the lives of all the Indians from the beginning of their creation ... [My father] was killed by the hand of a savage foe, whose life or soul is not worthy of a dog. ... Truly the blood of the martyred ones cries out for vengeance and shall the voice of anguish be hushed?"[2]

Almost without exception, Colorado papers picked up Miss Meeker's call for retaliation. Denver's *Daily Times* said "either they [the Utes] go or we go, and we are not going. Humanitarianism is [only] an idea. The Western Empire is an inexorable fact. He who gets in the way will be crushed." The *Boulder Banner* put it more directly: "The only solution of the [Indian] problem is extermination." Out-of-state papers chimed in. The *Cheyenne Leader* called for the slaughter of all Utes. "There will just be that many less to move." The government must act now, the Wyoming paper demanded, "unless the sniveling crocodile-teared, jelly-hearted sentiment that spreads over the East ... influences the government to call back the dogs of war. ... The miners and cow-boys are impatient for an opportunity to wipe out old scores, and they will do it in such a way that new scores will not be created."[3] The *Kansas City Times* called for a "retributive blow of telling severity" against the Utes that "will exterminate the whole tribe."[4]

When eastern politicians and press dared to criticize Colorado for wanting to rid itself of the Utes, Colorado's sole congressman, Representative Belford, returned the fire by reminding a few of his congressional colleagues of their less-than-heroic history. On his travels to and from Washington, Belford said that he had "crossed five states made up whole of lands stolen from the Indians. ... And now gentlemen stand here [in Congress] 'in the name of God and humanity' and say, 'while our fathers robbed and plundered the Indians, we want you to belong to the goody-goody class of people in the West.'"[5]

No one ever charged Governor Frederick Pitkin with belonging to such a class. The governor, aided by the press, went out of his way to inflame public fears and ignite up war. Pitkin sent telegrams to mining towns throughout the state warning of the impending war with the Utes. To the town officials in Ouray, he warned, "keep close watch on the Indians" and "reorganize your local militia" in preparation for an attack. To officials in the mining town of Silverton, he wrote, "The Indians are off their reservation seeking to destroy your settlements by fire, [they] are game to be hunted and exterminated like wild beasts. Send this word to the [other] settlements." And to insure that his constituents recognized the danger, he strongly recommended officials throughout the San Juan mining district to "act together for common defense ... "[6]

The army, Pitkin believed, must simultaneously protect the mining communities and finish off the Utes. To Secretary of War George McCrary, Pitkin wrote, "Colorado will furnish you, immediately, all the men you require to settle permanently this Indian trouble ... " And if the federal government refused to act, Pitkin offered up "25,000 brave men at my disposal." The army must severely punish the assassins of Meeker and Thornburgh, or "the consequences cannot be foretold."[7] In the face of evidence to the contrary, and to further alarm General Pope, commander of all U.S. Army forces in Colorado, he claimed other Ute bands and the Shoshone would soon go on the warpath to assist the White River band. Pitkin expanded the fabrication by adding, "We have war here in its most barbarous form." Ouray County, he said, faced the "danger of being massacred."[8] In order to protect the "two hundred miles of settlements exposed to massacre," Pitkin asked Pope for arms, ammunition, horses, and federal troops.[9] And to add political pressure to his calls for military action, Pitkin exaggerated the situation in a telegram to the interior secretary: "The government is doing nothing to defend our settlements. ... The Government [must] recognize that a war with barbarians now exists ... It can be terminated only by the most vicious and uninterrupted warfare."[10] And finally, to insure that the public fully understood the danger they faced, Pitkin released to the press copies of all his communications to local and federal officials.

Pitkin's clear strategy was to eliminate the Utes. The Indian Bureau and particularly Schurz, he thought, were too much influenced by the "eastern sentimentalists," and their adherence to Grant's "Peace Policy." Only the U.S. military, with or without the assistance of the Colorado militia, could remove from Colorado the major impediment to the state's full economic potential. In a letter to Jay Gould, the eastern railroad tycoon, Pitkin revealed the real reason he wanted the Utes moved or, if necessary, "exterminated." Referring to Gould's expressed desire to extend a rail line into Colorado, Pitkin wrote, "I trust all obstacles to [the railroad's] accomplishment may be speedily removed. We are struggling to get Indians removed from Colorado." "The insecurity to capital caused by the Indian presence," Pitkin noted, "keeps miners and capital away.

Frederick W. Pitkin, Colorado governor,
1879–83. Pitkin was an enemy of the
Utes and proponent of their "extermination."
(Courtesy of the Denver Public Library,
Western History Collection, #H-77)

If twelve million acres are thrown open to settlers, cities and towns will spring up almost immediately doubling railroad traffic in this state. We trust eastern sentiment may aid in accomplishing this result."[11]

The army needed no encouragement from Governor Pitkin to go after the Utes and "avenge the deaths of Thornburgh and Custer." General Sheridan blamed the battle not on Thornburgh, of course, nor on Meeker, but on the "savages." The well-intentioned, but impractical agent may have precipitated the battle by his "mismanagement and ignorance of the Indian character" and by his implementation of inappropriate "ironclad ... industrial theories." But the blame must rest, the general said, with the "savages who know nothing but war and the chase."[12] Sheridan called for an all-out attack against the White River renegades, including any Indians, Utes or otherwise, who came to their assistance. He advised Sherman that the army should accept nothing short of an unconditional surrender. Sherman agreed with his western commander and wired back that "no expense or effort should be spared to punish them severely." But he also cautioned Sheridan not to act on unfounded rumors about an all-out war emanating from Pitkin and General Pope. As far as Sherman knew, the trouble was confined to the White River band. "I have advised Governor Pitkin and General Pope to go slow ... until they can gather facts instead of rumors. Pope I think has been tearing his shirt a little more than was necessary. He usually wants more [troops] and accomplishes less than most people."[13] But to be safe, Sherman prepared his army to meet any future Ute raids with a larger, better-armed force. "There will be no halfway measures this time," Sherman told his western commander. "If necessary I will send every man from the Atlantic coast "to go after the Utes.[14] Sherman, like all senior army commanders, distrusted any attempts by the meddlesome Schurz and his farcical Peace Commission to investigate the battle and massacre, and to arrange a settlement with the Utes—a rumor circulating through Washington. For the army, there was nothing to investigate. In Sherman's learned opinion, the Indian Bureau had years to civilize the savages and had failed to do so. The Utes should either be removed or "exterminated," preferably the latter. But in either case, it was a job for the army and not Schurz's incompetent Indian Bureau.

Believing at first Pitkin's reports that all the Utes would join the White River band to defend against the army invasion, Sheridan ordered additional troops to move into Colorado. He transferred 530 soldiers to Colonel Merritt's command on the White River, with other units from Fort Robinson in Nebraska sent in reserve to Rawlins in the event Merritt requested additional reinforcements. In anticipation, if not in the hope of an all-out Ute war, Sheridan also moved 650 cavalry and infantry troops, plus Cheyenne scouts and pack trains, from New Mexico and Texas to Fort Garland, to keep an eye on the southern Utes whose leader, Ignacio, was thought "surly" and "ill-natured," according to one army commander.[15] Sheridan alerted army posts in Utah, the Dakotas, Arizona, and Oklahoma (Indian Territory) to prepare to move into Colorado on short notice. He warned his commanders, without evidence, that other Indian tribes, specifically the Shoshone in Wyoming and the southern Ute bands, were preparing to come to the aid of Jack's warriors now (two days after their withdrawal) some fifty miles south of the agency. And to add urgency to the mission, Sheridan wired Colonel Merritt that if the Utes did not surrender unconditionally, "they will be exterminated ... the attack on Maj. Thornburgh was a piece of the basest treachery and we will respond."[16] Three days after Meeker's death, one-third of the entire U.S. Army had either entered Colorado or surrounded it.

The army, poised to strike against the Utes with or without any further provocation, found itself, however, hobbled and without direct civilian authority to attack. Schurz demanded of the war secretary that he halt the army's advance against the Utes in order to protect the lives of the women hostages. Under orders from President Hayes to keep his army encamped at White River, Sherman fumed while Schurz tried to arrange a temporary peace and the release of the women.

Immediately after receiving word of the massacre and the capture of the hostages, Schurz appointed a special agent to proceed immediately to the Ute camp to arrange a truce and the release of the women hostages. For this delicate mission, he selected Charles Adams, a German-born Civil War veteran and former Ute agent at White River and Los Piños. Adams had the respect of the Utes, the military, and, as former adjutant general of the Colorado Territory, the state's citizens. Schurz instructed his special agent to tell the Utes that the army would not attack if they released the hostages, and that there would be an investigation of the killings at White River. If they refused, however, the army would hunt them down.

After a difficult trip from his home in Colorado Springs and with a stop at Los Piños Agency for provisions, guides, and interpreters, including thirteen

Utes from Ouray's band, Adams located the White River Utes at the junction of the Grand (Colorado) River and Plateau Creek, near the present town of Grand Junction. Adams found the hostages in good condition except for the sixty-four-year-old Arvilla Meeker, who had suffered a flesh wound to her hip on the day of the massacre. When questioned by Adams at the Ute camp as to their treatment by the Indians, the women said they had been treated well. They specifically praised Susan, Ouray's sister and wife of Chief Johnson, for her kind attention during the twenty-four-day ordeal. No, they had not been harmed or "violated" in any fashion, they responded when specifically questioned by Adams.

During a long evening meeting, Jack explained to Adams why he and his braves had engaged Thornburgh's troops. Both Meeker and Thornburgh told them the army would not enter the reservation, Jack said, and they broke their promise. Johnson told the special agent that Meeker had been sent to the agency by the government "to bring trouble about in order that the people [the whites] could get the land." He threatened that if Adams did not call off the army, they would kill the women, and go over to Gunnison and strike there. Jack asked Adams how they could believe his promise to call off the army if they handed over the women. The choice was theirs, Adams responded, Either they release the women now with his promise to halt the army, or face the military consequences. Adams also assured the chiefs of a fair investigation of the incidents at Milk Creek and the agency.

The talks continued the next morning. The chiefs finally agreed to Adams's assurances and released the women.[17] The special agent then departed immediately to meet with Merritt who, two days earlier, had received orders from Sheridan to halt his advance against the Utes. Adams wired Schurz in Washington to report that the Utes had released the women and added, "it is hard to say who should be punished. ... I think also that the Utes should be given credit for their good treatment of the captives and the delivery of [them] to me. ... "[18]

With the release of the women, the eastern press congratulated Schurz, and particularly Adams, for their efforts to bring about a peaceful solution to what might otherwise have escalated into a full-scale war. The *Providence Journal* reminded its readers of the government's treaty obligations with the Indians, that they needed to "be treated fairly," and applauded Schurz for standing up to those who wished to retaliate against the Utes.[19] Hundreds of citizens across the country wrote Schurz, urging him to continue waging his "peace policy." The president of the Universal Peace Society commended Schurz for his "good work" against the army's attack-dog policy. A Philadelphia resident wrote to express her support of the peace arrangement with the Utes against "those who cry our for extermination." "Oh," she concluded, "that the Government would for once keep its word with the Indians." The author enclosed an editorial from the *Philadelphia Daily Transcript* saying the Battle of Milk Creek was no reason for the secretary to give up on the idea of providing Indians with individual land allotments. It further stated there were many tribes, formerly "wild Indians," who had transformed themselves into successful farmers and who "no longer follow the chase."[20]

Such expressions of eastern "sentimentality," however, carried no weight at army headquarters, nor did the eastern defense of the Utes find a sympathetic ear in Colorado or elsewhere in the West. Towns around the Ute reservation, at Pitkin's constant urging, organized armed militias. One spokesman for the militia in Lake City said, "If the government would let us get at 'em, we'd clean them up in a month and make good Indians of every one of them, like Chivington did with the Cheyennes." In Ouray, citizens condemned Washington for not ordering the military "to exterminate the Utes" and for forbidding white settlers "to go into the reservation and attack them."[21]

The local agent at Los Piños, Wilson Stanley, however, came to the defense of the Utes. He reminded Ouray citizens that the Uncompahgre band had always remained peaceful with their troublesome white neighbors, and the Indians had no intention of going on the warpath to assist their Ute brethren to the north. The agent charged that the local whites who called for "extermination" constantly spread false rumors in their attempt "to make trouble." Did not the Utes themselves have treaty rights with the United States, he asked? Stanley wrote Commissioner Hayt about the false rumors and the call for war in Ouray, "if whites were as honest as some Ute leaders, we could call ourselves 'Christian People.'" He went on to say, "I am absolutely disgusted at the conduct of the white people." Referring to the Milk Creek battle, he concluded, "[I] am not at all surprised that the Indians, do occasionally, turn upon the traducers and robbers of their rights. The worm will squirm when tread upon ... when goaded to displeasure [;] and why not an Indian, one of God's people ... [the Indians] demonstrate none of white man's hypocrisy and cant."[22] For his defense of the Utes, Stanley caught the ire of Ouray's acerbic editor, who called Stanley and all Indian agents "a useless and contemptible class of men. ... a greater tax upon the country than the Indians themselves ... " The editor charged the local agent with being "either a fool or a liar. He may take his choice of terms." Fighting both the army and Colorado's governor, however, Schurz believed he could do without an agent stirring up trouble with the locals in Ouray and sent Stanley packing back to his farm in Illinois.[23]

The army cared little about treaty obligations or the Indian agents who wished to defend them. It wished only to avenge the death of Thornburgh and his troops.[24] In mid-October, an impatient General Sheridan complained to Sherman that the army lost soldiers to protect Meeker, "and now we are left with our hands tied and the danger of being snowed in [this winter] ... I am not easily discouraged, but it looks as though we [have] been pretty badly sold out in this business." "Who is going to punish the Indians," he asked, "and how long are we to wait at the agency for it to be done?"[25]

Governor Pitkin, too, wanted war. He continued to stir up trouble in the press and threatened Washington with his own solution to Adams's "peace" mission. In a letter to Schurz, and with a copy sent to a Denver newspaper, Pitkin renewed his offer to settle the entire matter quickly by calling on the Colorado militia. He also suggested that Ouray's Uncompahgre band's participation in the bloodshed at Milk Creek was "further evidence that our frontier settlements are liable to become the scenes of more massacres." The *New York Times* observed correctly that Pitkin "and Colorado's 'leading citizens' seem more anxious for a general Indian war than for the surrender of the captives and ... the murderers of Thornburgh."[26] Schurz, who had managed to hold the U.S. Army off with one hand, now had to contain Pitkin's militia with the other. He wired back to Pitkin that there was absolutely no evidence to suggest that the Uncompahgre Utes had participated at either the Milk Creek battle or agency massacre. He further reminded the governor of the hostages' rescue. "If not interfered with," Schurz informed Pitkin, "the captives will be delivered to safety in a few days and agent Adams will bring in those responsible for the killings." Further, the secretary admonished the governor, "we are endeavoring to prevent a general war with the Ute tribe, which would be a better way to protect your border settlements than a general attack upon the Indians by armed citizens as your dispatch seems to suggest."[27]

With the federal and state military forces under control, at least for the time being, Adams led the released hostages on a three-day overland journey to Ouray's camp at the Los Piños Agency. Ralph Meeker joyfully greeted his mother and sister and escorted them, Mrs. Price, and her children on another arduous journey by wagon and train to Denver and finally to their home in Greeley. At the rail station, a cheering crowd greeted the surviving heroes of the White River Massacre. Ralph thanked Schurz for sending General Adams to arrange the peace. "I am sure I would never have seen mother [and Josephine] alive again," and for that, he wrote the secretary, "I am ... profoundly and increasingly grateful."[28]

Pitkin refused, however, to give up on his military solution. He continued to call for all-out war against the Utes on the eve of the Peace Commission's investigation. They must not make peace with the Utes, the governor wrote Schurz. "Their trophies are not banners but scalps."[29] That Pitkin did not order his state militia to finish off the White River band, as he had threatened, had less to do with his desire to demonstrate restraint than the fact that he possessed no funds to strengthen his undermanned and overextended Colorado militia.

Nor did Pitkin's fight with the secretary win unanimous approval in the state. The *Colorado Gazette* editorialized that the controversy "between the governor and the secretary of interior is a disgrace to the state. The governor stands charged with misrepresenting facts for the purpose of getting possession of Ute territory. The people of Colorado don't want to resort to such an end. We believe it can be obtained by more respectable means."[30] The *Gazette*, and probably a minority of Colorado's citizens, now looked to the Peace Commission for a "respectable" way by which the state could take possession of the Ute reservation. Pitkin, of course, had little faith that "Granny" Schurz, with his usual sympathetic and "sentimental" treatment of the Utes, would find a way to rid Colorado of the Utes.

The three-member Peace Commission composed of Adams, Chief Ouray, and Army Gen. Edward Hatch opened its proceedings in mid-November of 1879 at the Los Piños Agency under heavy guard from a small army detachment and fifty armed Ute police specially selected by Ouray. Both Adams and Ouray posted guards, less to protect the commissioners than to protect the chief from angry Utes contemptuous of his willingness to meet with Washington's peace representatives. In its forty-one meetings over the span of two months, the commission took testimony in closed session from twenty Utes, various army officers present at Milk Creek, and Josephine Meeker.

Adams referred to the battle as a "fair fight," without blaming either the Utes or the army, though he did observe that had Thornburgh proceeded to the agency without his main body of troops, as originally planned, the whole trouble could have been avoided.[31] Josephine Meeker, not unexpectedly, also laid blame on the army. She testified that "if the solders had not come and threatened the Indians with [jail] ... and threatened to kill other Indians at White River, the agent and employees would not have been massacred."[32] Colorow said Thornburgh instigated the battle, while Jack testified that Meeker's lies started the trouble. Adams dropped the matter, holding the Utes harmless for the battle.

But for Adams, the massacre was an entirely different matter. Those Indians who had engaged in the murder of the agent and his employees must be treated "as white men ... under similar circumstances." Schurz had already decided, though he had not stated it publicly, that the Utes must be removed from Colorado, if only for their own safety. It was the job of the Peace Commission, Schurz informed Adams, to lay the groundwork and make the case for their removal.

Regarding the massacre, the commission wanted to know the names of those involved. The Utes remained silent. Then to further his case against the Utes, Adams presented before the commission, with the Utes present, testimony Mrs. Price gave to Adams two weeks earlier in Greeley. In a letter to Schurz, Adams reported the details of Mrs. Price's testimony and his reasons for keeping the testimony hidden until peace had been restored.

"During the examination of Mrs. Price today at Greeley, I learned for the first time a fact which has been carefully concealed by her that she had been outraged several time times during her captivity and she also intimated that Mrs. and Miss Meeker had shared the same fate.

"Proceeding in my investigation under oath [,] I learned this to be the fact, Chief Douglas[s] himself having committed the crime on the body of Mrs. Meeker[,] an old lady 65 years old. The ladies are very anxious that for their own sake this fact should be concealed from the public. ... I am anxious that this matter should not become public, until I at least can endeavor to carry out the original object to settle the matter without further war. ...

"I shall immediately demand the surrender of Douglas[s], Johnson, and three others and[,] without wasting any time[,] can see at once whether their protestations have been sincere.

"At any event I shall secure Ouray's friendship and those that will follow him and if possible shall try to have them on our side if it comes to further hostilities.

"Meanwhile I shall have time enough to notify the settlers on the Gunnison [River] and [,] as General Hatch shall be with me [,] he can judge for himself as to the necessity of hurrying or delaying the movement of his troops. ... Those of the White River Utes who had nothing to do with either crime, I think Ouray will succeed in winning over to him, but I am confident now that about 25 of them should be hung [sic] or shot with Douglas[s] as the first one."

Adams also explained to Schurz why the testimony should remain sealed until peace was arranged:

"In order that it never can be said that I or yourself had endeavored to hush up the crimes of the Indians, I immediately on reaching Denver communicated the startling truth to Governor Pitkin under the seal of confidence, explaining as well the wish of the women themselves as the furious excitement this would raise in this State and whereby the southern Utes might be implicated also. ...
"I am trying to do the best I can in this matter, always keeping in mind the necessity of cutting down [the size of] the Reservation for the good of the Indians themselves.
"If the matter is settled without war [,] I think it can be arranged that most of the White River Utes remaining can be consolidated with the Uintahs in Utah and others, with Ouray's particular band ... settled on their own farms along the Uncompahgre and Gunnison. ... Nothing however would ... pacify the remainder and make them feel inclined to settle as the prompt payment of money due them under the treaty of 1873. ... Should the guilty not be surrendered, all I can do is to keep as many as possible ... at peace [;] and then after the [investigation] is finished, [convince Ouray] of the necessity of a smaller reservation to avoid such troubles in the future ... In conclusion I ... trust Ouray's wisdom and sagacity implicitly and will give him all the support I can, so as to make him stronger with his people if possible."[33]

Schurz wired back "that a failure of the Peace Commission would be a great disappointment as well as a disaster." "You must not fail," Schurz implored Adams, meaning that the guilty Utes would have to be handed over for trial. If they were not, he wrote, the Indian Bureau would withhold their rations "and maybe they'll yield when they begin to starve." And if they still refused, Schurz instructed Adams that he should threaten them with the army.[34]

Confident that the temporary peace could be maintained without further interference from Pitkin and with army troops in place in the event they were needed, Adams presented the testimony of the Meeker women and Mrs. Price at the commission hearing. An interpreter read the testimony to the Utes. The women named their three attackers (Johnson, Douglass, and another younger Ute, Persune) and also identified nine other Utes they had seen at the agency during the massacre.[35]

Word of the "outrages" leaked out to the press, either from Pitkin's office in Denver or more likely from an interpreter on the scene, and again the call for war resounded throughout Colorado. Schurz continued to urge Pitkin to be patient, assuring the governor that he, too, wanted the Utes removed. With the conclusion of the commission investigation, Schurz vowed to Pitkin that the Utes would be removed.

As the commission proceedings dragged on into December, Adams and his colleagues made no progress in persuading the Utes to hand over the twelve named Utes. Chief Ouray missed many of the meetings due to the debilitating effects of Bright's disease and, after arriving at the meetings in his carriage, had to have his Mexican servants carry him into the sessions. He was present, however, when Adams introduced the women's sworn testimony. No, Ouray said, the Utes would not hand over the twelve Utes for trial in Colorado. Adams, showing increasing impatience with the Utes' intransigence, told them, "the cowards who killed their white friends at the Agency and outraged the women who had been good to them—these men we want and will have." Ouray reacted bitterly and quickly. He refused to accept the testimony of white women. They had lied in their testimony just as the government had lied to the Utes and, besides, the men had their own squaws in camp. Ouray told the commission that the false testimony of the women was but another excuse for the government to take their land. "You want our land, and you want our country," Ouray told the commissioners. "You have tried before to get our country away from us and us from it. You have tried to take it in pieces; and now you are trying to get it all. We will not leave our country."

The chief listed other grievances. Meeker, he charged, was sent by the government to cause trouble. He "made the Utes work for his own glory and refused to feed them when they did not work ... He had no right to do that. The Government in our treaty said nothing about work, but agreed to give us these lands and to give us supplies, blankets, and food. They have violated the treaty and my men are angry." Ouray continued, "They had heard that Meeker

| A Peace and Removal

had sent for the soldiers to punish them for not working and coming to church; they always remember what Chivington did to the Cheyenne, and they tried to prevent soldiers from getting to the agency by killing them." Ouray admitted the White River Utes "went crazy" when they killed Meeker, his employees, and captured the women and children. "They should not have done that," Ouray admitted. The twelve men must not be tried in the racist climate of Colorado or New Mexico, but in Washington. "If you agree to that I will send for them, and give them to you."[36]

It was not a promise Ouray could deliver. He possessed neither influence with the White River band nor did he even know their specific whereabouts. Jack had moved his lodges sixty miles downriver from the old agency, and then went off into Utah to hunt. Colorow, with fifty-four lodges, had camped west and south of the old agency. Only a few White River Utes dared come into Ouray's camp for fear of the army's proximity. Ouray told Adams he might arrange to hand over a few of the twelve Utes, an offer to which Schurz responded through Adams: Hand all of them over or none of them. When Ouray refused on principle and for lack of authority to comply with the demand, and with the twelve Utes still at large, the secretary ordered an end to the Peace Commission meetings at Los Piños Agency. Schurz took the matter to the president's cabinet and, upon Schurz's recommendation, President Hayes directed the secretary to draft a peace treaty removing the Utes from Colorado.[37] Congress, in the meantime, called for an investigation of the battle and the massacre and summoned the chiefs, the Meeker women, and select military officers to Washington. Ouray hoped that in Washington, far removed from the impassioned climate in Colorado, the Utes might receive a fair hearing to explain the Meeker incident.[38]

For once Pitkin went along with Schurz's plan. With assurances from the secretary that the Utes would be removed from the state, Pitkin privately called upon local officials to avoid demonstrations against the Utes. Pitkin wrote one local official to assure him the Utes were "on their way out." "Things are working right," the governor reported, "and if we make no blunders we shall come out all right. Keep things level [peaceful] in Alamosa. Don't publish this."[39] Yet he continued to maintain pressure on Schurz through statements to the eastern press. He reminded eastern readers of the *New York Daily Graphic* that mining continued to be the main generator of Colorado's wealth and employment. Why, he asked, should valuable Ute land "be kept sacred as a hunting ground for the Ute murderers of Meeker, Thornburgh and their associates?" "Citizens of Colorado sincerely hope that our [eastern] countrymen, whose ancestors ... regarded the Indians armed with bows and arrows as bad neighbors, will sympathize with us when we entertain the same opinion today about Indians armed with Winchesters."[40]

The Pueblo Chieftain picked up on Pitkin's harangues against the Peace Commission. "Has it come to this that a great nation of forty million people must treat with a band of lousy, roaming red devil cut throats, and wink at the crimes that would make a demon blush?" If the government refused to punish the Utes, then the job should be turned over to Colorado. "Vengeance should be the watch word from this time until the last footprints of the fiendish Utes are obliterated from the soil of Colorado." As for the Peace Commission, the newspaper editorialized, "the very name stinks in the nostrils of an outraged people ... Let us hope that Congress has enough manhood left [unlike 'Old Granny' Schurz] to cut this matter short ... and turn the whole business over to the army where it properly belongs, and let the Utes be notified that if they don't surrender the agency murderers ... the whole power of government will be invoked to exterminate them."[41]

General Sherman let it be known at the annual dinner of the New England Society, a group generally sympathetic to the Indians, that if the Utes didn't deliver up the twelve participants in the massacre, the entire tribe must "take the consequences"—their disappearance "from the face of the earth."[42]

Rosie Meeker added to the western chorus of criticism against Schurz and the eastern press. On a lecture tour, she criticized the government for encouraging Indian idleness and directed a scathing attack on traders who sold arms to the Indians and "the eastern sentimentalists" who wished to welcome the Utes back east so that they might better study "the lovely disposition of the savage." Her father's last words, she said on her tour throughout the state, were, "'They are unreliable and a treacherous race.'" In a letter to the *Denver Tribune*, widely circulated throughout the state, she called on Colorado's miners and cowboys to see to it that the Ute delegation not leave Colorado alive "by simply putting a necktie rope around the neck of each one of them." In Washington "they'll be feasted before they are returned to their reservation with gifts of blankets and arms." It was really a puzzling question, Ms. Meeker wrote, "who are the most delighted over the White River Massacre, the people of the East or the Indians?" She charged Schurz and his Department of Interior

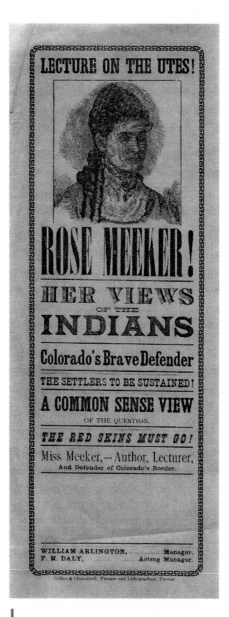

Advertisement for Rose Meeker's
1880 lecture tour after the murder
of her father, Nathan Meeker.
(Peter R. Decker collection)

cronies with capturing the eastern press and pulpit, while stealing thousands of dollars from the Indians. No wonder Schurz favored the Indians and wouldn't bring them to justice. "The time has come when Colorado must defend itself against the Indians as well as the Indian Bureau." The latter's "dishonesty and failure has never been equaled since sin took its abode with man. The most atrocious system is despised by an outraged public, and cursed by the widows and orphans of the victims of their criminal stupidity."[43]

With the hope of fairer treatment in Washington, the Ute delegation, composed of representatives of the White River, the Uncompahgres, and one southern band arrived in Pueblo, Colorado, in early January 1880 for the train to Washington. An angry crowd of three thousand greeted them with chants: "Hang the red devils. Shoot the murdering fiends." Before an army protective guard could get them safely onto the train, the whites pelted the Indians with stove coal, all the while calling for a lynching of the Ute leaders. When the train stopped in Kansas City, Chief Johnson gave himself up to an army guard in the hope his surrender would end the investigation and save the White River band from the hands of the army and the Washington politicians. As the Ute delegation proceeded under guard to Washington, army officials immediately incarcerated Johnson at Fort Leavenworth and held him without charges.[44]

In appearances before congressional committees, the Ute chiefs repeated their testimony given at Los Piños. As their colleagues from the East sat silent, western senators attempted, through their questions, to demonstrate that all the Utes, including those from Utah and the southern bands, had united in attack against the army. The battle, the senators wished to prove, was not a miscalculation by either Agent Meeker or the army, but rather a purposefully designed ambush against the lawful entry of the army called to defend the life of a government official and make legitimate arrests of unlawful Indians. Jack denied any premeditated battle plans. "I tried to stop the fight," Jack told his inquisitors, charging the army fired first. The senators remained unconvinced. Ouray reminded the senators that the army had invaded their reservation and, like Jack, he refused to name those involved in the massacre. The senators fumed.

In the hearing before the House Indian Affairs Committee, an eastern congressman asked Ouray, "Did not the Utes believe this trouble [at the agency] was brought on to get them [the White River Utes] off their land?" "They seem to think that way," Ouray hedged in his response, without implicating the government.[45] But once again, Ouray refused to implicate tribal members for the "outrages."[46] The committee then called upon Commissioner Hayt for his views. While Hayt disagreed with Ouray's suggestion and Jack's explicit charge that Meeker had purposely instigated the trouble on orders from the government, Hayt did defend the Utes and their treaty rights. Noting that Ute annuities had been withheld as punishment, Hayt testified, "I am sorry to say that it seems to be a great fault with most of our treaties [with the Indians] that they look out very sharply for the United States but not so sharply for the Indians." Yes, Hayt continued, individual crimes had been committed and the guilty must be punished. After the guilty were handed over to the government, the Utes would need to be moved out of Colorado to make room for a growing Colorado population. Hayt suggested that the Utes be sent to the Indian Territory where they would "civilize faster" and be fed cheaper. In the event the Utes went on the warpath in the territory, Hayt concluded, the flat terrain would allow the army to use its deadly artillery more effectively. The committee hearings concluded within days, without anyone other than Hayt coming forward to defend the Utes' treaty rights to its reservation.[47]

Within Colorado, the state legislature overwhelmingly passed a resolution demanding the Utes' expulsion from the state. Colorado lawmakers barely defeated a bill entitled "An Act for the Destruction of Indians and Skunks." Had it passed, the state would have offered up a bounty of $25 to anyone in possession of either a dead skunk or an Indian scalp. In Washington, Colorado's Senator Hill demanded that Schurz force the Utes out of Colorado, if for no other reason that former treaties forbade railroads from crossing reservation lands. These treaties should never have been made in the first place, Hill wrote the secretary, and since they did not own their lands, the time had come to move the Utes out of the way. Either the secretary of interior would negotiate a sale "or the government or someone else [the army] must resort to more extreme measures."[48]

The only effective defender of the Utes remained Schurz. He clearly recognized that for their safety, indeed for their survival, they needed to be removed from Colorado into Utah and possibly into New Mexico. And to prevent any further violence while he planned for their removal, Schurz was careful not to blame the army, while remaining sensitive to the political pressures put upon the president and the Indian Bureau by Colorado's small but influential congressional delegation. In his annual report Schurz avoided direct criticism of the martyred Meeker. He performed well as an agent, Schurz reported, and "when

| "THE UTES MUST GO!"

he endeavored to plow land for agricultural purposes ... he did it for the benefit of the Indians, not for himself." The real cause of trouble, Schurz noted, was the Ute "fondness ... for their old wild habits [of hunting abundant game], their disinclination to submit to any civilizing restraint, the evil influence exercised upon them by whites upon [the reservation] borders," and the "mischievous" White River leaders who couldn't control their band during the "temporary excitement." To insure the survival of the Utes, they must be moved.[49]

To this end, Schurz drew up a nonnegotiable agreement for the Utes to sign. The Uncompahgre Utes were to be moved to land at the junction of the Gunnison and Grand (Colorado) Rivers (present-day Grand Junction) "if sufficient quantity of agricultural land shall be found there," and if not, to adjacent lands. The White River band was to resettle within the Uintah Reservation in Utah. As for the southern bands, they were to be removed to unoccupied lands on the La Plata River or "adjacent" lands, including New Mexico. The centerpiece of the agreement made provision at all locations for all Ute family heads to receive title to a quarter section of arable land and an additional quarter section of grazing ground (with supplemental lands to single persons over eighteen and orphans) when "the necessary laws are passed by Congress." In return for surrendering their lands, the government promised to pay the Utes, in addition to the $25,000 agreed to in previous treaties, $60,000 a year in annuities "forever," to be prorated among the bands: one-third to the three southern bands,[50] one-half to Chief Ouray's Uncompahgres and, as punishment to the White River band, the remaining one-sixth interest. The Utes were also promised "forever" an additional $50,000 a year in cash for per capita distributions, and a one-time $350,000 appropriation to cover the expenses for necessary surveys, appraisals, a census, new buildings (including schoolhouses), farm implements, sawmills, gristmills, wagons, and livestock at the new reservation locations. Additional funds were included in the bill for the distribution to those headmen who demonstrated "good sense, energy, and perseverance" in their pursuits of "civilized life and understanding." The bribery funds also extended to Chief Ouray, whose $1,000 a year "salary" was extended an additional ten years. A special five-member commission would be appointed to locate and survey the appropriate lands and oversee the peaceful removal of the bands. The agreement further stipulated that those charged with the murder of Meeker must be turned over for trial or the agreement would be null and void. Representatives of all the bands put their mark to the agreement

*Ute delegation (Captain Jack, third from left) invited
to Washington to negotiate the 1880 peace agreement.
(Courtesy of the Colorado Historical Society, #F-7098)*

before returning to Colorado. Ouray, however, refused to sign—a defiant gesture that had no effect since, with or without his signature, the Utes could either consent or face the harsh military consequences.

The agreement met with a mixed reaction in Colorado. The state's newspapers applauded the agreement provision to remove the northern bands, but strongly opposed the continued presence of the southern bands in Colorado, even if confined to isolated and marginal land. Governor Pitkin, on the eve of his reelection bid in October of 1880, found occasion to play the race card again. When a party of four Utes near Gunnison killed a drunken teamster in retaliation for his shooting of an Uncompahgre Ute, the son of a sub-chief, Pitkin again viciously attacked Schurz and his "worthless" peace settlement. He renewed his call for the Utes' extermination and made no effort to calm the inflamed passions of Gunnison residents, nor did he discourage them from organizing a vigilante posse. He further threatened to send the militia into the Uncompahgre's camp, wipe out the Utes, and make moot any further attempts to relocate the "savages." An army officer, stationed at the new army post established on the Uncompahgre over the summer to keep whites off the reservation, reported to his commander at Fort Leavenworth, "I cannot help express the belief that Western Colorado newspapers are determined to create trouble with the Indians if they can."[51] One official in Pueblo, however, reported to Schurz that Colorado citizens were "not so worked up over the presence of the Indians in the state" as he would be led to believe by the press. "Governor Pitkin ... uses the matter as a strong card to catch votes. The immigration of the Missouri bushwhackers [Democrats and ex-Confederate guerrillas] during the [summer] season has endangered his chances for reelection, and so he tried to use the Utes as a prop to help him out of his ... difficulty." Delay any decision, the official advised Schurz, until after the 1880 election when the matter with Pitkin will be settled "one way or another."[52]

But Schurz recognized the imminent danger. A newspaper reporter wired Schurz, appealing to his party loyalty, that the Gunnison incident could cause trouble for Colorado Republicans. "It will make a difference against us of a thousand votes if they are not removed at once."[53] Without congressional approval to move the Utes immediately, unwilling to await the outcome of Pitkin's likely reelection, and fearing the situation might immediately implode, Schurz pressured the hotheaded and impatient governor indirectly through the president and directly by telegram. He requested that Pitkin control the "lawless" vigilantes in Gunnison and went on to warm Pitkin that such "an aggressive action [use of the militia] would only lead to war."[54] Fortunately for the Utes, Pitkin thought it more politically expedient to use his under-manned and overextended militia against the striking miners in Leadville than to send them into the reservation to implement his "final solution."[55]

In Washington, opposition to the peace agreement came from an unexpected quarter—the Board of Indian Commissioners—a group appointed by the pres-ident to review Indian policies and "protect" Indian rights. One member, who opposed the agreement as too solicitous to the Utes, observed that "barbarism must yield to civilization, flee before it, or sooner or later be overcome by it." "The Anglo-Saxon race will not allow the car of civilization to stop at any line of latitude or longitude on our broad terrain. If the Indian in his wildness plants himself on the track, he must be crushed by it."[56] That Anglo-Saxons had originally placed the Indians on the track seemed never to have occurred to the commissioner.

Another "friend" of the Utes, John Wesley Powell, who had spent a winter among the White River band Utes prior to his exploratory expedition down the Colorado River in 1868, urged their removal as the first step in the progress toward civilization. At the invitation of Senator Teller, the renowned Indian ethnologist testified before a Senate committee that the White River band needed to start anew in Utah so that they would be separated from what is "most sacred to them" (their homeland). This, he argued to the surprise of some Indian reformers, would help them assimilate and bestow upon them the necessary tenets of Anglo-Saxon culture. "The progress of civilization and the establishment of homes for millions of civilized people should not be retarded because of the interests and superstitions of a small number of savages." The Indians should be moved with "the widest charity" away from barbarism "[by] inducing them to take lands and property in severalty." The move would also separate the Utes from the army, nothing but "a source of trouble and loathsome disease."[57]

The *New York Tribune* echoed those who supported the Utes' removal. The newspaper, a reliable mouthpiece for the nation's economic and financial interests, editorialized that since the Utes had failed to take advantage of the resources of their reservation, they did not deserve what had been put aside for them by treaty. The elimination of the large Colorado reservation would provide "a powerful impetus" for the development of the nation's untapped natural resources.[58] The *Tribune's* competitor, The *New York Times*, attacked Schurz while indirectly defending the Utes and their treaty rights. The Meeker massacre was used by the government as an excuse "to despoil the whole tribe of their ancestral homes" in the interests of peace. The whole "agreement" was a sham, "negotiated" at gunpoint. The Utes had "as good a legal title to their entire reservation as any home-owner in New York," the *Times* editorialized. "It is precisely such compulsory arrangements" with the Indians "in which greed masquerades as generosity" that had caused costly and cruel wars. Meeker, the newspaper reminded its readers, forgot the reservation belonged to the Utes, not to him. The editorial concluded that the agreement "is claimed as a triumph of humanity and justice" and many friends of the Utes were anxious for its success, but only because of the alternative—extermination. In the end, Colorado "called for extermination and compromised on confiscation."[59]

Helen Hunt Jackson, a nationally known outspoken critic of the Indian Bureau with considerable influence among eastern reformers, particularly the clergy, called Schurz's plan nothing more than a policy of convenience supported by the power of the sword. Jackson, who described herself as "a woman with a hobby," said that the granting of individual allotments (lands in severalty) to the Utes was duplicitous, a way to steal both money and land from the Indians. Besides, the secretary, in violation of Ute treaty rights, had no right to withhold annuities from all the Utes, much less to relocate the vast majority of the Utes as punishment for the transgressions of a few. If, as Jackson argued with considerable logic, the Colorado reservation belonged to the Utes, as Schurz admitted, what legal authority did the government have to compel the Indians' removal from one reservation to another? The secretary's argument was filled with "sophistry and dishonesty," she asserted, designed to expropriate from the Utes their rightful and legally protected lands.[60]

Congress, at the urging of its western members and anxious to be rid of the Ute problem, paid little attention to "reform" sentiment. It supported the agreement, but not before insisting upon some major changes: no citizenship for the "savages" and punishment for the entire Ute tribe, rather than holding individuals responsible. If, in their idiosyncratic tribal manner, the Utes wished to hold land in common, then they should be punished in common.

At Senator Teller's urging, Congress altered some critical wording in the agreement as it related to the ultimate relocation of Utes. Where, for example,

Schurz's original draft had called for both the Southern Utes and the Uncompahgre to be removed to separate river valleys within Colorado "or lands adjacent to" them, Congress amended the language and extended the receiving area to include lands "in the vicinity of" these valleys. The semantic alteration provided latitude (and longitude) for the commission to look beyond the borders of Colorado, specifically into New Mexico and Utah. Teller wanted all the Utes out of the state, the bands separated from each other so as to "break up their tribal relations," to keep them under army guard and, if necessary, to take their horses to insure they lacked the means "to roam." "Put him in one place," Teller argued, "and keep him there ... "[61]

New Mexico reacted vehemently to the possibility of becoming a dumping ground for the displaced Utes. There is no record of Utah's reaction, but few politicians in Washington or Colorado cared what Brigham Young and his disciples thought about expanding the territory's Indian population. In Colorado, conspiratorial theories abounded that the Mormons had all along encouraged, with the aid of arms and ammunition, the Ute attack on the army. One Denver paper noted the "general feeling among our people that Mormon emissaries are at the bottom of the Ute problems. If this should prove to be true, and we are inclined to credit these rumors, there would be no better time than the present to settle with those libelous rascals at Salt Lake and wash out the stain of polygamy. Between the Utes and the Mormons, we have no choice."[62] For Colorado's citizens, the Utes and the polygamists deserved each other.

The longest and most contentious debate surrounded Schurz's pet proposal—giving individual property allotments to the Utes, the first tribe to be the recipient of lands "in severalty." It was a concept important to the reformers who wished to move the Indians to a higher level of "civilization." Schurz's plan for the Utes was part of a larger national policy to dismember the reservation system into which Indians had been placed with too little supervision and control. Schurz and the Indian reformers came to recognize that the old reservation system had not worked, and that while the Indians had moved from savagery to barbarism, they had failed to advance to the third stage of civilization. "To fit the Indians ... for civilized life," Schurz proposed, the government must begin to allot "lands in severalty" to the Utes with fee simple title and sell the lands they cannot use to assist the "development of the country." With individual rather than tribal ownership, the Indians would immediately learn individual initiative as they farmed and raised stock, all the while assisted and encouraged, as before, by government employees. "The enjoyment and pride of individual ownership of property is one of the most effective civilizing agencies," Schurz argued. And, the theory went, as the Indians became more self-sufficient, the savings in the cost for annuities to the government would be passed on to the Utes in cash. The army would no longer be needed as policemen, a mission they had never liked, the railroads could purchase rights-of-way, and the public treasury would be saved the expense of feeding and fighting the Indians.[63]

Schurz also advanced the popular argument that by granting individual allotments, the policy would financially benefit both the collective assets of the Indians and those of the West's expanding white population. For with available land increasingly scarce for new settlers, it was no longer acceptable, Schurz observed, to withhold large tracts from white farmers and miners "so as to maintain a savage aristocracy in the enjoyment of their chivalrous pastimes." Such a system Schurz thought "incompatible with the progress of civilization and injurious to the material interests of the country."[64] Excess land not selected by allotment would then be available to white settlers, with the sales income credited to the each band's account. "This done," Schurz announced, "the Indians will occupy no more ground than ... white people; the large reservations will gradually be opened to general [white] settlement and enterprise, and the Indians with their [land] possessions, will cease to stand in the way of the development of the country" thus removing the constant friction between the whites and the Utes. A win-win situation for everyone, Schurz declared, particularly for the Indians, whose allotments could not be taxed and, after twenty-five years, would be eligible for sale by the Indian owners. With "the formal discontinuance of their tribal existence," Schurz summarized in his report to Congress, the Indians would become "farmers like other [white] inhabitants ... under the laws of the land."[65]

The Indian Bureau, with the support of the reformers, asked Congress to implement by legislation that which they had formerly failed to accomplish through education—an Anglo-Saxon value system.

Critics in Congress went after Schurz and his plan. The secretary had failed to root out the corruption in his department, specifically his Indian commissioner, Hayt, who, Congress charged, had covered up a suspicious land transaction with a business friend in Arizona. As for the secretary's allotment plan, it was, for its opponents, a mechanism "to get Indian lands and open them for settlement." After the Indians received their allotments and the rest of the land was put up for sale to the highest bidder, some congressmen argued, the Indian would quickly be surrounded by a "wall of fire, a cordon of white settlements, which will gradually hem him in ... and eventually crowd him out"[66]

Senator Teller, long an admirer of Colonel Chivington and his attack at Sand Creek, led the opposition in the Senate. To set the tone for his argument, Senator Teller reminded his colleagues, "We ought never to forget that we are dealing with savages—and we should never deal with savages as we deal with civilized people."[67] He argued that while the allotment plan might save the reputation of the Indian Bureau, it would do little to "civilize" the Utes. Giving them title to land would not change their tribal customs. Let them first be "civilized" and afterward make arrangements for lands in severalty at some time in the future. Teller told his Senate colleagues that when in thirty or forty years the Utes would have sold off their lands "they will curse the hand that was raised ... to secure this kind of legislation; and if the people who are clamoring for it understood Indian character, and Indian laws, and Indian morals, and Indian religion, they would not be here clamoring for it at all."[68]

Teller's defense of Ute culture and their adherence to tribal ownership was disingenuous. Beneath his rhetoric, he believed that the granting of individual allotments was both an unnecessary and wasteful gift of valuable land, land that should more properly be saved, not for the Indians, but for white settlers who could and would make better use of it. Teller recognized no inconsistency in arguing, as he had for years, that all public lands must be privatized, but not Indian lands.[69] The senator understood all too well that it was far easier to take Indian land under the present system than for whites, twenty-five years in the future, to have to deal with individual Indians and new laws protecting their assets. Teller failed in his efforts to strike the allotment clause from the agreement. He had, however, gained the satisfaction that it would take years before Congress passed the appropriate laws implementing the system.

Schurz's original proposal also failed to include compensation to the white families who had lost husbands and sons at the White River Massacre, a matter of some concern to Senator Teller. The families believed they were as deserving of compensation, if not more so, than the Utes. The Meekers led the procession of those demanding compensation. They had suffered not only the loss of their patriarch, family members reminded the Colorado press, but the women had been "outraged" by Nathan Meeker's "murderers." That the Meeker family finances remained in disarray only added to the urgency of their request. Rosie's lecture tour, on which she defended her father and publicized the Indian "outrages" against her sister and mother, helped raise some money for Arvilla. Ralph Meeker started collecting notes for a book about his family's travails. And in an effort to assist the family, Schurz arranged a stenographer's job for Josie at the Interior Department. From discretionary funds, Schurz also paid her for four months' work as cook at the agency. But he thought it inappropriate to compensate the Meekers and other families out of the funds designated for the Utes. Mrs. Meeker pleaded with Schurz to arrange for an appropriation for herself, her daughter, and Mrs. Price. We are, she wrote Schurz, "all thrown helpless upon the world," and added that had the army acted sooner, her husband "would be alive today."[70] Ralph Meeker also called upon Schurz for assistance. He complained to the secretary that some newspapers had blamed his father for the massacre. "How hollow and hypocritical [was] the entire political crusade" to "slander" his father and the entire Meeker family. He attempted to excuse his mother and sister's prior statements to the press attacking Schurz and his department for inaction, and then asked Schurz to arrange for an appropriation to the family.[71] Mrs. Dresser, who had lost her two sons at the agency, also sought help from Teller. At the senator's insistence, the revised agreement included an additional $3,500 (debited against the payment designated for the White River band) to compensate Arvilla and Josie Meeker, Mrs. Price, and other families of the "murdered" agency employees. Teller also inserted the requirement that three-quarters of the adult Ute males sign the agreement and, of course, that the twelve White River "murderers" be handed over to the authorities.

When Congress approved the revised agreement in June 1880, no one bothered to explain to the Utes some of the semantic alterations that would come to affect their ultimate destination. To their relief, the Utes did learn they would not immediately be forced to accept lands in severalty, a concept so foreign to their culture it remained almost incomprehensible. But they understood all too well the loss of their homeland, with its sacred sites, familiar hunting grounds, and ancestral history. In the end, as Ouray recognized, they had but two choices. Stand and fight, or move and survive. As a realist, Ouray recognized that the Utes could no more halt the whites taking their land than an animal could withstand gunfire at close range. When it came time to sign the agreement, Ouray selected the second option and urged all of the Utes to do the same. He had done what he could—they had not been exterminated.

Where Ouray expressed more sorrow than anger with the agreement, Schurz took satisfaction that he had, with Ouray's assistance, saved the Utes from annihilation. The secretary praised Ouray for understanding and then adjusting to a problem not of his own making. "He comprehended perfectly the utter hopelessness of the struggle ... against the progress of civilization" and he had no choice "but to accommodate ... to civilized ways or perish." By cooperating with the government, Ouray made the transition as painless as possible.[72]

Schurz expressed disappointment with Teller's deletion of his allotment plan, but he remained optimistic that the Utes could be removed without bloodshed. He did not wish to repeat the mistake made with the Ponca Indians when, in 1877, he forced their removal from the Dakotas, causing a heavy loss of life. Of his department's efforts with the Utes, Schurz said with pride and with a heightened sense of realism, "We prevented something that might have been worse." The Indians could not survive amidst white migration into Colorado. "There is nothing more dangerous to an Indian reservation than a rich mine" and fertile agricultural land.[73] And in response to harsh criticism from the *Philadelphia Telegraph,* a mouthpiece for Indian reformers, Schurz took credit, and rightfully so, for the Utes' survival. In his memoirs Schurz reminded his readers that after the Thornburgh attack and the massacre he "single handed and alone" stood "between the Utes and destruction ... If I had removed my hand from them for a day, war would have been inaugurated and we should have seen the last of the tribe. I can say without exaggeration that I alone saved them and ... they can [only] be saved in the future by removing the source of irritation ... large numbers of whites crowding around them."[74]

As Schurz left office with the election of President James Garfield, three-quarters of the Utes still needed to sign the agreement and then be moved, peacefully and without bloodshed, he hoped, to their new homes.

SEVEN | *Removal*

With a gun pointed to their heads and recognizing the futility of engaging the U.S. Army in further warfare, Ute leaders reluctantly signed the peace agreement in 1880. Except in very general terms, the White River, Uncompahgre, and southern bands did not know where they were being moved, or when or how, if at all, they would be compensated for their "ceded" land. They also recognized that if those involved in the White River Massacre did not surrender, the Utes would lose everything promised under the peace agreement—land, annuities, and compensation—while being left homeless and unprotected. An Uncompahgre sub-chief expressed the Hobbesian choice he faced at the time he placed his mark on the peace agreement, "It was the best we could do, though not what we wanted."[1]

The government demanded those Indians responsible for the massacre be handed over, the agreement signed by three-quarters of the Utes, and the Indians moved into their designated boxes. On a reservation, with the army nearby, they would stay put and out of harm's way. The government also anticipated that the agreement's generous appropriation to encourage agricultural endeavors would change the Utes' attitude toward farming.

Secretary Schurz, who was soon to leave office, faced the immediate problem of how to keep whites off the reservation once they learned the Utes would be removed. With reports from local military commanders in Colorado, General Pope wired Sheridan's headquarters in Chicago, "miners are armed and ready for a fight."[2] General Adams warned Schurz that so many whites had crowded around the reservation in anticipation of the Utes' departure that he feared a major outbreak of violence. Adams called the delay "a powder keg ready to explode."[3]

The problem became particularly acute in the Uncompahgre Valley, close to the town of Ouray. To protect the reservation from the influx of whites, the army had, at Chief Ouray's request, hastily built a small installation, Fort Crawford, in the summer of 1880. Initially, the 250 infantry and cavalry troops had orders to protect a survey team sent to delineate the reservation boundary north of town. But when word spread that the Uncompahgre Utes would soon be moved to Utah, white settlers anticipated the move by invading the reservation to stake out mineral deposits and farm sites. The intruders, observed a visitor to the area, were for the most part "men dishonorably discharged from the Army, crooks, desperadoes, and still others who had left their country for their country's good ... "[4] The local papers, which continued to call for the Utes' immediate removal, encouraged the trespassers. And within a month of the cease-fire, the army found itself occupied with halting trespassers and arresting those found on the reservation without authorization.

The army's primary mission, however, remained to escort the Uncompahgres to their new reservation, at a location yet to be determined. The local commander, Col. Ranald Mackenzie, a Civil War veteran and former Indian fighter, thought the Utes peaceful, well-behaved, and "very independent ... richer than any Indians I have ever seen ... scarcely begging at all."[5] He observed that he had experienced more problems with white intruders and a high desertion rate among his soldiers than he did with the peaceful Utes.

Schurz, too, worried about the white intruders instigating further conflicts with the Utes. He began the arrangements to move them and to gather the necessary Indian signatures for the treaty's ratification. Over the summer he appointed a new and important five-member peace commission to identify the specific destinations for the individual Ute bands. He also awaited impatiently the delivery of the twelve Utes identified as instigators of the White River Massacre, realizing that if the "guilty" Utes remained at large, the peace process would unravel in the hands of his congressional critics. To that end, he put increasing pressure on the Utes to deliver up the men by withholding rations to all the Utes at the two Colorado agencies. The tactic, not unexpectedly, failed. Yet despite his frustration, Schurz recognized that if the Utes were to survive, the peace process must be kept on track. To that end and in one of his last acts as interior secretary, Schurz certified to Congress in the fall of 1880 that "after [the commission's] investigation, it is our belief the guilty are either dead or have fled beyond the limits of the U.S. [to Canada to join with Sitting Bull and his renegade Sioux]." Congress accepted the recognized falsehood if only to be rid of the Ute problem and to clear the way for Schurz's commission to get on with its work.

Schurz remained optimistic that the agreement could be completed. Through his agent with the Uncompahgres, Schurz worked hard to convince Ouray that it was in the best interest of the Utes to remove themselves voluntarily from Colorado. He would, he assured Ouray, treat them fairly and arrange for a new reservation in Utah of sufficient size for the Uncompahgres. The reservation, Schurz added, would be located at a safe distance from white settlements. After his meeting with Ouray in Washington, Schurz reported that the chief "spoke like a man of a higher order of intelligence and larger view, [a man] who had risen above the prejudices and aversions of his race ..." Schurz said Ouray expressed himself well in English, contrary to reports of the chief's poor English, and "he comprehended perfectly the utter hopelessness of the struggle ... [and] nothing was left to them but to accommodate themselves to civilized ways or perish." Ouray, Schurz said, fully recognized the necessity of cooperating with the government and "he depended on me to bring about [the] removal under conditions favorable to his people." Schurz praised Ouray for his acquiescence, a "noble savage with chivalrous impulses and fine sentiments," an Indian who stood above the "barbarous habits" of his tribe. Schurz believed Ouray to be "by far the brightest Indian I have ever met," something of an uninformed observation given the secretary's limited contact with other chiefs. Yet for all of Schurz's respect for Ouray and the secretary's national reputation as a strong and adamant defender of all Indians, in his opinion they remained, with only a few exceptions, "barbarous" and "uncivilized." The Utes needed to be moved out of the way of civilized society until they had attained a "higher level of civilization."[6]

For Schurz, the area around present-day Grand Junction in western Colorado was an appropriately remote location. The secretary had sent three commissioners to the area to locate a new reservation for Ouray's Uncompahgre band. He detailed two other commissioners, including chairman George Manypenny, a Pittsburgh industrialist-reformer and a recognized long-time friend of the Indians, to the La Plata River valley (near present-day Durango) to seek a permanent home for the southern bands. The fifth commissioner, Alfred Meacham, a strong defender of Indian rights despite having almost lost his life in a Modoc massacre some years earlier, Schurz sent off to attempt a permanent and peaceful settlement with the most contentious of the bands, the White River Utes.

In one sense, Manypenny had the easier task. The Southern Utes already occupied much of the land thought appropriate for them. A major move, the Indian Bureau believed, would be unnecessary. White settlers who had only recently moved onto Ute land in the La Plata valley and the surrounding area complicated the situation, however. The miners, shopkeepers, and farmers would not remove themselves voluntarily, Manypenny recognized, and to include white settlements within the boundaries of a new reservation would only endanger the Utes and further escalate racial hatred in southern Colorado. To circumvent another violent outbreak against the Utes, Manypenny advised that the Colorado acreage promised the Utes in the agreement be cut in half. Additional acreage, he suggested, might be found for the Utes in northern New Mexico. The Southern Utes, he noted, had for centuries lived, often peacefully, within the San Juan River basin and the outlying Hispano towns north of Taos and Santa Fe and had only recently vacated the area to be closer to the new agency in southern Colorado at Ignacio. Manypenny recognized that while the peace agreement called for the Southern Utes to be placed in La Plata valley, the additional wording of "in the vicinity of" allowed Manypenny a certain geographical latitude that could encompass northern New Mexico. No one, of course, bothered to ask the authorities in New Mexico. And when word reached the territory's governor, Lew Wallace, he informed Schurz's replacement, Samuel Kirkwood, that one to two thousand whites had already settled in northern New Mexico and that it would be "unwise to plant Indians upon them." Such a movement of Utes was certain to be met, the governor wrote, by an armed force of white ranchers, timbermen, and miners.[7]

Regardless of whether New Mexico wanted the 1,300 Southern Utes, whites in Colorado wanted them gone. The state legislature petitioned Congress on various occasions to remove the Utes. Cattlemen in southern Colorado continually charged the Utes with livestock theft and threatened to shoot any Indian on sight. The *Durango Record* editorialized that the Utes should be removed at once to New Mexico. The *Durango Democrat* added fuel to the racial fire when it attacked the Department of Interior for protecting its "government pets," calling them nothing more than a bunch of "thieves and killers." The Indian Bureau, the paper went on to say, "is now, as it has always been, the friend of the red devil and the enemy of the pioneer." Our Indian policy is "an entire failure," it wrote, and called for a vigilante army of "our cowboys, miners and pioneers ... [to] march against them and not return until every dirty, miserable devil of them has bit the dust and the tribe has been annihilated."[8]

The ultimate location and size of the Southern Ute Reservation was further complicated by a new rail line through the Ute reservation destined for Durango. The Denver and Rio Grande railroad headed by Gen. W. J. Palmer asked permission of neither the Utes nor the government to lay tracks or build construction camps within the reservation. Commissioner Manypenny reported to Washington that the Utes were ready to do battle against the unprotected railroad crews. "It is a trying time for the Utes," Manypenny wrote Secretary Kirkwood, "and it will be a marvel if something does not occur to produce a disturbance."[9] Palmer promised to compensate the Utes and halt the white settlements along his rail line, but the railroad's permanent presence added to yet another rationale for a smaller reservation.

The railroad incursion crystallized for Commissioner Manypenny the limits of what he could accomplish. The land is "so essential to the prosperity and development of this part of Colorado," Manypenny said on behalf of the commission, "that it is beyond human reason to believe it will long be permitted to remain under the control of [Indians] who only cultivate at most 600 acres."[10] The reservation would have to be cut by half if for no other reason than "for the safety of the Indians" who must be separated from "the constant annoyance of evil-disposed persons." Further, because the Southern Utes "are essentially wild Indians," who refused "to adopt the new mode of life contemplated by the agreement," Manypenny said that they would never utilize but one-fourth of the land awarded to them. "I see no other way than to modify the agreement," Manypenny concluded, than to cut the size of the reservation to a smaller "strip of land one hundred miles long and fifteen miles wide" where—with new buildings, irrigation ditches, plus "100 gentle milk-cows and seven bulls"— the Utes could begin their new lives. "The Indians must be convinced that this new agreement is in their best interest."[11]

The matter was not resolved until 1895 when the government, after ten legislative sessions lasting fifteen years and over the objections of the Colorado legislature, allowed the Southern Utes to remain in Colorado, but on a drastically reduced reservation of six hundred thousand acres located south of Durango. The Capote and Muache bands accepted individual allotments, finally authorized in 1906, on the eastern portion of the reservation. The Weeminuche band on the western half of the reservation refused allotments and continued to own its land in common.

The physical relocation of the Northern Ute bands presented a different set of problems. While the government agreed that they must be removed from the state, where to place them and how to compensate the different bands caused lasting feuds between the bands and Washington. About a third of the seven hundred or so White River Utes had joined the Uncompahgres. The remainder of the band had either voluntarily moved over to Utah or, like Jack's lodges, remained in or near the White River before they were ordered to move in with the eight hundred Uintahs in Utah. To encourage their removal, the Indian Bureau told band members they would receive their cash ($19 per capita) and annuity payments only after their removal to Utah. And because the White River Utes were presumed directly responsible for the deaths of Thornburgh and Meeker, the government would deduct from the band's cash settlement those payments destined to the families of the massacred white victims.

The Uncompahgres, the largest of the Ute bands with about 1,500 members, expected to be given a new reservation at or near the confluence of the Gunnison and Colorado Rivers (present-day Grand Junction) in western Colorado. Two commission members, Otto Mears and John D. Bowman, visited the site in the fall of 1880 only to discover the area to be "unsuitable" for Indians. "Nothing can be accomplished here," the commissioners reported, "without irrigation ... a very expensive proposition." But what may have influenced the commissioners more than the area's "lack of fertility" was the increasing pressure from white settlers who recognized the area's farming potential. They looked for help to Mears, the commissioner ultimately responsible for selecting a new site for the Uncompahgres.

Mears had befriended the Uncompahgres, particularly Chief Ouray, ever since his arrival in Colorado in the 1860s. A Civil War veteran, Mears used his government connection to launch profitable businesses throughout western Colorado. He supplied wheat to the government garrison at Fort Garland and poured his profits into building and operating toll roads throughout the San Juan Mountains and the San Luis and Arkansas Valleys. Later he expanded his business to supply meat to the Los Piños Agency and, through political connections in Denver, acquired a mail contract for service into the San Juans. He ingratiated himself with the Uncompahgre band, particularly with Chief Ouray, upon whom he showered gifts.

But Mears had personal profits in mind, not the Utes' welfare. He became fluent in their language, gained the trust of Chief Ouray, and often advised the chief in his negotiations with Washington. It was Mears who broke the deadlock in the negotiations over the 1873 treaty by suggesting the Uncompahgre chief be awarded an annual $1,000 salary for life in return for ceding the San Juan mining district. Critics of the deal claimed Mears's mercantile company received in return lucrative trading contracts from the Indian Bureau. Some even suggested Mears received a kickback from Ouray for the "salary" arrangement. Always on the lookout for a quick profit, he cheated the Indians as readily as he did the government. On one occasion, an agent reported, Mears held back fifty head of government cattle designated for the Indians, told the agent not to brand them, then told the government they had died after selling the cattle to a Denver merchant. If the agent ever reported the incident, Mears threatened to have the agent fired. Mears once told an acquaintance, "I don't care a damn how much 'Uncle Sam' gets beat, but I hate like hell to get beat myself."[12]

Never one to pass up an opportunity to profit from his friendship with the Utes and his contracts with the government, and ever on the lookout for more lucrative endeavors, Mears recognized the opportunity for a trading bonanza in the Grand Valley. He knew that with proper irrigation, the Grand Valley could become a farmers' paradise where he would, under the proper arrangements, personally profit. The prospects of a profitable trade with white farmers and miners far outweighed the uncertainty of future Indian contracts from the government. In addition, farmers and miners would flock to the vacated valley on new roads he would build, again with lucrative government contracts. To insure that the Grand Valley would be free of any Indian presence, Mears informed Senator Teller that the valley was "gold country," reason enough for Teller to insist upon finding a home for the Utes elsewhere, specifically in Utah. No friend of the Indian, Teller demanded the tribe be broken up, shipped off to different locations (outside of Colorado), and their ponies taken away. Only after the army prevented their "predatory life" could the government make any progress in teaching "the savages" agriculture.[13]

Another member of the commission charged Mears and Bowman with using their positions for personal profit. They care "as little for the welfare of the Indian as they do for barking coyotes ... Their only interest in the Commission is that it may give them earlier opportunity than the outside world for pushing this or that speculation."[14] When asked many years later why he deemed the Grand Valley "unsuitable" for the Utes, Mears answered as if ordained by God. "It was in my blood," he said, "to want to see new furrows writhing from the plow ripping through the warm earth that had lain undisturbed since creation." And since all wealth, said Mears taking a page from Adam Smith, "comes from the soil" and the Utes refused to farm it, "they have to move on."[15]

The decision found easy acceptance in Washington, where Teller repeatedly introduced bills in the Senate to have the Utes removed from Colorado. Pitkin, too, never let up in his identically themed writing campaign to Schurz. Only the Uncompahgres' Indian agent, W. H. Berry, attempted to correct the commissioners' false claim of the Grand Valley's "unsuitability." He reminded Washington how the Utes had for centuries migrated to the area's mild climate to escape the harsh winters on the White River. They knew the area well and had lived and survived in the Grand Valley for at least three hundred years. The secretary, however, sensitive to Pitkin's wishes, instructed the commissioners to search for a more suitable site in the "vicinity" of Utah the following spring. So with the Uncompahgre agent, Berry, five chiefs, and two hundred army troops, the two commissioners proceeded to the junction of the White and Green Rivers in Utah to discover land "more satisfactory than we had anticipated" and distant from "the interests of other people."[16] Adjacent to the 2 million-acre Uintah Reservation, the commissioners carved out 1.9 million acres for the Uncompahgres, naming it after Chief Ouray. The name notwithstanding, the Uncompahgre leaders sent word to Washington through the commissioners they did not wish to relocate, especially next to a band (the Uintah) they believed inferior. Washington responded unequivocally: you will move, or be removed.

Warned that the army might have to use force to move the Uncompahgres and some stragglers of the White River band, Sherman alerted his commanders. In a letter to Sheridan, the army chief reminded his western commander of the White River debacle and advised him not to repeat the mistake of sending too small a force. "No more such accidents as resulted in the death of Major Thornburgh," he wrote. And to the secretary of war, Robert Lincoln, Sherman informed his civilian commander that if the Utes must be moved by force, as seemed likely, "the military must be in complete control without the interference from the Interior Department and its Indian Bureau." Speaking with some authority in these matters, Sherman added, "Divided responsibility always results in confusion and disaster."[17]

Besides the Utes' ultimate destination, there was the matter of compensation. The 1880 peace agreement called for, in addition to the $60,000 in annuities, an annual cash payment to the Utes of $50,000 to be dispersed on a per capita basis "for ever." This was to be added to the $25,000 annual payment guaranteed under the 1873 treaty. An additional one-time congressional appropriation of $350,000 for "The Removal and Settlement of the Utes" included funds for: (1) per capita cash payments to the Uncompahgre and White River bands for vacating their lands; (2) the construction of replacement structures on the new reservations; (3) cash reimbursement to individual Utes for permanent improvements such as buildings, corrals, and sheds; and (4) an "inducement" fund set aside for "meritorious Indians" who assisted the government in securing the needed three-quarters of adult Ute males for the agreement's ratification. Individual Uncompahgres received small cash payments before they departed for Utah; but to insure that their leaders would not balk, the Indian Bureau withheld additional payments, including reimbursements to those owning "improvements," until after their arrival in Utah. As for the White River band, the commission froze their smaller cash outlay, as punishment for the massacre, until they had settled peacefully among the Uintahs. The Southern Utes received no compensation for remaining in place on a smaller reservation. Nor did the Uintahs receive additional compensation for having to share their homeland with the White River band, for whom they had little affinity or respect. The payment of funds to the separate bands for different obligations (including bribes) left the Indian Bureau with an accounting nightmare that has lasted to this day. As for the Utes themselves, they had no way to know if the promised cash and annuity amounts matched the cash or goods received, nor any confidence that the annuities would, in fact, be issued.

In addition to locating a new reservation for the Uncompahgres, the commission faced the immediate problem, in the summer of 1880, of securing the necessary Ute signatures for the agreement's ratification. Obtaining the signatures proved an unusually difficult task. The White River band had splintered into various sub-bands and dispersed through central and northern Colorado. For them, the appearance of a government agent raised the possibility of individual arrests. Faced with the likelihood of securing few signatures from the White River band, the commission focused its attention on the Uncompahgres and the southern bands. Get them to sign, the theory went, and the White River outlaws would be presented the agreement as a fait accompli. But the problem persisted. How to get the necessary signatures from the other bands? Virtually all the Ute leaders believed that neither the 1868 nor the 1873 treaties ceded to the government all the land Washington claimed. And some Utes thought the 1880 agreement made promises without assurances, in unclear language, and was translated by untrustworthy interpreters. Chief Ignacio, the Weeminuche leader and nominal head of the Southern Utes, remained suspicious of the entire peace arrangement and let it be known that his band would refuse any settlement until he personally approved the new reservation boundary. In August of 1880, Chief Ouray traveled south to meet with Ignacio to urge the southern leader's assistance in collecting signatures. But the trip proved too exhausting for Ouray. He lived barely long enough to make his appeal. He fell victim to Bright's disease, a liver ailment he had suffered for at least five years, and died among the Southern Utes at the age of forty-seven. Ignacio and his sub-chiefs quickly buried Ouray in a cave south of the Indian agency.

An army officer present at the time of Ouray's death stated, "The Indians took sole charge of him during his sickness, not permitting the whites [or Ouray's Mexican servant] to have anything to do with him. There were three doctors present, but the Indian medicine man held his powwows so continuously that his white rivals could only occasionally get into the tent ... The funeral was conducted as that of any other [Ute] Indian, no ceremony, no pomp. When life was extinct, they wrapped the body in a blanket, threw it across a horse, and ... it was conveyed to the place of burial. ... No one whatsoever was permitted to accompany the burial party, and no one knew, nor could find out, the place of burial." Some weeks later the Indian commissions and army officers were taken to the burial site. "They found the body deposited in a natural cave, the entrance to which had been walled with rocks. The body was found to be in such a state [of decomposition] that the effort to removal was abandoned. There was no stone or mark to indicate the grave, nothing

*Chiefs Ouray and Ignacio pictured here
shortly before Ouray's death in 1881.
(Courtesy of the Denver Public Library,
Western History Collection, #X-30601)*

except a little distance [away] the putrefying carcasses of five horses that had been killed by the grave, for his service in the Happy Hunting Grounds."[18]

The chief's death presented problems for the commission. While all the bands did not universally respect Ouray, particularly the Southern Utes, he had promised to gather support for the agreement among all the Utes, especially among the Uncompahgres, the largest of the bands. To help secure their approval in Ouray's absence, Mears stepped in to assist the government. He paid two silver dollars to each Indian who put his mark to the agreement. The Uncompahgres overwhelmingly signed the affidavits. Commissioner Manypenny, hearing of the payments, wrote to Secretary Schurz immediately before he left office and charged Mears with bribery. Schurz's successor, Kirkwood, called Mears back to Washington for an explanation. With Senators Teller and Hill in attendance, Mears explained that the Indians thought silver in hand was worth more than the promise of a payment. The secretary asked Mears if he doled out government money. No, Mears replied, he paid the entire sum from his own pocket. The secretary told him that "he was perfectly right in doing as he did" and to submit a bill to the government "and he would see to it that it was paid." The secretary also asked Mears if he thought he could persuade the Uncompahgres to move. "If given enough troops," Mears responded. Kirkwood promised a sufficient force.[19]

Among the Southern Utes, Manypenny had collected what he reported to be enough votes to ratify the agreement. The commissioner figured that because each male vote represented five inhabitants (a questionable assumption) and with 573 signatures (from an estimated total population of 3,850), three-quarters of the adult male population had given their approval. Neither Manypenny's shoddy arithmetic nor Mears's bribes prevented the commission from certifying the Utes' confirmation. The only major task remaining for the commission was to get the Northern Utes moved into their new outdoor boxes.

A minority of the White River band, dispersed in isolated pockets throughout northern Colorado and primarily those loyal to Jack, presented a problem. How to get them to move permanently to Utah? The commission hoped that the carrot of individual cash payments to the Utes and the promise of annuities once they arrived at the Uintah Reservation would eliminate the need for force. Also, the government hoped that releasing Chief Johnson from the Fort Leavenworth jail would encourage the remainder of his band to move peacefully to Utah. A local lawyer had come to Johnson's defense, writing

"THE UTES
MUST GO!"

Schurz that Johnson was ill, and either he should be charged with a crime or released. Unwilling to bring the chief to trial without witnesses, since the Meeker women were unwilling to undergo the ordeal, Schurz arranged for his release and insisted the action be kept "confidential" to insure the chief's safe return to his band.[20] But Johnson refused to return to White River band and instead asked for, and was granted, membership among the Uncompahgres, with whom his sister, Chipeta, lived. However, he provided no assistance to the commission, which was left with the unresolved problem.

The commissioner responsible for the White River Utes, Alfred Meacham, worked to arrange for those few Indians with improvements to receive government reimbursement; he also wanted new structures in place on the Uintah Reservation before Jack's lodges moved into Utah. For all of Meacham's genuine concern, the press attacked him as it did all who came to the aid of the Utes. One newspaper called Meacham "a coward of nature, a thief by instinct, a hypocrite by choice."[21] Senator Hill pressed Schurz to replace him with a good "Colorado man."[22] Meacham received no better treatment from Jack and his followers, who absolutely refused, under any condition, a permanent move to Utah. The war chief refused to recognize the peace agreement, and he threatened a battle if forced to move. He and his lodges had traveled to Utah in the late summer of 1881 to collect their rations, but they had not intended to make their home among the Uintahs. Meacham predicted, "[they] will ... return to White River for the hunting season and come back to Uintah to winter." They demanded compensation for their improvements, Meacham added, and recommended payment of $3,200 as "the most sensible and economical way of settling the White River question." But Jack refused any inducements to move to Utah and, according to Meacham, continued to "defy the government" and "interfere with the negotiations over compensation." The chief, said the commissioner, "is a dangerous and ambitious demagogue who ought to be removed from among his people." Meacham recommended settling their claims by providing the Utes with wagons, harnesses, plows, and seed as an inducement to a peaceful resettlement. It would help immensely, Meacham added, if some of the sub-chiefs received some bribes.[23]

The Uncompahgres, under the leadership of Chief Ouray, had remained peaceful and, on almost all occasions, had accommodated themselves to the Indian Bureau after the troubles at White River. Their agent, W. H. Berry, wrote in his annual report in the fall of 1880 that he found them to be "loyal, peaceable, and well disposed towards the whites and the government." They desired "permanent peace," Berry reported, and he found them to be "willing, tractable, and loyal people." As always, they "spend much time hunting which takes time away from their farming responsibilities." The biggest hindrance to their advancement continued to be those "unprincipled white men," who were always prepared to stir up trouble. But if the Uncompahgres are fairly and justly treated, Berry advised, they could "be advanced to civilization."[24]

Within years of Ouray's death, the Uncompahgres became intractable. In a council with Agent Berry and Commissioner McMorris, Sappovonare, Ouray's replacement, announced that the band would not move.[25] They would "as soon die as go to [Utah] and starve ... [and] will resist," reported an army spy among the Utes at Fort Crawford to his commander.[26] Recognizing that force might have to be used but possessing no authority to order the army, a commission member asked Washington for instructions. Interior Secretary Kirkwood conferred with the Secretary of War Lincoln and, with the War Department's approval, wrote back to the commissioner, "If the Indians will not go without force, request the officer in command [Mckenzie] to compel removal." If the Indians will not move because they have not received compensation for their improvement, "assure the Indians that money will be paid them at the new agency. If the refusal is absolute, have [the] military proceed at once."[27]

At first Colonel Mckenzie attempted to convince the Uncompahgres to move voluntarily. He understood their reluctance, but the colonel had his orders. He met with the Uncompahgre chiefs and informed them that they must move to their new agency promptly; if they continued in their disobedience, force would be used. When one unidentified chief proposed various alternatives, Mckenzie stood firm, "All I want to know is whether you will go or not. If you will not go of your own accord, I will make you go. When you have sufficiently discussed this matter and have arrived at a conclusion, send for me. Remember, you are to go, at once."[28] With a gun pointed at their heads, the Utes had no option but to agree to move. Agent Berry issued the 361 Ute families two weeks' rations, plus extra sugar, coffee, and tobacco. The next day (August 28, 1881) with their possessions loaded onto their backs and leading their horse travois, 1,458 men, women, and children set out on the 350-mile march into Utah.

*Hospital (far left), guard house (center),
and soldiers quarters (far right) at Fort
Crawford on the Uncompahgre River,
close to the Los Piños Agency, circa 1880.
(Courtesy of the Denver Public Library,
Western History Collection, #Z-1393)*

*Ration day at the Los Piños Agency on the Uncompahgre
River, with U.S. soldiers in attendance, circa 1880.
(Courtesy of the Colorado Historical Society, #F-50181)*

More than a thousand army troops stood guard at a distance. Other troops, a company of the Fourth Cavalry, were posted in the Grand Valley to insure the Utes did not linger on their way to Utah. The army, however, expected less trouble from the Utes than from the white settlers who followed on the heels of the departing Uncompahgres.[29] Some whites actually advised the Utes to stay and defy the army in order to start an inevitable war. The conflict, and even its threat, would require the army to remain at Fort Crawford, a boon to the local merchants who fed and liquored the soldiers. When Mckenzie asked what he should do with the thousands of intruders flooding onto the vacated reservation, Washington ordered they should not be disturbed. The new squatters must be allowed to remain on the land, one commissioner wrote to Secretary Kirkwood, for then the Ute "will be much easier controlled in his new location" knowing they had no land upon which to return.[30] The Indians left peacefully and without incident.

For more than five hundred years, the Utes had survived undisturbed in the Uncompahgre Valley and the surrounding area. Manifest Destiny had finally caught up with them. The mountains with their minerals and the valleys with fertile farmland could no longer provide protection. Overwhelmed by the threat of military force, the Utes could only look over their shoulders as they left behind the land that had fueled and nourished them for centuries. With more than eighteen thousand head of ponies, sheep, and goats, the Uncompahgre packed up their teepees, food, clothing, and personal possessions and slowly made their way by foot and horseback across the Colorado River and into Utah. For the Utes, as for all Indians, the land they left behind had provided life's sustenance and memories, including their most sacred sites—the burial grounds of their ancestors.

The move to the new reservation took a month to complete. On their arrival, as promised, they received $7,700 as compensation for their improvements ($5,000 to Chipeta, Ouray's widow). The cash, however, did not compensate for the shortage of rations and annuities. The Indian Bureau were constructing, or had already completed, structures for the agent and his staff (a physician and his family, a clerk, blacksmith, miller, farmer, and carpenter), including a schoolhouse, barn, various workshops, equipment and storage sheds, and a mess hall. The facility would soon be equipped with a sawmill and gristmill, wagons, harnesses, and farm machinery to support the livestock, including a new herd of three hundred milk cows, a breed unfamiliar to the Utes.[31]

By issuing new equipment and additional livestock, the Indian Bureau in Washington continued to hope that the Utes would, in a new setting, surrender their old hunting habits for the ways of white agriculturalists. The Indian agents remained skeptical. One agent reported, "With the exception of a very few, perhaps a half dozen, they have never cultivated even a garden patch, but have relied for their living on the chase and the supplies furnished by the government. They will not readily adapt themselves to their new condition [or] ... make successful tillers of the soil." A few will make the transition to farmers, but even they will "make slow progress." They need to be rid of some useless horses, the agent said in the manner of the deceased Meeker, and "take up the plow ... but it is fool hearty to think they will do so voluntarily."[32]

In Utah, immediate friction arose between the White River Utes and the industrious Uintahs. The agent in Utah, John J. Critchlow reported the "indolent" White River band cared "nothing of farming or ... civilized pursuits"; and "what is worse," he wrote, "many of them have no desire to learn. ... they laugh at the Uintahs for farming, and say they ought to fight [,] and then Washington would furnish them with plenty to eat."[33] In addition to the ridicule from the White River band, the Uintahs felt unfairly treated when the Colorado Utes band moved in on top of them without their assent and without compensation. Besides, the agent reported, the Uintahs looked upon the 665 White River Utes with both disdain and distrust, seeing them as an inferior and wild band of interlopers. "The peaceful and industrious Indian has [been given] less consideration than the turbulent and vicious [ones]. ... We feed the White River murderers and compel the peaceful Uintahs to largely care for themselves. This ... induces the Indians to believe that if they are to get favors from the government [,] they must refuse to work, refuse to be orderly and peaceful, and must commit some depredations or murder, and then a commission will be appointed to treat them, pay them in goods, provisions, and money to behave themselves. This looks to an Indian very much like rewarding enemies and punishing friends, and gives him a singular idea of our Christian civilization ... which has so much the appearance of rewarding vice and punishing virtue."[34]

In the end, the Indian Bureau moved the Ute bands into different locations without bloodshed. However, Washington failed to alter the Utes' attitudes about farming. In this regard, not much had changed since the death of Meeker. But Washington faced the more immediate and important problem of how to keep the Utes in their new designated pens. If they returned to Colorado for hunting, even seasonally, they would wander amidst the whites as they had moved atop the Uintahs. For as the interior secretary warned the secretary of war upon hearing the White River Utes planned to return to Colorado in the fall of 1881, "If the White River Utes shall be permitted to leave, it will be impossible to keep the Uncompahgres [in place] & the whole treaty is made a nullity ... "[35]

To insure that they remained in Utah, the army, in conjunction with the Interior Department, immediately planned for a new military post (insensitively named for the fallen Thornburgh) adjacent to the two Utah reservations. And about the time the Uncompahgres arrived at their new reservation (named for Chief Ouray), most of the White River Utes departed the Uintah Reservation to hunt on their old grounds in Colorado. Chiefs Jack and Colorow informed the agent that they and their lodges could not be enticed back to Utah by rations, monies owed them by treaty, or even bribes. For the army it was like trying to herd butterflies into a wheelbarrow.

Jack, good to his word, refused to return. And when whites in northwest Colorado hollered to the state's politicians, the secretary of interior authorized the arrest of Jack for being off the reservation without written permission. That the 1880 peace agreement, or any treaty with the Utes, did not require such permission failed to stop the Indian Bureau or the army in its pursuit of Jack, considered an outlaw and "troublemaker" by the authorities. Jack, the agent in Utah wrote Washington, "will start trouble on the White River and its vicinity" and may be attempting to arrange an alliance with the Shoshone tribe to the north. Jack and his followers (estimated at 190 Utes) must be returned to Utah. "If not, others from the Uintah Reservation will follow them." Nothing less than "unconditional submission" must be demanded, he declared.[36]

The army liked nothing better than to go after Jack. He had led the Utes at the Battle of Milk Creek, continued to brag about his outnumbered, young braves halting the well-armed army force from entering the reservation, and expressed in Washington no remorse for the death of Major Thornburgh. Indeed, he bragged to various Indian agents about killing the army major, and expressed nothing but contempt for the Indian Bureau, their broken promises, and the ineptitude of U.S. soldiers. To no one's surprise, the Indian Bureau and the army put out the word to be on the lookout for Jack.

Rumors of Jack's whereabouts circulated throughout Colorado, Wyoming, and Washington. One unconfirmed report placed him with the

Sioux in the Dakotas, and another reported him in Rawlins as a teamster. The wildest rumor had him stalking the governor outside his office in Denver. But when an army spy in Wyoming confirmed the appearance of Jack on the Shoshone Reservation near Fort Washakie, the army moved into action.

A detachment of the Third Cavalry stationed at the fort received orders on April 28, 1882, to hunt down Jack, capture and return him to the Uintah Reservation. Accompanied by six soldiers, Lt. George H. Morgan, the company commander of Troop H, went to a two-story log structure where Jack was reported to be hiding. As a precaution, the lieutenant ordered his small detachment to surround the Indian house as he cautiously approached the front door. Anticipating no problem, he had not drawn his revolver. He shouted up the stairs to Jack to come down. Silence. Then after a second command, Jack responded.

"What do you want?" the Ute war chief asked in good English.

"You must come with me. The Great White Father wants to see you," the lieutenant answered.

Jack, recognizing his trap, rushed down the stairs holding a knife and bolted out the door. The lieutenant drew his pistol and threatened to shoot if Jack did not stop. He kept running. Lieutenant Morgan fired three times at Jack's legs, trying to wound him. He missed. Just before the war chief escaped into a nearby teepee, a mounted trooper took aim at Jack with his carbine and shot him in the arm. Inside, Jack gathered up his own carbine and some ammunition.

From a distance, the troops surrounded the teepee. The army officer ordered two soldiers to tie several lariats together and sling a loop over the teepee and pull it over on Jack. From his hiding place, the Indian immediately recognized the ploy. Jack ran from the back of the teepee to another where he took cover from the soldiers' volley of bullets among some bales of buffalo robes. As Jack suffered his wound silently and bled slowly, the troops waited.

The soldiers tried again to pull down the second teepee but failed. The lieutenant shouted to Jack to surrender. No response. Thinking that Jack had lost consciousness from loss of blood, the army officer ordered his sergeant to advance slowly and cautiously on the teepee. As the soldier approached the front opening, Jack fired and dropped the sergeant with a well-aimed bullet through the heart. The other troops fired into the teepee as they sought cover among some trees.

Clearly Jack would not surrender peacefully. The lieutenant sent two troopers back to the post with the dead sergeant and a message to Maj. J. W. Mason, the post commander, for reinforcements. Mason and his troops hastened to the lieutenant's position with a mountain howitzer. They placed the howitzer in front of the teepee and fired. Immediately after the shell exploded, the troops rushed the teepee, collected into a salt bag the few body parts of Jack they could identify, and burned what little remained of the buffalo hide structure. The post commander filed his official report the following day to army headquarters reporting on his "measurers which resulted in the capture and death of Indian Jack."[37]

Two weeks later, the *Laramie Sentinel* reported Jack's death to its delighted readers. In an attempt at humor, the editor reported that the howitzer shell, "owing to some fault in its construction ... burst with great havoc near Captain Jack's bosom and a few inches north of his liver. So great was the shock to his system that the only feature that could be recognized was a copper-colored seed wart which he had acquired three years ago." The news report continued, "His death, however, was not officially announced until a cavalry officer brought in a lobe of liver that he had found in a tree near by. It was then stated authoritatively that Captain Jack was dead. The military ... never jumps to conclusions. When a vital organ is found in the limb of a neighboring tree, the remains under discussion seem to be lacking a vital organ, the military authorities jump to the conclusion that the man is hopelessly injured." As "a warrior and a liar he was the envy and admiration of the Ute nation." But now he was dead with his brain "scattered over four acres of sage brush." How secure whites could now feel "when we know that an Indian has passed away in this manner." As for Jack's friends, they too could be assured he was not buried alive. "Those who saw his remains will always feel certain that death was instantaneous and painless. His body will lie in state in a cigar box, until the time ... he will be interred with ... a corn planter."

And then this final message to its readers, "We believe that the mountain howitzer is destined ... to become an important factor in the civilization of the Indian and the amelioration of mankind."[38]

Industrial capitalism with its mountain howitzers had finally subdued the Utes. The tribe had lost in less than three decades the land they considered home for longer than seven centuries. And in the process of disconnecting the Utes from their land, Anglos managed to destroy the centuries-old balance between human habitation and the natural environment. The United States replaced the delicate balance with a system so ferocious in its appetite and imperial in its design that it could not accomodate those "savages" who wished only to be left alone. In the end, the conquerors had finally cleansed the landscape of a physical and cultural barrier that had stood stubbornly in the path of "civilization."

"Capt. Ute Jack is made a good Indian near Fort Washakie, WY. T."
Illustration from Leslie's Magazine.
(Courtesy of the Smithsonian Institution, National Anthropological Archives, James Taylor Album, #6233)

Epilogue

Not long ago, I visited Meeker, Colorado, an attractive agricultural community of 3,200 surrounded by lush wheat fields and prosperous livestock ranches. This county seat is home to the Rio Blanco County Historical Society and White River Museum, housed in two of the log buildings Colonel Merritt had constructed for his occupying troops in 1879. To enter the museum is to visit your grandmother's attic. Photographs of the pioneer settlers, their saddles, harnesses, and sturdy wagons remind visitors of the county's ranching heritage. An arrowhead collection serves as a reminder of the first residents. So also do the uniforms and weapons of the soldiers sent to remove them. To the back of the museum sits, prominently displayed, a Moline single-bladed plow, painted black. It is the farm implement Nathan Meeker ordered to transform the Ute horse pasture into a vegetable garden and grain field. The sign does not hint of how the town father's actions led to the battle, his own death, the death of his employees, the death of Indian and army soldiers, or the removal of the Utes from their homeland.

The town no longer hosts its annual "Meeker Days," whose weekend events once glorified its namesake—the heroic and proud agent who stood firm against Indian "savagery." Today the "Range Call" festivities have replaced the Meeker celebration with horse races, a rodeo, and a pageant. The latter depicts the loss of Indian braves and army soldiers, not as an unavoidable "incident," but as a tragic battle and a brutal massacre that could and should have been avoided. Maybe, the pageant suggests, Agent Meeker had not served well either the Indians for whom he was responsible or the army troops he summoned to his defense. There is more thought given today to the amends that can be made, have been made, and are still under consideration in federal claims court.

Elsewhere, however, Meeker's reputation survives unscathed. In 1970, the National Cowboy Hall of Fame inducted Nathan Meeker into their Hall of Great Westerners. He is cited for "his unswerving beliefs in Christian morality, honest work, and individual freedom," and for being a man "whose principles and actions contributed so significantly to the development of the West."[1]

I wanted to see for myself the real legacy of this "Great Westerner." Leaving Meeker, I drove north along the route of the old Indian trail and wagon road, now paved, which led up to the Milk Creek battlefield and on north across the Yampa to Rawlins. My guide for the day, Joe Sullivan, a retired rancher and president of the county historical society, pointed out some Ute rock art as we climbed slowly through the narrow Coal Creek Canyon and on up to Yellow Jacket Pass. Far off to our east were the snow-covered peaks of the Flat Tops Wilderness area. To the west were the Danforth Hills, named for Meeker's predecessor at the agency. The arid hill country through which we drove was broken by shale outcroppings and covered with sage, oak brush, and a scattering of thirsty piñons. The country had probably changed little from the time the Utes lived and hunted here, though Ute fires had kept the country cleared of the sage brush that, more recently, has spread with over-grazing. To the uninitiated, it appeared to be a rough country with an even tougher climate. As we passed a dilapidated sheep corral, Joe informed me that the area's once-thriving sheep industry had all but disappeared—a casualty of international free trade. Now cattle had replaced the "woollies" on the land-scape and so, too, had a few, small second-home log cabins built by urban refugees. Mostly, though, the country sat quiet and devoid of human habitation.

We dropped down off the pass into a grass valley, the battlefield site. A series of private owners have, over the years, transformed the valley into a large and lush hay meadow. A system of delicate and intricate irrigation ditches, common in this dry, high-plateau region, laces the valley. Milk Creek, with its shallow, late-summer flow, divided the view. A New Holland hay swather sat idle next to an abandoned wooden shed and barn that had, long ago, sheltered the horses of the children who had attended the nearby one-room schoolhouse.

Joe pointed out to me the rock outcroppings behind which the Utes awaited Major Thornburgh's troops. Just ahead of us was the trail, barely discernible, on which Lieutenant Cherry scouted a shortcut to the agency and where he waved his hat at Captain Jack before the bloodshed commenced. We could see below us, about a quarter of a mile downstream on Milk Creek, the cottonwood grove where an Indian bullet had taken Thornburgh's life. The rifle pits where the troops had held out, awaiting relief, had disappeared, covered over by years of farming.

We walked down to the stone monument commemorating the army soldiers who died in the battle. Buried there were the bodies of nine U.S. soldiers and three civilian employees who worked alongside the army troops. Their vainglorious dead commander, Thornburgh, had been carried back and buried at Fort Fred Steele and was later exhumed and reburied in Omaha, Nebraska. His fallen troops, however, rest in an unmarked grave. Only recently were the bodies discovered, causing considerable controversy as to what to do with them. The private landowners refuse to have their land disturbed, while army veterans have called for a proper reburial of the their troops. Meanwhile the soldiers lie in their mass grave while the army continues to drag its bureaucratic feet.[2]

Overlooking the battlefield and next to the soldiers' granite monument has been placed a newer monument, the one the Utes visit, the memorial to their fallen heroes. In 1993, the Utes and the Rio Blanco County Historical Society arranged for the memorial to be placed alongside the army memorial, an arrangement not allowed, until very recently, on federal property. "The Utes were humans too," Joe quietly explained, "and they deserve our recognition."

Among the survivors, if not beneficiaries, of the Ute War, Otto Mears continued to build and profit from toll roads and railroads through the Utes' former homeland. The Colorado legislature memorialized the "Pathfinder of the San Juans" with a stained-glass window in the state capitol after handing Mears the contract to erect the structure. He later moved to Pasadena, California, where, the self-described "capitalist" retired with his considerable wealth. Governor Pitkin enjoyed the kudos of grateful citizens for his efforts to remove the Northern Utes. Within years, Colorado named a county in his honor, the seat of which, Aspen, is rather better known today as a playground for the rich and famous than as the Utes' former hunting grounds. Carl Schurz eased into a well-deserved retirement to lecture and write his memoirs. He considered his efforts on behalf of the Utes one of his crowning achievements. He had reigned in the army's plan to annihilate the Utes, but he never acknowledged that he and others had failed to consider seriously the option of leaving the Utes in Colorado with or without land allotments. Schurz's replacement as secretary of interior under President Chester Arthur, Senator Henry Teller, garnered the enthusiastic support of westerners as one of their own. The *Laramie Sentinal* lauded his appointment with the observation: "If the truth be known, he believes with General Sherman that the best Indian is a dead Indian, and that they have no more right to the splendid western domain than the panthers and coyotes ... "[3] He demonstrated compassion for Josephine Meeker, whom he hired in 1881 as a "copyist" and later as his assistant private secretary in Washington. She died of pneumonia within the year. Teller evidenced no such compassion for the remaining Southern Utes in Colorado, toward whom he continued his efforts at removal. He failed not for lack of effort but because neighboring states refused to accept them. Teller did succeed, however, in establishing an Indian boarding school in Grand Junction, Colorado. When Ute children contracted white diseases and died off in astounding numbers, the school closed before it could inculcate students in the benefits of a white value system. Teller, a decidedly stronger advocate for silver than for Indian welfare, faded from the political scene when, in the 1890s, the nation opted for the gold standard.

The U.S. government, however, had not yet finished reconfiguring the Ute reservations. In 1886, in a move to save administrative and military costs, Washington combined the Ouray and Uintah Reservations into one unit, insensitive to the disparate histories and cultures of the three Ute bands, all the while keeping an eye on them from Fort Thornburgh. When well over half of the Uncompahgre and White River bands, unhappy with their land and irregular rations, made an effort to move to the Cheyenne River Indian Reservation in South Dakota, the army hunted them down and drove them back into their Utah pen. In 1887, Congress finally enacted its allotment policy, so dear to Schurz and Indian reformers, with passage of the Dawes Act. It proved to be as unpopular as it was ineffective. The Utes, as well as other tribes, quickly discovered that as much as Washington wished to push the Indians toward "the habits of civilization," it was difficult to sustain a livelihood on semiarid parcels too small and dry to sustain a prairie dog colony. In addition, the entire concept of individual ownership violated the Utes' concept of tribal holdings. In 1895, the Weeminuche band, under Chief Ignacio's leadership, found the allotment idea so alien to their tradition that they moved to the western end of the Southern Ute Reservation, where they established their own Ute Mountain Reservation. They refused to accept any allotments. In Utah and within the remaining portion of the Southern Ute Reservation, where allotments were made and often forced upon individual Utes, the parcels carried the prohibition against selling the land for twenty-five years. Lands not allotted, or about 85 percent of the reservation, were declared "excess" by Washington and thrown open to white settlers.[4] It is no wonder that the Utes, along with other tribes, took to the soon-to-be-banned Ghost Dance, which promised to the faithful a better life and an empowerment to rid the world of whites. And to further convince the Utes that agreements were made to be broken, Washington lopped off more than fifty thousand acres from the Southern Ute Reservation to carve out Mesa Verde National Park and another million acres from the combined Uintah/Ouray Reservation to create the Uintah National Forest. The Utes did receive some compensatory lands and cash in the 1930s and 1950s, but the payments, said the Utes, failed to match the government's original promises.

Ironically, the Southern Utes today are recognized primarily for their wealth. The 1,400–member tribe sits on one of the biggest supplies of natural gas in the United States. The Utes retained the mineral rights on the entire reservation, including "excess" lands sold to whites, creating immense legal battles with private landholders and the Department of Interior. But through a series of court settlements and astute reinvestments in real estate, joint energy ventures, and securities, the tribe has assembled a $1.45 billion energy conglomerate, making it one of the richest tribes in the nation. It is one of the very few tribes whose wealth doesn't hinge on gambling.[5]

From where I write in southwestern Colorado, just down from the serene hilltop where my discovery of arrowheads several years ago spawned this book, I find it difficult to imagine the bloody horror played out over a century ago on a similarly pastoral setting. If the Battle of Milk Creek was one of the most decorated in U.S. military history, what must the Utes have suffered? And how had the Indians honored their heroes? I do not know. But a Ute told me their spirits live here, in a country no longer their own.

Endnotes

KEY:

CHS: Colorado Historical Society
DPL: Denver Public Library Society
GM: City of Greeley Museums (archives)
GPO: Government Printing Office
LOC: Library of Congress
M: Microcopy Number
NA: National Archives
R: Roll Number
RG: Record Group Number

Preface

[1] Michael Fellman, *Citizen Sherman: A Life of William Tecumseh Sherman* (New York: Random House, 1999), 263.

[2] Stephen Ambrose, *To America: Personal Reflections of an Historian* (New York: Simon and Schuster, 2002).

[3] Some U.S. foreign policy "experts" today use the same Hobbesian "historical inevitability" argument, referring to themselves as "tragic realists."

[4] Isaiah Berlin, "Historical Inevitability," in *The Proper Study of Mankind: An Anthology of Essays* (New York: Ferrar Straus and Giroux, 1998), 185.

Introduction

[1] See letter from Agent J. J. Critchlow, Uintah Agency (Utah), to the commissioner of Indian Affairs, 30 January 1882, NA, RG 74, M 666, R 517.

[2] Quoted in Carolyn Marchant, "Reinventing Eden: Western Culture as a Recovery Narrative," in *Uncommon Ground: Toward Reinventing Nature*, ed. William Cronin, (New York: W. W. Norton and Company, 1995), 143.

[3] Clark Spence, ed., *The American West, A Source Book* (New York: Crowell, 1966), 108.

[4] From *North American Review of Reviews* (January 1856), quoted in David Haward Bain, *Empire Express: Building the First Continental Railroad* (New York: Penguin, 1999), 51; also William Goetzmann, *Exploration and Empire: The Explorer and the Scientist in the Winning of the American West* (New York: Alfred A. Knopf, 1966).

[5] Francis Paul Prucha, *The Indians in American Society: From the Revolutionary War to the Present* (Berkeley: University of California Press, 1985), 12.

[6] For Jefferson's view on the Indians, see Anthony F. C. Wallace, *Jefferson and the Indians: The Tragic Fate of the First Americans* (Cambridge, Mass.: Harvard University Press, 1999), 18–19.

[7] Ibid., 19–20.

[8] Elizabeth A. Fenn, "Biological Warfare in Eighteenth Century North America: Beyond Jeffrey Amherst," *Journal of American History* (March 2000): 1552–58.

[9] See Theda Perdue and Michael Green, *The Cherokee Removal: A Brief History with Documents* (Boston: Bedford/St. Martin's, 1995), 113–14.

[10] For a review of Jackson's policies, see Robert V. Remini, *Andrew Jackson and His Indian Wars* (New York: Penguin, 2001).

[11] Donald Meinig, *The Shaping of America: A Geographical Perspective on 500*

Years of History: Continental America 1800–1867 (New Haven, Conn.: Yale University Press, 1993), 77.

[12] Ray Allen Billington, *Land of Savagery, Land of Promise: The European Image of the American Frontier in the Nineteeth Century* (Norman, Okla.: University of Oklahoma Press, 1981), 105.

[13] For the theme of Indian inferiority see Robert F. Berkofer, *The White Man's Indian: Images of the American Indian, from Columbus to the Present* (New York: Random House, 1978).

[14] The delineated categories are explained in William Channing Woodbridge, *Rudiments of Geography* (Hartford, Conn.: Oliver D. Cooke and Company, 1822).

[15] See Francis Parkman's review of Cooper's collected works in *The North American Review* 74 (1852): 150–51, 155.

[16] From the *Cheyenne Daily Leader*, 3 March 1870, quoted in Dee Brown, *Bury My Heart at Wounded Knee: An Indian History of the American West* (New York: Henry Holt and Company, Inc., 1970), 189.

[17] Not until 1924 did Indians gain the right to vote. For a discussion on the connection between racism and power, see George Frederickson, *Racism: A Short History* (Princeton, N.J.: Princeton University Press, 2002), 156.

[18] The Uncompahgre name derived from the red-colored headwaters of the river that originates today in present-day Ironton Park above the city of Ouray, Colorado.

[19] The Utes also used fire as a form of communication, a weapon against other tribes, and as a means of clearing areas for ease of travel. Shepard Krech III, *The Ecological Indian: Myth and History* (New York: W. W. Norton, 1999), 104–7. For diet and hunting habits, see William Sturtevant, ed., *The Great Basin*, vol. 11, *Handbook of North American Indians*, (Washington, D.C.: Smithsonian Institution, 1986), 64–93, 336–47; also David G. Noble, *Ancient Colorado: An Anthropological Perspective* (Denver: Colorado Council of Professional Archeologists, 2000), 44–45.

[20] See John Wesley Powell's report on his observations among the Utes during the winter of 1868–69 in his "Notes on the Utes," original manuscript at the Smithsonian Institution, a copy of which is included in the Goss Collection at the Southern Ute Cultural Center and Museum (Ignacio, Colorado), item 830. See also Donald Worster, *A River Running West: The Life of John Wesley Powell* (New York: Oxford University Press, 2001), 262, 289. Powell, who studied the Utes and their language, frequently defended the Indians against those who wished to expropriate their land. Unlike most nineteenth-century Americans, he did not consider Indians "a contemptible species of vermin to be exterminated."

[21] See Anne M. Smith, *Ethnography of the Northern Utes*, no. 17, *Museum of New Mexico Papers in Anthropology* (Sante Fe: Museum of New Mexico Press, 1974); also Smith's *Ute Tales* (Salt Lake City: University of Utah Press, 1992); and William Wroth, ed., *Ute Indian Arts and Culture*, (Colorado Springs:

Colorado Springs Fine Arts Center, 2000). For Ute contact with the white trappers, see William Goetzmann, *Exploration and Empire*, 67–70.

22 Joseph Campbell, *The Power of Myth* (New York: Broadway Books, 2001), 73.

23 Quoted in Don. C. Fowler and Catherine S. Fowler, *Anthropology of the Numa: John Wesley Powell's Manuscripts on the Numic Peoples of North America, 1868–1880* (Washington, D.C.: Smithsonian Institution Press, 1971), 37–38.

24 See Powell, "Notes on the Utes." Powell reported that among the White River band, it was believed that women who could no longer bear children were destined to become witches, wrapped in a snakeskin. To prevent such a fate, it was common for women to commit suicide by starvation. Powell's observation about the status of women, particularly as it relates to their role in council meetings, is at odds with that presented by Catherine M. B. Osburn in *Southern Ute Women: Autonomy and Assimilation* (Albuquerque: University of New Mexico Press, 1998), 21–22.

25 See Powell, "Notes on the Utes," for the importance of a chief's historical knowledge of his band.

26 For a discussion of both ethnic cleansing and genocide, see Norman M. Naimark, *Fires of Hatred: Ethnic Cleansing in Twentieth Century Europe* (Cambridge, Mass.: Harvard University Press, 2002).

ONE: *From Spanish Neighbors to an American Reservation*

1 For details on this borderland cultural polyglot, see James F. Brooks, *Captives and Cousins: Slavery, Kinship, and Community in the Southwest Borderlands* (Chapel Hill, N.C.: University of North Carolina Press, 2002). For the Ignacio-Manzanares meeting, see 304–5, 358.

2 For a discussion of Spain's policy of "paternalistic pacification," see Jerry Adelman and Stephen Aron, "From Borderlands to Borders: Empires, Nation-States, and the Peoples in Between in North American History," *American Historical Review* (June 1999).

3 Spanish colonists found themselves surrounded by the Apache to the south and southwest, the Navajo to the west, the Utes to the northwest, and the Comanche to the northeast. See Frances L. Swadesh, "Structure of Hispanic-Indian Relations in New Mexico," in Paul M. Kutsche, ed., *The Survival of Spanish American Villages* (Colorado Springs: The Research Committee, Colorado College, 1979), 55–56; and David J. Weber, *The Spanish Frontier in North America* (New Haven, Conn.: Yale University Press, 1992), 192.

4 See Joseph P. Sanchez, *Explorers, Traders, and Slavers: Forging the Old Spanish Trail, 1678–1850* (Salt Lake City: University of Utah Press, 1997); and Herbert E. Bolton, ed., *Pageant in the Wilderness: The Story of the Escalante Expedition to the Interior Basin* (Salt Lake City: Utah State Historical Society, 1950).

5 For an account of the Dominguez-Escalante expeditions, see Herbert E. Bolton, ed., *The Story of the Spanish Exploration in the Southwest*, 1542–1706 (New York: Charles Scribner's Sons, 1916); Bolton, *Pageant in the Wilderness;* and Ted J. Warner, ed., *The Dominguez-Escalante Journal: Their Expedition Through Colorado, Utah, Arizona, and New Mexico in 1776*, 2nd ed. (Salt Lake City: University of Utah Press, 1995), 38.

6 Of the 1,646 baptisms of non-Pueblo Indians in northern New Mexico between 1700 and 1800, 5 percent were Utes, 55 percent were Apache, 20 percent were Navaho, 12 percent were Comanche, and 8 percent were from another tribe. Of the 2,210 baptisms in New Mexico of non-Pueblo Indians between 1800 and 1880, only the Navajo baptisms exceeded the number of Ute baptisms. See Brooks, *Captives and Cousins*, 123–25, 146, 235.

7 See William deBuys, *Enchantment and Exploration: The Life and Hard Times of a New Mexico Mountain Range* (Albuquerque: University of New Mexico Press, 1995), 68–70; Alvar W. Carlson, *The Spanish-American Homestead: Four Centuries in New Mexico's Rio Arriba: Creating the North American Landscape* (Baltimore: John Hopkins University Press, 1990), 159–63; Alfonso Ortiz, ed., and William Sturtevant, gen. ed., *Southwest*, vol. 9, *Handbook of North American Indians*, (Washington, D.C.: Smithsonian Institution Press, 1979), 198–99; and Leslie Poling-Kempes, *Valley of the Shining Stone: The Story of Abiquiu* (Tucson: University of Arizona Press, 1997).

8 L. R. Bailey, *Indian Slave Trade in the Southwest: A Study of Slave-Taking and the Traffic in Indian Captives* (Los Angeles: Westernlore Press, 1966), 152–53. With the arrival of the Mormons in Utah, the Utes discovered another buyer's market.

9 For a discussion of the affects of disease upon North American Indians, see Charles C. Mann, "1491," *Atlantic Monthly*, March 2002, 41–53. My estimates are based on a Ute population of 8,500 in 1900, considered the low point of the Ute population, and estimating a 50 percent mortality rate. See also Shepard Krech III, *The Ecological Indian: Myth and History* (New York: W. W. Norton, 1999). Krech estimates a population decline of between 60 to 70 percent in the American Southwest during the seventeenth century and then a "downward trend" into the eighteenth and nineteenth centuries; see page 86.

10 See P. David Smith, *Ouray: Chief of the Utes* (Ridgway, Colo.: Wayfinder Press, 1986), 46–47.

11 See Thomas G. Andrews, "Tata Atansio Trujillo's Unlikely Tale of Utes, Nuevomexicanos, and the Settling of Colorado's San Luis Valley," *New Mexico Historical Review* 75 (January 2000): 4–41. For the influence of the horse among the southern Plains Indians, see Pekka Hämäläinen, "The Rise of the Plains Indian Horse Culture," *Journal of American History* 90, no. 3 (December 2003), 833–62.

12 For a detailed description of the Indian-Hispanic relations during the colonial period, see the rich and detailed discussion in Frances L. Quintana,

Pobladores: Hispanic Americans of the Ute Frontier, 2nd rev. ed. (Notre Dame, Ind.: University of Notre Dame Press, 1991). Quote from page 172.

13 Charles Kappler, comp., "Treaty with the Utah, 1849," in *U.S. Indians Affairs: Laws and Treaties*, vol. 2 (Washington, D.C.: GPO, 1904–41), 585–88.

14 Some Indians did take up Spanish surnames to hide their Indian identity, gain immediate citizenship, and avoid being displaced from their land. See William Wroth, ed., *Ute Indian Arts and Culture*, (Colorado Springs: Colorado Springs Fine Arts Center, 2000), 11.

15 Quoted in David Rich Lewis, *Neither Wolf Nor Dog: American Indians, Environment, and Agrarian Change* (New York: Oxford University Press, 1994), 35.

16 Quoted in Anne M. Smith, *Ethnography of the Northern Utes*, no. 17, *Museum of New Mexico Papers in Anthropology* (Sante Fe: Museum of New Mexico Press, 1974), 7.

17 Quoted in Joseph G. Jorgensen, *The Sun Dance Religion: Power for the Powerless* (Chicago: University of Chicago Press, 1972), 36.

18 Charles Wilkinson, *Fire on the Plateau: Conflict and Endurance in the American Southwest* (Washington, D.C: Island Press/Shearwater Books, 1999), 150.

19 Donald W. Meinig, *Continental America, 1800–1867*, vol. 2, *The Shaping of America: A Geographical Perspective on 500 Years of History*, (New Haven, Conn.: Yale University Press, 1993), 180–81.

20 *Rocky Mountain News*, 26 March 1863.

21 Evan S. Connell, *Son of the Morning Star: Custer and the Little Bighorn* (San Francisco: North Point Press, 1984), 176.

22 Alvin M. Josephy Jr., *The Civil War in the American West* (New York: Random House, 1991), 230.

23 Quoted in Rodman W. Paul, *The Far West and the Great Plains in Transition: 1859–1900* (New York: Harper and Row, 1988), 132.

24 Denver called itself the "Queen City of the Plains," but one English observer called it "more plain than queenly" and definitely "undistinguished." See G. W. Steevens, *The Land of the Dollar* (Edinburgh and London: William Blackwood and Sons, 1900), 199; quoted in Rodman Paul, *The Far West*, 298.

25 Sidney Jocknick, *Early Days on the Western Slope of Colorado* (Denver: Carson-Harper, 1913), 27.

26 Quoted in Elmer Ellis, *Henry Moore Teller, Defender of the West* (Caldwell, Idaho: Caxton Printers, 1941), 48.

27 Charles C. Royce, "Indian Land Cession in the U.S.," in *18th Annual Report of the Bureau of American Ethnology, 1896–97* (Washington, D.C.: GPO, 1899), see appendix, 365.

28 From Samuel Bowles, *The Switzerland of America* (Springfield, Mass.: Samuel Bowles and Company, 1869); quoted in W. Storrs Lee, *Colorado: A Literary Chronicle* (New York: Funk and Wagnal, 1970), 250–55.

29 See A. C. Hunt (governor of Colorado Territory) to commissioner of Indian Affairs, 20 September 1868, NA, RG 75, M 234, R 200.

30 Curiously, the signatures agreeing to the treaty show five signatures from the Muache band, including Ouray, the chief of the Tabaguache (Uncompahgre) band. Ignacio, chief of the Weeminuche, did not sign the treaty. For a list of the signatures by band, see Kappler, "Treaty with the Utah, 1849," 993–95.

31 Quoted in Marshall Sprague, *Massacre: The Tragedy at White River* (Boston: Little, Brown, and Company, 1957), 92.

TWO: *"Conquer by Kindness"*

1 Robert W. Mardock, *The Reformers and the American Indian* (Columbia, Mo.: University of Missouri Press, 1971), 4.

2 Secretary of Interior Columbus Delano, *Annual Report of the Secretary of Interior,* in *Executive Documents, 1873–74* (Washington, D.C.: GPO, 1874), iii–iv.

3 George E. Ellis, *The Red Man and the White Man in North America from Its Discovery to Its Present Time* (Boston: Little, Brown, and Company, 1882), 585.

4 Quoted in Robert F. Berkhofer Jr., *The White Man's Indian: Images of the American Indian from Columbus to the Present* (New York: Alfred A. Knopf, 1978), 173.

5 Mardock, *The Reformers*, 5.

6 *The Colorado Herald* (Central City, Colorado), 13 April 1870.

7 Quoted in George W. Manypenny, *Our Indian Wards* (1880; reprint, New York: Da Capo Press, 1972), 399.

8 (New York: Random House, 1999), 266.

9 Ibid., 267–70.

10 Quoted in Brian W. Dippie, *Vanishing Americans: White Attitudes and U.S. Indian Policy* (Middletown, Conn.: Wesleyan University Press, 1982), 148.

11 Sherman quote in Donald W. Meinig, *Transcontinental America, 1850–1915,* vol. 3, *The Shaping of America: A Geographical Perspective on 500 Years of History,* (New Haven, Conn.: Yale University Press, 1998), 159. For a discussion of Sherman's Indian views, also see Fellman, *Citizen Sherman* and James M. Merrill, *William Tecumseh Sherman* (New York: Rand McNally and Company, 1971). Lt. Gen. Philip Sheridan, the commander of the U.S. Army in the West, believed his troops "protected the hearty pioneer" who "redeemed from idle waste ... a home for millions of progressive Americans." See Lt. Gen. Philip H. Sheridan, *Record of Engagements with Hostile Indians, 1868–1882* (Washington, D.C.: GPO, 1882), 103.

12 Quoted in Robert Marshall Utley, *Frontier Regulars: The United States Army and the Indian, 1866–1891* (Lincoln, Nebr.: University of Nebraska Press, 1984), 22.

[13] Grant to George Stuart, 26 October 1872, quoted in Jean Edward Smith, *Grant* (New York: Simon and Schuster, 2001), 524.

[14] William Tecumseh Sherman, *Memoirs of General W. T. Sherman* (New York: Library of America, 1990), 927.

[15] See Indian Commission's "Report to the President," 7 January 1868, in *Annual Report of the Commissioner of Indian Affairs, Annual Report of the Secretary of Interior*, 40th Cong., 3rd sess., 1868–1869, H. Doc. 1, serial 1366, 502–3.

[16] Quoted in Jan Pettit, *Utes: The Mountain People*, rev. ed. (Boulder, Colo.: Johnson Books, 1990), 104.

[17] For accounts of crimes blamed on the Indians see Val McClellan, *This Is Our Land*, vol. 1 (New York: Vantage, 1977), chapter 2.

[18] John Gregory Bourke, *On the Border with Crook* (Lincoln, Nebr.: University of Nebraska Press, 1971), 425.

[19] See Frances L. Quintana, *Pobladores: Hispanic Americans of the Ute Frontier*, 2nd rev. ed. (Notre Dame, Ind.: University of Notre Dame Press, 1991).

[20] Report of A. J. Alexander, Eighth Cavalry, to Lieutenant Sartle at Fort Garland, Colorado, letters dated 4 September and 18 September 1871, NA, RG 75, M 234, R 202.

[21] Editorial, *Laramie Times*, reprinted in the *Ouray Times*, 20 September 1879.

[22] Quoted in P. David Smith, *Ouray: Chief of the Utes* (Ridgway, Colo.: Wayfinder Press, 1986), 96–97.

[23] *Boulder News*, 13 September 1872.

[24] *Denver Tribune*, 26 March 1873.

[25] Smith, *Ouray*, 105–6.

[26] Board of Indian Commissioners, *Annual Report of the Board of Indian Commissioners*, (Washington, D.C.: GPO, 1872), 94.

[27] See Commissioner of Indian Affairs, *Annual Report of the Commissioner of Indian Affairs*, (Washington, D.C.: GPO, 1873), 106–7.

[28] William Saunders, unpublished manuscript (courtesy of Mr. P. David Smith), 86.

[29] See Agent Charles Adams to Governor McCook, 1 April 1871, NA, RG 75, M 234.

[30] Reported by Sidney Jocknick, *Early Days on the Western Slope of Colorado* (Denver: Carson-Harper, 1913), 359.

[31] Thomas A. Dawson and F. J. V. Skiff, *The Ute War: A History of the White River Massacre* (1879; reprint, Boulder, Colo.: Johnson Books, 1980), 176–77.

[32] By 1873, the government no longer made "treaties" with Indians, since after 1871 tribes were no longer considered "foreign powers." Treaties were replaced by "agreements" and still subject to congressional approval.

[33] The compensation to the Utes came to about $.13 per acre at a time when the government asked $1.25 per acre for less-valuable homestead land.

34 The agreement was concluded in 1874 but not ratified until 1875, the year the Los Piños Agency moved to the Uncompahgre Valley.

35 The spring exists to this day; it is now known as Orvis Hot Springs and is located three miles south of Ridgway, Colorado.

36 See statement of Ignacio, translated by John Moss, October 1876, n.d., NA, RG 75, M 234, R 236.

37 See Annual Report of Charles Adams to American Unitarian Association, 26 September 1873, American Unitarian Association "Letterbooks."

38 Taken from the 1881 appraisal of Ouray's farm included in "Civilization" File, NA, RG 75.

39 For a firsthand description of Ouray's house and dress, see William Henry Jackson, *Time Exposure: An Autobiography of William Henry Jackson* (New York: Van Rees Press, 1940).

40 Quoted in P. David Smith, *Ouray*, 87–88.

41 Martha A. Sandweiss, *Print the Legend: Photography and the American West* (New Haven, Conn.: Yale University Press, 2002), 228.

42 Jocknick, *Early Days on the Western Slope*, 117–20; also "Report of Agent Henry Bond to Commissioner of Indian Affairs," 4 October 1875, NA, RG 75, M 234, R 205.

43 See Maj. A. J. Alexander, Eighth U.S. Cavalry (Fort Garland) to Lieutenant Sartle, 4 September 1871, NA, RG 75, M 234, R 202.

44 William Saunders, unpublished manuscript (courtesy of Mr. P. David Smith), 85.

45 Trask to "Friend Lowe," 23 May and 11 August 1871, American Unitarian Association "Letterbooks."

46 Jocknick, *Early Days on the Western Slope*, 33–38.

47 J. B. Chaffee to U.S. Long Branch, 28 July 1871, American Unitarian Association "Letterbooks." After his Indian service, Trask preached briefly in New Salem, Massachusetts, and then took up an engineering career in Orange, Massachusetts. He died in 1909 and willed his body to Harvard Medical School and his small estate to the Society for the Prevention of Dumb Animals.

48 Adams to McCook, 1 April 1871, NA, RG 75, M 234, R 201.

49 Adams to Rush Shippen, 9 November 1872, American Unitarian Association "Letterbooks."

50 Littlefield to commissioner of Indian Affairs, 1 July, 22 July, 23 August, 30 September, 25 December 1871 and 16 January, 1 April 1872, NA, RG 75, M 234, R 201 and 202.

51 Annual Report of Charles Adams to American Unitarian Association, 26 September 1873, American Unitarian Association "Letterbooks"; and Agent Bond to F. H. Smith, Board of Indian Commissioners, 28 September 1874, American Unitarian Association "Letterbooks."

52 Charles Adams to Rush Shippen, secretary of American Unitarian Association, 1 August 1872, American Unitarian Association "Letterbooks."

53 See Danforth to Edward P. Smith, commissioner of Indian Affairs, 9 January 1875, NA, RG 75, M 234, R 205.

54 See Thompson (Denver) to Edward P. Smith, commissioner of Indian Affairs, 16 June 1875, and report of Danforth to Edward P. Smith, commissioner of Indian Affairs, 21 June 1875, NA, RG 75, M 234, R 205.

55 See Danforth to E. P. Smith, commissioner of Indian Affairs, 1 March 1875, American Unitarian Association "Letterbooks" and Danforth letter to Rush Shippen, 3 October 1876, American Unitarian Association "Letterbooks." Also see Commissioner Hayt to the secretary of interior, 25 January 1878, NA, RG 75, M 234.

56 See Carl Wittke, "Carl Schurz and Rutherford B. Hayes," *Ohio Historical Quarterly* 65, no. 4 (October 1956).

57 Secretary of Interior, *Secretary of Interior Annual Report* (Washington: D.C.: GPO, 1879).

58 Quoted in Peter Nabokov, ed., *Native American Testimony: A Chronicle of Indian-White Relations from Prophecy to Present, 1492–1992* (New York: Penguin, 1999), 236.

59 The most notorious instance involved Secretary of War Belknap who was charged with taking kickbacks from a contractor supplying the Indians.

THREE: *"Father Meeker"*

1 Contemporaries describe the young Meeker as a tall, thin, gangling youth, very serious, precocious, and always ready with an opinion. Meeker's closest friend, J. L. Chester, a fellow seven years his senior, wrote Meeker in response to his longing to be back in Euclid, "Let me cheer you, Meeker. I wish that instead of going to N.O. [New Orleans] you had mended your way to the north. Gladly I would have received you[,] and everything that I have should have been shared with you. You should have gone to my school with me, should have ate and slept with me and we would not have been separated. No, I love you, and always did. You are a strange fellow, Meeker, but for this I love you the more." See Chester to Meeker, 4 January 1838, CHS, Folders 25 and 26, Meeker "Papers."

2 Nathan Meeker diary, 16 April 1843, CHS, Folder 73, Meeker "Papers."

3 Ibid., 6 April 1843.

4 Quoted in Russel B. Nye, *Society and Culture in America, 1830–1860* (New York: Harper and Row, 1974), 28–29.

5 See Meeker diary, 20 March and 26 March 1843.

6 Ibid., 2 December 1844.

7 Ibid., n.d. but included in entries for late 1845.

8 For their early correspondence, see CHS, Meeker family correspondence, Meeker "Papers." Ralph Meeker recalled his mother as "shy as a wood-robin."

9 Meeker diary, 28 August and 17 September 1843.

10 See CHS, Folder 12 "Trumbull Phalanx," Meeker "Papers." Meeker invested $275 for nine shares in the venture, capitalized at $25,000. But serving as both auditor and librarian for the phalanx, Meeker believed his "talent" salary would more than compensate him for his lack of "capitalist" position. The Meekers believed that Arvilla's salary would, as a teacher and "talent," supplement their family income.

11 Meeker to J. L. Chester, May 1845, n.d., CHS, Folder 45, Meeker "Papers."

12 See Meeker diary, 13 June and 24 June 1847. Ralph Meeker, many years later in a letter to a friend, explained the reason for Trumbull's failure. It failed, he said, "because of the unhealthiness of the place and the lack of earnest cooperation on the part of the grabbers and schemers who would do everything but work." Ralph Meeker to "Friend Houston," 21 April 1910, CHS, "Ralph Meeker" Folder, Meeker "Papers."

13 Meeker diary, 31 January 1848.

14 Ibid., 25 February 1843.

15 Nathan Meeker, *The Adventures of Captain Jacob D. Armstrong* (New York: DeWitt and Davenport, 1852), 70.

16 Meeker diary, 10 February 1843.

17 Ibid., 28 February 1852.

18 Meeker to Hawthorne, CHS, correspondence file for early 1853, Meeker "Papers."

19 See Greeley to Meeker, 18 February 1850, DPL, "Greeley Letters," Meeker "Papers."

20 See Meeker diary, 19 March 1853.

21 By 1860, the U.S. Census listed Meeker with assets of $1,270 in real estate and $500 in personal property, a comfortable situation for the time.

22 Meeker to [unidentified] Meeker, n.d., CHS, Folder 49 with 1864 correspondence, Meeker "Papers."

23 Meeker to Lurana Meeker, 19 March 1868, CHS, Folder 352, Meeker "Papers."

24 Quoted in William Dudley, ed., *Native Americans: Opposing Viewpoints* (San Diego: Greenhaven Press, 1998), 134.

25 Quoted by Rodman W. Paul, *The Far West and the Great Plains in Transition: 1859–1900* (New York: Harper and Row, 1988), 11–12; for an account of Greeley's 1859 trip to the West, see his *Overland Journey from New York to*

San Francisco in the Summer of 1859 (San Francisco: H. H. Bancroft and Company, 1860), 152–53.

26 See DPL and CHS, promotional brochures, "Union Colony" folders, Meeker "Papers."; also *New York Tribune*, 8 December 1869 and 23 January 1870.

27 See numerous letters in DPL and CHS, "Union Colony" folders, Meeker "Papers."

28 Meeker to General Palmer, 15 December 1869, CHS Folder 57, Meeker "Papers."

29 Quoted in Irving Stone, *Men to Match My Mountains: The Opening of the Far West 1840–1900* (Garden City, N.Y.: Doubleday, 1956), 352.

30 From an editorial by George A. Hobbs in the *Genesco* (Illinois) *Republic*, quoted in David Boyd, *A History: The Greeley and Union Colony of Colorado* (Greeley, Colo.: The Greeley Tribune Press, 1890), 52–63.

31 For a list of the original members and those who came to the colony, see James F. Willard, *The Union Colony at Greeley, Colorado*, vol. 1, *University of Colorado Historical Collections Colony Series* (Boulder, Colo.: University of Colorado, 1918), 171–91.

32 Greeley to Meeker, 26 December 1870, DPL, "Greeley Letters," Meeker "Papers."

33 Letters from Greeley to Meeker, 5 April, 1 September, 30 October, and 12 November 1871. DPL, "Greeley Letters," Meeker "Papers."

34 See Ralph Meeker to "Friend Houston," 21 April 1910, DPL, Meeker "Papers."

35 Greeley wrote Meeker, "You may hold on to the $1,000 [loan] another year and pay the interest in getting my [new] trees started." Greeley to Meeker, 1 September 1871, DPL, Meeker "Papers."

36 *New York Tribune*, 16 October 1872.

37 Greeley to Meeker, 25 February 1872, DPL, Meeker "Papers."

38 Greeley to Meeker, 9 March and 18 March 1872, DPL, Meeker "Papers."

39 Boyd, *The Greeley and Union Colony*, 377.

40 See William E. Pabor letter, CHS, File 102, Meeker "Papers."

41 Greeley to Meeker, 8 May 1872, DPL, Meeker "Papers."

42 Greeley to Meeker, 29 March 1872, DPL, Meeker "Papers."

43 Greeley to Meeker, 7 November 1872, DPL, Meeker "Papers."

44 See Meeker to Storrs, 27 September 1873, DPL, Meeker "Papers."

45 In 1877, the valuation of Meeker's properties totaled $705.00 with taxes of $27.88. In 1876, he had sold off a portion of the land (12.5 acres) given to him by the colony in appreciation for his services as president. See DPL, "Greeley Colony" Files, Meeker "Papers."

46 Nathan Meeker to Arvilla Meeker from Philadelphia, 5 October 1876, CHS, Meeker "Papers."

47 Charles Storrs to Meeker, n.d. (winter 1877), DPL, Meeker "Papers."

[48] The colony spent $412,000 for the four irrigation canals, which were in constant need of repair and not always functional.

[49] Quoted in Marshall Sprague, *Massacre: The Tragedy at White River* (Boston: Little, Brown, and Company, 1957), 18.

FOUR: *"They Deserve a Lesson"*

[1] Meeker to Teller, 27 May 1878, DPL, Teller "Letters," emphasis added.

[2] See Carl Wittke, "Carl Schurz and Rutherford B. Hayes," *Ohio Historical Quarterly*, 65 no. 4 (October 1956). Ralph Meeker wrote a series of articles for the *New York Herald*, competitor to Horace Greeley's *Tribune*, detailing widespread incidents of bribery within the mismanaged Indian Bureau.

[3] Meeker to Hayt, 17 January 1878, DPL, Meeker "Papers."

[4] Pitkin quoted in Robert Emmitt, *The Last War Trail: The Utes and the Settlement of Colorado* (Boulder, Colo.: University Press of Colorado, 2000), 21–22, 26.

[5] The complaint arose because grain rations, destined for the White River Agency, were locked in storage by the Union Pacific Railroad in Rawlins awaiting payment of the freight bill. The White River Utes blamed Danforth for the withholding of rations in Rawlins. Washington's delay in payment may have been an Indian Bureau strategy in 1878 to force the White River Utes to join with Ouray's band and the southern Utes into a single agency on the Uncompaghre, a "control" plan proposed by General Pope but never implemented. The Utes, particularly Chief Ouray, adamantly opposed the relocation plan. See William Stickney, *Memorial Sketch of William Soule Stickney by His Father* (Washington, D.C.: School of Music Press, 1881), 151–227.

[6] C. B. Clements to Teller, 28 January 1878, DPL, Teller "Papers."

[7] "Indians and Farmers," *Springfield Republican*, n.d., DPL, Meeker "Papers."

[8] Teller to Meeker, 3 January 1878, DPL, Meeker "Papers."

[9] Senator Chaffee to Meeker, 21 March 1877, DPL, Meeker "Papers."

[10] Superintendent of Instruction to Meeker, n.d., CHS, Folder 96, Teller "Letters."

[11] The Chinese were the target of racial violence in numerous mining towns and Denver where their community was burned. Teller advocated the exclusion of the Chinese from the United States, a popular position for most Coloradans. See Patricia Ourada, "The Chinese in Colorado," *Colorado Magazine* 29, (1952).

[12] Teller to Cooper, 17 January 1878, DPL, and Z. L. White letters to Meeker, 13 March and 29 March 1877, CHS, Folder 70, Teller "Papers."

[13] Danforth to Shippen, 6 September 1877, American Unitarian Association "Letterbook."

14 Danforth to Shippen, 24 February 1878, American Unitarian Association "Letterbook."

15 Nathan Meeker, "The Utes of Colorado," *The American Antiquarian* 4 (April 1879), 225–26.

16 Arvilla Meeker to Ralph Meeker, 12 December 1878, DPL, Meeker "Papers."

17 Secretary of Interior, *Annual Report of the Secretary of Interior*, (Washington, D.C.: GPO, 1878). Schurz at this time started the Carlisle Indian School in Pennsylvania to educate Indian youths.

18 See Danforth report in Commissioner of Indian Affairs, *Annual Report of the Commissioner of Indian Affairs*, (Washington, D.C.: GPO, 1877). Copy of report in the American Unitarian Association "Letterbook" for 1877.

19 In one letter to the American Unitarian Association, Danforth complained about meager funding for the White River Agency and the Indian Bureau regulations that forced Utes, in search of needed supplies and arms, off the reservation into the hands of a "poor class of Whites." The Utes are "unfairly treated," Danforth wrote in a letter to Rush Shippen, 3 October 1876, American Unitarian Association "Letterbook."

20 See Adams to Edward M. McCook, governor of Colorado Territory, 1 April 1871; Littlefield to Gen. E. S. Parker, commissioner of Indian Affairs, 22 July 1871; Littlefield to F. A. Walker, commissioner of Indian Affairs, 1 April 1872; and Littlefield to Edward P. Smith, commissioner of Indian Affairs, 11 September 1873, all in NA, RG 75, M 234.

21 Quoted in David Rich Lewis, *Neither Wolf Nor Dog: American Indians, Environment, and Agrarian Change* (New York: Oxford University Press, 1994), 44.

22 U.S. Senate, *Report of the Ute Commission*, 46th Cong., 3rd sess., 1880, Exec. Doc. 31, serial 1943.

23 Nathan Meeker to Josephine Meeker, 13 May 1878, GM, "Nathan Meeker Correspondence." Josephine (Josie) had attended a secretarial school in Denver before joining her father at the agency. Later in the summer of 1878, Meeker also offered Josie the added responsibility of caring for the agency's boarding house (for the single, white employees). As he mentioned in a letter to Arvilla, the additional job would give Josie the opportunity "to make some [more] money." See Nathan Meeker to Arvilla Meeker, 15 May 1878, GM.

24 Nathan Meeker to Ralph Meeker, 10 July 1878, CHS, Folder 19, Meeker "Papers."

25 Annual Report of Meeker to the commissioner of Indian Affairs, included in the Secretary of Interior, *Annual Report of the Secretary of Interior*, (Washington, D.C.: GPO, 1878), 18–19.

26 Report of Agent Critchlow, 1872, quoted in Lewis, *Neither Wolf Nor Dog*, 41.

27 Emmitt, *The Last War Trail*, 123–24.

28 U.S. Senate, *Report of the Ute Commission*, 137.

[29] Meeker also believed, but without any evidence, that whites used the horse races as occasions to procure Ute girls to go off with them to the white settlements on the Little Snake River where, for "a commission," their procurers arranged for the girls to have sex with white settlers.

[30] The cattle were branded "USID" (U.S. Indian Department), a mark whites translated to mean "You Steal, I Divide."

[31] Ida Greeley to Meeker, 2 April 1878, DPL, Meeker "Letters."

[32] The savings also included some funds from Josephine's teacher salary, possibly supplemented by Arvilla's assistant teacher salary ($150 per year).

[33] Nathan Meeker to Ralph Meeker, 1 November 1878, GM, "Meeker Letters."

[34] Quoted in Joseph G. Jorgensen, *The Sun Dance Religion: Power for the Powerless* (Chicago: University of Chicago Press, 1972), 58.

[35] Meeker to Shippen, 10 March 1879, American Unitarian Association "Letterbooks."

[36] Quoted in Emmitt, *The Last War Trail*, 72–74.

[37] Meeker to Thornburgh (with copy to Hayt), 1 March 1879, quoted in Emmitt, *The Last War Trail*, 96.

[38] Meeker to Thornburgh, 17 March 1879, in U.S. Senate, *Report of the Ute Commission*, 55.

[39] See Meeker to Hayt, 9 December 1878 and 3 February 1879, in U.S. Senate, *Report of the Ute Commission*, 125 and 135.

[40] Hayt to Meeker, 3 February 1879, U.S. Senate, *Report of the Ute Commission*, 125 and 135.

[41] Nathan Meeker to Arvilla Meeker, 5 October and 7 October 1876, DPL, Meeker "Letters."

[42] Meeker to Hayt, 2 July and 11 August 1879, NA, RG 75, M 234.

[43] Meeker to Thornburgh, 7 July 1879. NA, RG 75, M 234.

[44] Copy of Teller's wire given to and reprinted in the *Rocky Mountain News*, 6 July 1879.

[45] Schurz to secretary of war, NA, RG 75, M 666, R 513.

[46] Val McClellan, *This Is Our Land*, vol. 1 (New York: Vantage, 1977), 223.

[47] Thornburgh quoted in McClellan, *This Is Our Land*, 224–26.

[48] Meeker wrote his son of the accident and said, "It is by no means likely that I shall live long enough to find the shoulder wholly recovered." Nathan Meeker to Ralph Meeker, 11 August 1879, GM, Meeker "Letters."

[49] Meeker wrote two letters to Hayt on 11 August 1879. One is included in U.S. Senate, *Report of the Ute Commission*, 46, the other in NA, "Letters Received," RG 75, M 666, R 513.

[50] Hayt to Meeker, 15 August 1879, NA, RG 75, M 234.

[51] Quoted in U.S. Senate, *Report of the Ute Commission*, 246.

[52] For an account of Jack's meeting with Pitkin, see House, *Ute Commission Investigation of 1879*, 46th Cong., 2nd sess., 1879, Exec. Doc. 84, serial 1925, 68.

[53] Quoted in Marshall Sprague, *Massacre: The Tragedy at White River* (Boston: Little, Brown, and Company, 1957), 164. In 1876, Rep. J. H. Belford (Colorado) introduced the first bill into Congress to have the Utes removed from Colorado.

[54] Annual Report of Meeker to the commissioner of Indian Affairs, included in the Secretary of Interior, *Annual Report of the Secretary of Interior*, (Washington, D.C.: GPO, 1879).

[55] Meeker to Hayt, 8 September 1879, U.S. Senate, *Report of the Ute Commission*, 43.

[56] For Johnson's account of the incident, see House, *Ute Commission Investigation of 1879*, 7–8.

[57] Meeker to Hayt , 10 September 1879, "Letters Received," NA, RG 75, M 666.

[58] Jack's testimony included in House Committee on Indian Affairs, 46th Cong., 2nd sess., January 1880, Misc. Doc. 38, serial 1931, 199.

[59] Quoted in Emmitt, *The Last War Trail*, 157.

[60] Meeker to Byers, 10 September 1879, CHS, Pitkin "Papers."

[61] Copy of Pitkin to General Pope, 11 September 1879, CHS, Pitkin "Papers."

[62] Normally the 120-mile trip took three to four days and often longer in the winter. All mail addressed to the agency came from Rawlins once a week. There were no settlements between Rawlins and the agency except for the Bagg Ranch on the Little Snake River and Peck's store on the Yampa.

[63] Copy of communication from Indian Bureau to Department of War in "Letters Sent," Department of Interior, 14 September 1879, NA, RG 75, M 666, R 513.

[64] See Emmitt, *The Last War Trail*, 156.

[65] David Boyd, *A History: The Greeley and Union Colony of Colorado* (Greeley, Colo.: The Greeley Tribune Press, 1890), 356.

FIVE: *A Battle and a Massacre*

[1] Quote from Lt. Gen. Philip H. Sheridan, *Record of Engagements with Hostile Indians, 1868–1882* (Washington, D.C.: GPO, 1882), 103.

[2] Quotes from Michael Fellman, *Citizen Sherman: A Life of William Tecumseh Sherman* (New York: Random House, 1999), 260, 275–76.

[3] On occasion, the army often confused which fort or post fell under whose geographical command. For example, when Sheridan, on Grant's authority, issued orders for the "nearest military command" to send "a sufficient numbers of troops" to proceed to the White River Agency, the order went first to General

Pope's headquarters (Department of Missouri) at Fort Leavenworth (Kansas) in the belief that Colorado came under its military jurisdiction. It did, but Fort Fred Steele (Wyoming Territory) with its "nearest" troops came under the jurisdiction of General Crook and his command (Department of the Platte) at Omaha Barracks in Nebraska. Robert Marshall Utley, *Frontier Regulars: The United States Army and the Indian, 1866–1891* (Lincoln, Nebr.: University of Nebraska Press, 1984), 22. According to Utley, a second lieutenant received in salary $1,400 per year, sergeants $22 per month, and privates $14 per month. All soldiers received their pay in paper currency, which then had to be converted into specie at a discount.

4 According to one army officer in the 1870s, "drink was often the compelling reason for enlistment in the Army. Payday was irregular—sometimes once in two months, sometimes, because of absences in the field, once in four or six months. The soldier's pay ... on $13 a month, and at times reduced by fines, might account on payday to a considerable sum. Payday was often a debauch, an orgy of drunkenness. ... There was much desertion as well on payday." See General James Parker, *The Old Army: Memoirs: 1872–1918* (Philadelphia: Dorrance and Company, 1929), 16–17.

5 The sutler, a civilian licensed trader, supplied fresh produce and mercantile goods to the soldiers and their dependents. Other civilian employees at the post included a sawyer, engineer, blacksmith, saddler, laundress, and wheelwright.

6 Letter included in Commissioner of Indian Affairs, *Annual Report of the Commissioner of Indian Affairs*, (Washington, D.C.: GPO, 1879).

7 President Hayes had commanded a brigade under General Crook in West Virginia during the Civil War. Hayes had shown exceptional courage and had proved himself, in Crook's estimate, "as brave a man as ever wore a shoulder strap." John Gregory Bourke, *On the Border with Crook* (Lincoln, Nebr.: University of Nebraska Press, 1971), 321.

8 Communications from Thornburgh to Crook's command at Omaha Barracks, 16 September 1879, NA, RG 75, M 666, R 513.

9 The civilians included teamsters, blacksmiths, guides, a sutler, farriers, saddlers, and two musicians (excluding four military trumpeters).

10 Dr. Grimes carried in his medical wagon a variety of instruments and medicines required by army regulations. His equipment included a lance, scalpel, forceps and scissors, rolls of adhesive plaster, some needles, waxed thread, a hypodermic injection syringe, and tourniquets. Medicines included quinine, opium, and cathartic put up in small doses, some chloroform, laudanum, camphor, solution of morphine, iodine, chlorides, spirits of ammonia, and various assortments of creams, oils, and ointments. For snakebites, a not uncommon occurrence on the high plains, possibly because of the antidote, the army prescribed a strong dose of whiskey. The manual informed soldiers how "the action of the [snake] poison seems to counteract the effects of the whiskey," and as the soldiers were delighted to learn about their favorite medicine, "a very large quantity may be

taken without causing intoxication. No time should be lost in administering the spirits." Edward S. Farrow, *Mountain Scouting: A Handbook for Officers and Soldiers on the Frontier* (New York: E. S. Farrow, 1881), 52.

11 U.S. Army RG 393 (Records of the U.S. Army Continental Command), Part I, entry 3726, Department of the Platte, Headquarters Records, "Letters Sent," vol. 27. Emphasis added. The telegram was originally sent to Fort Fred Steele and delivered by messenger two days later to Thornburgh. If Crook believed Thornburgh to be in danger of an Indian attack, which seems unlikely, the general would have most certainly so informed his field commander.

12 Mark E. Miller, *Hollow Victory: The White River Expedition of 1879 and the Battle of Milk Creek* (Boulder, Colo.: University Press of Colorado, 1997), 33–34.

13 Quoted in George Manypenny, *Our Indian Wards* (1880; reprint, New York: Da Capo Press, 1972), 426–27 and Miller, *Hollow Victory*, 38.

14 Quoted in Miller, *Hollow Victory*, 43–44.

15 The meeting reported in House, *Ute Commission Investigation of 1879*, 46th Cong., 2nd sess., 1879, Exec. Doc. 83, serial 1925, 62.

16 From Payne's testimony before the House Committee on Indian Affairs, 46th Cong., 2nd sess., January 1880, Misc. Doc. 38, serial 1931, 67, 172.

17 Miller, *Hollow Victory*, 49–50.

18 Jack, in testimony two months later before a House Investigating Committee, said the presence of his braves was intended to halt the army's move toward the agency and that he thought a fight would be and could be averted. When asked who fired the first shot, Jack responded, "I don't know from which side, and in a second or so many shots were fired, that I knew I could not stop the fight, although I swung my hat to my men and shouted, 'Don't fire; we only want to talk;' but they understood me to be encouraging them to fight." House Committee on Indian Affairs, Misc. Doc. 38, 14.

19 Robert Emmitt, *The Last War Trail: The Utes and the Settlement of Colorado* (Boulder, Colo.: University Press of Colorado, 2000), chapter 6.

20 Both communications in Miller, *Hollow Victory*, 70–71.

21 Ibid., 77–78.

22 Ibid., 92

23 The white commanding officer of the Ninth Cavalry recognized the excellent morale, discipline, and high enlistment rate of the unit. The "buffalo soldiers" performed with distinction at Milk Creek despite their traditional lack of adequate supplies and equipment, always a problem for the unit because of racial prejudice displayed by senior army authorities against black units. Later cited for bravery by Dodge, he wrote of his troops "good soldiers and reliable men." NA, RG 75, M 666, R 514; also Miller, *Hollow Victory*, appendix D, 207.

24 Message of Dodge to Army Headquarters in Omaha, 8 October 1879, NA, RG 75, M 666, R 513.

25 The extraordinary distance covered in record time by the forced march soon became part of the curriculum at West Point.

26 Message written on 2 October 1879 and not delivered until at least two days later. Agent W. M. Stanley probably wrote the message for Ouray, who lost an uncle and a nephew in the battle. See William Saunders, unpublished manuscript (courtesy of Mr. P. David Smith), 105.

27 Ten soldiers, one civilian guide, and two civilian teamsters had been killed. The wounded included thirty-nine soldiers (including the surgeon) and five civilians. Later, the army awarded the Medal of Honor to eleven soldiers involved in the battle, including a black sergeant from the Ninth Cavalry. The Indians acknowledged thirty-seven dead suffered at both the battle and at the agency. It is estimated that around three hundred animals (almost all army horses and mules) were killed in the course of the battle. For human and animal losses, see Miller, *Hollow Victory*, appendix B.

SIX: *A Peace and Removal*

1 *Rocky Mountain News*, 8 October and 11 November 1879.

2 *New York Tribune*, 9 October 1979.

3 *Denver Daily Times*, 14 October 1879; *Boulder Banner*, 10 October 1979; *Cheyenne Leader*, October 1879, n.d., reprinted in U.S. Senate, *Report of the Ute Commission*, 46th Cong., 3rd sess., 1880, Exec. Doc. 31, serial 1943, 269.

4 Reprinted in *Ouray Solid Muldoon*, 24 October 1879.

5 Quoted in Carl Ubbelohde, Maxine Benson, Duane Smith, *A Colorado History* (Boulder, Colo.: Pruett Publishing Company, 1995), 183.

6 For Pitkin's correspondence during this period, see CHS and DPL, Pitkin "Papers."

7 See *Denver Daily Republican*, 2 October 1879, copy in CHS, Pitkin "Papers." Pitkin had no state funds at his disposal to pay for the troops and, therefore, no way to enroll a force of 25,000 men; in addition, almost the entire state militia had been sent to Leadville, Colorado, to quell the riots and keep an eye on striking miners in Leadville.

8 Pitkin's papers reveal no evidence that the governor received confirmed, or even unconfirmed, reports of the Shoshone or other Ute bands coming to the assistance of the White River band. The Ute agent in Utah reported that the Uintah band had not been contacted for assistance. See John C. Critichlow correspondence with commissioner of Indian Affairs in Commissioner of Indian Affairs, *Annual Report of the Commissioner of Indian Affairs*, (Washington, D.C.: GPO, 1880), 272–73. Neither is there evidence that the White River

band ever made a request to Ouray for military assistance. Val FitzPatrick, *Red Twilight: The Last Free Days of the Ute Indians* (Yellow Cat Flats, Utah: Yellow Cat Publishing, 2000), 183–86.

[9] At the height of Pitkin's efforts to alarm the army, he received a report from the Indian agent at Los Piños on October 9, 1879, that the presence of the U.S. Army would only stir up more trouble. See CHS. Pitkin "Papers."

[10] Pitkin to Schurz, 12 October 1879, CHS, Pitkin "Papers."

[11] Pitkin to Gould, 23 October 1879, CHS, Pitkin "Papers."

[12] Robert W. Mardock, *The Reformers and the American Indian* (Columbia, Mo.: University of Missouri Press, 1971), see also Philip H. Sheridan, *Personal Memoirs of Philip Henry Sheridan*, vol. 2 (New York: C. L. Webster and Company, 1888), 536.

[13] Wires of General Sherman to General Sheridan, 2 October and 8 October 1879, NA, RG 75, M 666, R 213.

[14] Quote from Charles M. Robinson III, *Bad Hand: A Biography of General Ranald S. Mackenzie* (Austin, Tex.: State House Press, 1993), 263.

[15] Observation about Ignacio by General Hatch, NA, RG 75, M 666, R 515.

[16] Quoted in George W. Manypenny, *Our Indian Wards* (1880; reprint, New York: Da Capo Press, 1972), 432.

[17] Adams testimony before House Committee on Indian Affairs, 46th Cong., 2nd sess., January 1880, Misc. Doc. 38, serial 1931. See also account of the meeting in the *Denver Daily News*, 11 November 1879.

[18] Adams to Schurz, October 1879, (n.d), NA, RG 75, M 234.

[19] *Providence Journal*, 22 October 1879.

[20] Alfred Love, president of the Universal Peace Union, to Schurz, 31 October 1879, and Mrs. Mary Ann Longstreth to Schurz, 21 October 1879, LOC, Schurz "Papers", R 26.

[21] William Saunders, unpublished manuscript (courtesy of Mr. P. David Smith), 129–30

[22] Stanley to Hayt, 15 October 1879, NA, RG 75, M 666, R 514.

[23] *Ouray Solid Muldoon*, 24 October 1879. The two Ouray papers hesitated to print any articles favorable to the Utes that might antagonize the local business community. The papers paid their correspondents very little, arranging for them to have free food and lodging provided by advertisers in return for free advertising space in the papers. For a description of this arrangement, see Saunders manuscript. Schurz may also have fired Stanley for a drinking problem. Saunders called the agent "a pleasant, weak-faced politician from Illinois," fond of his whiskey.

[24] Sherman said in October 1879 that if those responsible for the massacre did not surrender, the army should confiscate the entire northern

reservation and confine all the Utes to the southern part except those who "chose, like Ouray, to become citizens and denizens of Colorado, each family with its own piece of land." (See Sherman to Schurz, 12 October 1879, LOC, Schurz "Papers." But when the Utes refused to hand over the guilty Indians, Sherman, like Sheridan, called for their elimination.

25 Sheridan to Sherman, 17 October 1879, NA, RG 75, M 666, R 513.

26 *New York Times*, 1 October 1879.

27 Pitkin wire to Schurz, 23 October 1879, CHS, Pitkin "Papers"; Schurz's response to Pitkin 23 October 1879, LOC, Schurz "Papers."

28 Ralph Meeker to Schurz, 20 December 1879, LOC, Schurz "Papers."

29 Pitkin to Schurz, 1 November 1879, LOC, Schurz "Papers."

30 *Colorado Gazette*, 1 November 1879.

31 Adams to Schurz, 24 October 1879, in U.S. Senate, *Report of the Ute Commission*, 14.

32 Thomas A. Dawson and F. J. V. Skiff, *The Ute War: A History of the White River Massacre* (1879; reprint, Boulder, Colo.: Johnson Books, 1980), 111.

33 Adams to Schurz from Denver, 4 November 1879, NA, RG 75, M 234; for testimony about "outrages," see also House, *Ute Commission Investigation of 1879*, 46th Cong., 2nd sess., 1879, Exec. Doc. 84, serial 1925.

34 Schurz to Adams, 24 October, 5 November, and 8 November 1879, LOC, Schurz "Papers."

35 Marshall Sprague, *Massacre: The Tragedy at White River* (Boston: Little, Brown, and Company, 1957), 281, quotes Josie Meeker as saying that the Utes thought it "a pretty good thing to have a white squaw" during the women's captivity and that it was an Indian custom, if not an honor, to rape a captive. Sprague presents no source for Josie's opinion nor any evidence for the Indian "custom."

36 Saunders manuscript, 138. Saunders was present at Los Piños during the hearings as a reporter for both the *Denver Tribune* and the *Ouray Times*. Though not allowed to attend the closed meetings, he gathered his information about the proceedings, no doubt, from an interpreter after the meetings.

37 See agenda items for December 1879 cabinet meeting in Rutherford B. Hayes Presidential Center Library.

38 *Denver Republican*, 23 December 1879.

39 Pitkin to mayor of Alamosa , 5 January 1880, CHS, Pitkin "Papers." In the same week, Pitkin approved new irrigation districts, appointed temporary county commissioners, dealt with Washington over contested land claims, issued holiday proclamations, arranged for prisoner exchanges with other states, granted pardons, and filled newly created state government positions (including the head of the new Colorado Asylum for the Insane). He also had time to write the newly elected officials in Gothic, Colorado, to congratulate them on

their new telegraph line. "Gothic is now in immediate communication with the civilized world."

[40] *New York Daily Graphic*, 24 November 1879.

[41] From the *Pueblo Chieftain* reprinted in the *Ouray Solid Muldoon*, 9 January 1880.

[42] Talk given by Sherman on 22 December 1879, mentioned in George Manypenny, *Our Indian Wards*, 432–33.

[43] Report of Ms. Meeker's tour reported in the *Ouray Muldoon*, 28 November 1879, reprinted from the *Denver Tribune*, 17 December 1879.

[44] *Pueblo Chieftain*, 7 January 1880.

[45] Adams reported in a letter to Schurz, 25 October 1879, that in his conversations with Ouray and the other chiefs they believed the government sought an excuse to invade and occupy the northern part of the reservation. See Senate, 46th Cong., 1879, Ex. Doc. 46, 2nd sess.

[46] House, *Ute Commission Investigation of 1879*, 46th Cong., 2nd sess., 1879, Exec. Doc. 84, serial 1925.

[47] Ibid.

[48] Interview with Senator Hill quoted in *Chicago Tribune*, reprinted in the *La Plata Miner* (Durango, Colorado), 10 January 1880.

[49] Secretary of Interior, *Annual Report of the Secretary of Interior*, (Washington, D.C.: GPO, 1879.)

[50] From this point forward, Washington made a clear and formalized distinction between the Southern Utes and the Northern Utes, a distinction carried forward to this day.

[51] Major J. S. Fletcher to Department of Missouri Headquarters at Fort Leavenworth, 19 November 1880, NA, RG 75, M 666, R 516.

[52] McHenry Green (Pueblo, Colorado) to Schurz, 22 October 1880, LOC, Schurz "Papers."

[53] Wire of an unidentified Associate Press reporter to Schurz, 13 October 1880, LOC, Schurz "Papers."

[54] See two letters of Schurz to Pitkin, 14 October 1880 and n.d., LOC, Schurz "Papers." Second letter undated but probably from late October 1880.

[55] Pitkin won the 1880 election by 5,000 votes out of 52,000 cast.

[56] Board of Indian Commissioners, *Report of the Board of Indian Commissioners*, (Washington, D.C.: GPO, 1879), 11–12.

[57] Frederick E. Hoxie, *A Final Promise: The Campaign to Assimilate the Indians, 1880–1920* (Lincoln, Nebr.: University of Nebraska Press, 1984), 24; also Donald Worster, *A River Running West: The Life of John Wesley Powell* (New York: Oxford University Press, 2001), 270–71, 277–78, 285, 453–55.

58 *New York Tribune*, 8 March 1880.

59 *New York Times*, 6 August 1880.

60 Helen Hunt Jackson, *A Century of Dishonor: A Sketch of the United States Government's Dealings with Some Indian Tribes* (Norman, Okla: University of Oklahoma Press, 1995), 251–53.

61 *Congressional Record*, 46th Congress, 2nd sess., 1880, pt. X: 2160–61

62 *Denver Daily News*, 2 December 1879.

63 Carl Schurz, "Present Aspects of the Indian Problem," *North American Review* 83 (July 1881), 6.

64 Quoted in Francis Prucha, *American Indian Policy in Crisis: Christian Reformers and the Indian: 1865–1900* (Norman, Okla.: University of Oklahoma Press, 1976), 159–60, and House, *Agreement with Ute Indians of Colorado*, 46th Cong. 2nd sess., 1880, H. Report 1401, serial 1937, 2–3.

65 Secretary of Interior, *Secretary of Interior Annual Report*, (Washington, D.C.: GPO, 1880).

66 House Committee on Indian Affairs, *Minority Report on Land in Severalty Bill*, 46th Cong. 2nd sess., 1880, H. Report 1576, serial 1938, 10.

67 *Congressional Record*, 46th Congress, 2nd sess., 1880, pt. X: (3), 2069

68 *Congressional Record*, 46th Congress, 2nd sess., 1880, pt. X.

69 Teller once observed, "There has never been a landlord in the history of the world as oppressive as a national landlord." Quoted in Elmer Ellis, *Henry Teller* (Caldwell, Idaho: Caxton Printers, 1944), 374.

70 Arvilla Meeker to Schurz, 7 January 1880, LOC, Schurz "Papers."

71 Ralph Meeker to Schurz, 11 February 1880, LOC, Schurz "Papers."

72 From Schurz' *Memoirs*, quoted in Sidney Jocknick, *Early Days on the Western Slope of Colorado* (Denver: Carson-Harper, 1913), 228–29.

73 Carl Schurz, *Speeches, Correspondence, and Political Papers*, vol. 4 (New York: Putnam, 1913), 93.

74 Schurz, *Speeches*, vol. 3, 504–5.

SEVEN: *Removal*

1 Quoted from Indian Commission: *Report of the Indian Commission to the Secretary of Interior January 20, 1881* (Washington, D.C.: GPO, 1881).

2 Pope to Sheridan, 8 May 1880, NA, RG 75, M 666, R 515.

3 Adams to Schurz, 20 May 1880, LOC, Schurz "Papers."

4 Sidney Jocknick, *Early Days on the Western Slope of Colorado* (Denver: Carson-Harper, 1913), 160. Two years later, many Uncompahgre Utes would hold the

white citizens of Ouray directly responsible for the loss of their land. See letter from the commander of the Sixth Infantry at Fort Thornburgh (Utah Territory) to Assistant A. G., Omaha, Nebraska, 7 May 1882, NA, RG 75, M 666, R 517.

5 See Charles M. Robinson III, *Bad Hand: A Biography of General Ranald S. Mackenzie* (Austin, Tex.: State House Press, 1973), 269.

6 From Schurz' *Memoirs* quoted in Jocknick, *Early Days on the Western Slope*, 228–31

7 Governor Wallace to Secretary Kirkwood 11 May and 12 May 1881, NA, RG 75, "Correspondence Relating to the Ute Commission, 1881–82," Letterbook.

8 *Durango Record* and the *Durango Democrat*, 4 June 1881, NA, RG 75, "Correspondence Relating to the Ute Commission, 1881–82," Letterbook.

9 Manypenny to Secretary Kirkwood, 24 June 1881, NA, RG 75, "Correspondence Relating to the Ute Commission, 1881–82," Letterbook.

10 William Wroth, ed., *Ute Indian Arts and Culture*, (Colorado Springs: Colorado Springs Fine Arts Center, 2000).

11 Manypenny's summary report to Congress, 11 November 1881, NA, RG 75, "Correspondence Relating to the Ute Commission, 1881–82," Letterbook.

12 See letter from Lieutenant Speer, Indian agent at Los Piños, to Edward M. McCook, territorial governor of Colorado, 11 November 1869, NA, RG 75, M 234, R 200; Jocknick, *Early Days on the Western Slope*, 100.

13 Congressional Record, 46th Congress, 2nd sess., 1880, pt. X: 2160–61.

14 J. R. French, a commission member, in a letter to Schurz, quoted in Loring B. Priest, *Uncle Sam's Grandchildren: The Reformation of the United States Indian Policy, 1865–1887* (New Brunswick, N.J.: Rutgers University Press, 1942), 252.

15 Michael Kaplan, *Otto Mears: A Paradoxical Pathfinder* (Silverton, Colo.: 1982), 48.

16 Commissioners to Kirkwood, 6 July 1881, NA, RG 75, "Correspondence Relating to the Ute Commission, 1881–82," Letterbook.

17 Sherman to Sheridan, 25 March 1881, and from Sherman to Lincoln, 7 April 1881, NA, RG 75, M 666, R 513.

18 A doctor had diagnosed the disease on Ouray's trip through Denver on his way to Washington earlier in the summer, though one white scholar believes, without evidence, that Ouray "was poisoned by Southern Ute enemies who distrusted Ouray ... " In 1925, Ouray was reburied at the Indian agency in Ignacio, Colorado. See C. W. Wiegel, "The Death of Ouray," *Colorado Magazine* 7, no. 5 (September 1930): 189.

19 Jocknick, *Early Days on the Western Slope*, 216–17. The charge of bribery was never confirmed and there appears to be no record of the meeting between Mears, Secretary Kirkwood, and Senators Teller and Hill. There is, however, no compelling reason to doubt Jocknick's account provided to him by Manypenny. No record of a reimbursement to Mears could be located.

[20] Schurz to Attorney Fenlon, 24 January 1881, Schurz "Papers," R 87.

[21] The *Dolores News*, quoted in Priest's *Uncle Sam's Grandchildren*, 61. Meacham was so disliked by whites for his defense of Indian rights, in addition to his support of temperance, that when he returned home for a visit in the winter of 1880–81 he had to be evacuated incognito under an army guard.

[22] Senator Hill to Schurtz, 11 November 1880, NA, RG 75, "Correspondence Relating to the Ute Commission, 1881–82," Letterbook.

[23] Meacham to Kirkwood, 24 August and 29 August 1881, NA, RG 75, "Correspondence Relating to the Ute Commission, 1881–82," Letterbook. The White River band had no treaty with the government or executive order guaranteeing their rights to any land at the Uintah Reservation, their forced destination.

[24] Annual Report of Agent W. H. Berry to Indian Bureau, 1 September 1880, Secretary of Interior, *Annual Report of the Secretary of Interior*, (Washington, D.C.: GPO, 1880).

[25] Sometimes spelled Sapovonaux or Sappovonare.

[26] Chris Gibson to Mackenzie, 21 June 1881, NA, RG 75, M 666, R 517.

[27] Wire of Commissioner McMorris to Secretary Kirkwood, 23 August 1881, and Kirkwood reply to McMorris, 24 August 1881, and Kirkwood wire to Mackenzie, 24 August 1881, NA, RG 75, "Correspondence Relating to the Ute Commission, 1881–82," Letterbook.

[28] Robinson, *Bad Hand*, 278.

[29] See one account of the army's problem with "holding back the civilians" in General James Parker, *The Old Army: Memoirs: 1872–1918* (Philadelphia: Dorrance and Company, 1929). See Meacham to Kirkwood, 23 July 1881, NA, RG 75, "Correspondence Relating to the Ute Commission, 1881–82," Letterbook.

[30] McMorris to Kirkwood, 12 September 1881, NA, RG 75, "Correspondence Relating to the Ute Commission, 1881–82," Letterbook.

[31] Inventory of structures, equipment, and livestock are listed in NA, RG 75, "Correspondence Relating to the Ute Commission, 1881–82," Letterbook.

[32] NA, RG 75, "Correspondence Relating to the Ute Commission, 1881–82," Letterbook.

[33] See Commissioner of Indian Affairs, *Report of the Commissioner of Indian Affairs*, (Washington, D.C.: GPO, 1881), 215.

[34] Agent's report included in Commissioner of Indian Affairs, *Report of the Commissioner of Indian Affairs*, (Washington, D.C.: GPO, 1881), 2.

[35] Interior Department to secretary of war, 24 September 1881, NA, RG 75, "Correspondence Relating to the Ute Commission, 1881–82," Letterbook.

[36] Agent J. J. Critchlow at the Uintah Agency to the commissioner of Indian Affairs, 30 January 1882, NA, RG 75, M 666, R 517.

[37] For an official account of the shooting of Jack, see reports of Second Lt. George H. Morgan and Major J. W. Mason (post commander of Fort Washakie), NA, RG 75, M 666, R 517.

[38] *Laramie Sentinel*, 6 May 1882.

Epilogue

[1] *Rocky Mountain News*, 3 May 1950.

[2] *Denver Post*, 12 May and 9 December 2002.

[3] The paper went on to editorialize that no one was better prepared to deal with the "lousy, treacherous, murderous savages" and "pampered pets" than the good senator from Colorado. *Laramie Sentinal*, 1 April and 8 April 1882.

[4] The resulting checkered land pattern remains to this day. It took years of litigation in state and federal courts to untangle conflicting land titles.

[5] *The Wall Street Journal*, 13 June 2003.

Index

Explore the West and Learn More

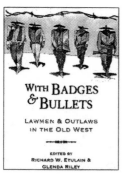
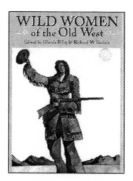
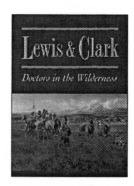

CPSIA information can be obtained at www.ICGtesting.com
Printed in the USA
LVOW07s0743310714

396883LV00001B/11/P